VOCABULARY ACQUISITION

VOCABULARY ACQUISITION
Implications for Reading Comprehension

Edited by

Richard K. Wagner
Andrea E. Muse
Kendra R. Tannenbaum

THE GUILFORD PRESS
New York   London

© 2007 The Guilford Press
A Division of Guilford Publications, Inc.
72 Spring Street, New York, NY 10012
www.guilford.com

Printed in the United States of America

This book is printed on acid-free paper.

Last digit is print number: 9 8 7 6 5 4 3 2 1

Library of Congress Cataloging-in-Publication Data

Vocabulary acquisition : implications for reading comprehension / edited by
Richard K. Wagner, Andrea E. Muse, Kendra R. Tannenbaum.
    p. cm.
    Includes bibliographical references and index.
    ISBN-13: 978-1-59385-338-9 (pbk.)
    ISBN-10: 1-59385-338-6 (pbk.)
    ISBN-13: 978-1-59385-339-6 (hardcover)
    ISBN-10: 1-59385-339-4 (hardcover)
    1. Reading comprehension.   2. Vocabulary.   I. Wagner, Richard K.
II. Muse, Andrea E.   III. Tannenbaum, Kendra R.
LB1050.45.V63 2006
372.47—dc22

                                      2006010631

About the Editors

Richard K. Wagner, PhD, is a Distinguished Research Professor and the Binet Professor of Psychology at Florida State University, and an Associate Director of the Florida Center for Reading Research. His major area of research interest is the acquisition of complex cognitive knowledge and skills, which he has pursued in two domains. In the domain of reading, his research has focused on the role of reading-related phonological processing abilities in normal and abnormal development of reading skills; in the prediction, prevention, and remediation of dyslexia; and in understanding origins of individual and developmental differences in reading comprehension. In the domain of human intelligence, his research has focused on the role of practical knowledge and intelligence in intellectual performance manifested outside the classroom setting. Dr. Wagner's work has addressed a variety of measurement issues and practical considerations involving assessment of constructs in the domains of language, reading, and intelligence. He is coauthor of a test of practical intelligence (Tacit Knowledge Inventory for Managers) published by the Psychological Corporation, as well as tests of phonological processing (Comprehensive Test of Phonological Processes in Reading) and reading (Test of Word Reading Efficiency), published by PRO-ED. He has been appointed to the Advisory Board of the National Institute for Literacy.

Andrea E. Muse, PhD, is a Research Scientist at the American Institutes for Research in Washington, DC. She currently serves as a reading and language expert on contracts funded by the Institute of Education Sciences, the National Center for Education Statistics, and the Department of Homeland Security. Dr. Muse received her PhD in developmental psychology from Florida State University, where she studied the acquisition of complex cognitive skills and their role in the development of normal and abnormal reading. While in graduate school, she worked as an educational consultant, evaluating a variety of programs focusing on topics such as teacher and superintendent training, literacy, and alternatives to suspension.

Kendra R. Tannenbaum, MS, is a doctoral candidate in clinical psychology at Florida State University and a graduate research assistant at the Florida Center for Reading Research. Her research and clinical interests include the assessment of vocabulary knowledge in children, the relations between vocabulary knowledge and reading comprehension, and the assessment and treatment of childhood psychopathology. She is the author or coauthor of several articles in peer-reviewed journals as well as a number of book chapters.

Contributors

Kendra Anderson, MA, EdS, Portage Public Schools, Portage, Michigan

Isabel L. Beck, PhD, Learning Research and Development Center, University of Pittsburgh, Pittsburgh, Pennsylvania

Marco A. Bravo, PhD, Elementary Education Department, San Francisco State University, San Francisco, California

Julie Buck, PhD, Psychology Department, University of Tennessee, Chattanooga, Tennessee

Joanne F. Carlisle, PhD, School of Education, University of Michigan, Ann Arbor, Michigan

Jill de Villiers, PhD, Departments of Psychology and Philosophy, Smith College, Northampton, Massachusetts

Laurel Disney, MS, Department of Teacher Education, Michigan State University, East Lansing, Michigan, and the Reading Clinic at Michigan Career and Technical Institute, Plainwell, Michigan.

Susan E. Gathercole, PhD, Department of Psychology, University of York, Heslington, York, United Kingdom

Erin Renee Harrell, BA, Florida Center for Reading Research, Florida State University, Tallahassee, Florida

Elfrieda H. Hiebert, PhD, Graduate School of Education, University of California at Berkeley, Berkeley, California

Valerie Johnson, PhD, Department of Communication Sciences, University of Connecticut, Storrs, Connecticut

Young-Suk Kim, MEd, Harvard Graduate School of Education, Cambridge, Massachusetts

Susan H. Landry, PhD, Children's Learning Institute, Department of Pediatrics, University of Texas Health Sciences Center at Houston, Houston, Texas

Christopher J. Lonigan, PhD, Florida Center for Reading Research, Florida State University, Tallahassee, Florida

Catherine McBride-Chang, PhD, Department of Psychology, Chinese University of Hong Kong, Hong Kong, China

Margaret G. McKeown, PhD, Learning Research and Development Center, University of Pittsburgh, Pittsburgh, Pennsylvania

Xiangzhi Meng, PhD, Department of Psychology, Peking University, Beijing, China

Andrea E. Muse, PhD, American Institutes for Research, Washington, DC

William Nagy, PhD, School of Education, Pacific University, Seattle, Washington

Jessica Yuen Wai Ng, Bssc, Department of Psychology, Chinese University of Hong Kong, Hong Kong, China

P. David Pearson, PhD, Graduate School of Education, University of California at Berkeley, Berkeley, California

Trevor Penney, PhD, Department of Psychology, Chinese University of Hong Kong, Hong Kong, China

Caroline Phythian-Sence, MS, Department of Psychology, Florida State University, Tallahassee, Florida

Michael Pressley, PhD (deceased), Department of Teacher Education, Michigan State University, East Lansing, Michigan

Christopher Schatschneider, PhD, Florida Center for Reading Research, Florida State University, Tallahassee, Florida

Hua Shu, PhD, State Key Lab for Cognitive Neuroscience and Learning, Beijing Normal University, Beijing, China

Karen E. Smith, PhD, Department of Neurology, University of Texas Medical Branch, Galveston, Texas

Catherine E. Snow, PhD, Harvard Graduate School of Education, Cambridge, Massachusetts

Kendra R. Tannenbaum, MS, Department of Psychology and Florida Center for Reading Research, Florida State University, Tallahassee, Florida

Richard K. Wagner, PhD, Department of Psychology and Florida Center for Reading Research, Florida State University, Tallahassee, Florida

Preface

Dramatic advances have occurred in our understanding of how children learn to read. These advances have been accompanied by changes in how reading is taught, both to children for whom learning to read is no more difficult than most other kinds of learning and to children for whom learning to read is among the most difficult challenges they will face. However, much of what has been learned has been about the processes by which readers access the sounds and meaning represented by printed symbols at the level of the individual word. Understanding how readers fully comprehend the meaning of connected text, and what might be done when this is the challenge, represents a more difficult undertaking. This volume addresses a central question for everyone interested in how individuals comprehend the meaning of what they read: What is known about vocabulary acquisition, and what are its implications for understanding reading comprehension?

Phythian-Sence and Wagner (Chapter 1) provide a primer on vocabulary acquisition. They summarize key findings about vocabulary development that may be of interest to researchers who primarily study reading comprehension rather than vocabulary. The following two chapters address relations between vocabulary development and reading for young children. Lonigan (Chapter 2) presents results from a training study that have implications for understanding a causal role for vocabulary development in subsequent reading: The effects of a vocabulary intervention also impacted phonological awareness, whereas a phonological awareness intervention did not have a corresponding effect on vocabulary. Landry and Smith (Chapter 3) describe an approach for improving young children's language skills and later reading competence by targeting language usage by parents.

The roles of morphological awareness and other metalinguistic skills in vocabulary development and reading are the topics of the next three chapters. Nagy (Chapter 4) argues that relations between vocabulary development and reading comprehension reflect their joint association with metalinguistic ability. Carlisle (Chapter 5) argues for fostering morphological processing as a means to develop both vocabulary and reading comprehension. McBride-Chang, Shu, Ng, Meng, and Penney (Chapter 6) describe relations between morphological structure awareness and both vocabulary and reading. This chapter also expands the study of vocabulary development and reading beyond English monolinguals to children with other native languages.

Following up on this theme, Snow and Kim (Chapter 7) consider the problem of vocabulary acquisition for English language learners. They report that the same factors that promote the development of a native language also promote the development of English as a second language, but that many English language learners are at a disadvantage because of limited development of English vocabulary. Bravo, Hiebert, and Pearson (Chapter 8) address the role of cognates in science learning. They argue for a more active approach to utilizing the high percentage of cognates in science vocabulary as a way of improving the science performance of English language learners. De Villiers and Johnson (Chapter 9) introduce the topic of the effects on vocabulary assessments of minority children who come from homes in which a dialect other than mainstream American English is spoken.

The next two chapters focus on vocabulary interventions. Beck and McKeown (Chapter 10) highlight advances in our understanding of challenges that must be met if an intervention is to develop vocabulary knowledge that is useful for comprehension. Pressley, Disney, and Anderson (Chapter 11) provide a review of landmark instructional research and an analysis of its implications for what kind of vocabulary instruction ought to be tried given current knowledge.

Gathercole (Chapter 12) argues for working memory as a key construct that needs to be considered in understanding both vocabulary development and reading comprehension. Schatschneider, Harrell, and Buck (Chapter 13) report a large-scale individual-differences study that shows developmental changes in relations between reading comprehension and fluency, memory, vocabulary, and other language skills. In the final chapter, Wagner, Muse, and Tannenbaum (Chapter 14) suggest several avenues for promising research on the underlying dimensions of individual and developmental differences in both vocabulary and reading comprehension. Advances in knowledge about underlying dimensions would have implications for developing better assessments and interventions.

Most of the chapters in this volume began as presentations at a conference on vocabulary development and its implications for reading comprehension that was held in Captiva, Florida. One of the most active conference participants was Michael Pressley, to whom this volume is dedicated. As influential as his writing has been, his real legacy will be the students he has trained. Mike was one of the rare scholars who excelled not only in making profound contributions to the literature but also in mentoring students. They may no longer hear his voice, but they will carry his words for many years to come.

Contents

CHAPTER 1

Vocabulary Acquisition
A Primer

CAROLINE PHYTHIAN-SENCE
RICHARD K. WAGNER

Acquiring the vocabulary we use for thinking and communicating is a linguistic achievement of nearly incomprehensible importance and complexity. The study of vocabulary acquisition and use is a scientific discipline characterized by compelling empirical data and a good bit of theorizing. But, as is the case with most areas of research, it is easier to identify what is unsettled and controversial than it is to identify clearly established knowledge. Our goal in this chapter is not to attempt to provide a summary of the field of vocabulary acquisition. Rather, we seek merely to provide a useful primer that describes some basics that could be of use to reading researchers. By way of organization, we focus on two fundamental issues: What do we know about how vocabulary is acquired, and what does it mean to "know" a word?

VOCABULARY ACQUISITION FROM BIRTH TO PRESCHOOL

Although it appears that infants learn to attend to and produce language with ease, acquiring a language in an immense task (MacWhinney, 1998; Thiessen & Saffran, 2003). Infants' early learning is probably facilitated by maturational constraints on perceptual and cognitive abilities that confine infants' attention to crucial elements of language that are necessary for its mastery (Newport, 1990). Neonates as young as 2 days old show preference

1

for their native language, indicating that at least some aspects of their mother's language probably are acquired prenatally (Moon, Cooper, & Fifer, 1993). Infants are able to perceive and discriminate adult speech sounds as early as 1 month of age (Eimas, Siqueland, Jusczyk, & Vigorito, 1971). By 4–6 months of age, infants can discriminate categorically distinct phonemes in their native language (e.g., /ba/ vs. /da/). Early experience with their native language and developing cognitive and perceptual abilities conspire to diminish infants' ability to discriminate novel speech sounds that are not found in their native language. By 10–12 months of age, clear evidence of a loss in ability to distinguish nonnative phonemes is apparent (Werker & Tees, 1999).

Moving from individual sounds to larger phonological units, 6- to 9-month-old infants begin to track the co-occurrence of sounds in syllables (e.g., *ba* and *by*) by using what appear to be rudimentary statistical cues (Newport & Aslin, 2000; Thiessen & Saffran, 2003). Similar statistical cues facilitate an infant's ability to track the co-occurrence of syllables that form words (e.g., *baby, daddy*). Stress cues appear to be used to isolate individual words from a continuous speech stream; this system works because the initial syllable of many English words is stressed (Thiessen & Saffran, 2003). Before the end of the first year, infants can discriminate not only sounds and syllables, but familiar and unfamiliar words. Eight-month-old infants can discriminate between words read to them in a story context and unfamiliar words after a 2-week delay (Jusczyk & Hohne, 1997).

Turning to production, infants begin social vocalizing and babbling vowels at 3 months, followed by the babbling of vowel and consonant combinations at 6 months, but it is not until 11 months that an infant's babbling begins to correspond with phonemes in his or her native language (Bates & Goodman, 1997; MacWhinney, 1998). Even though word-like vocalizations (e.g., *da-da*) may appear before an infant's first birthday, these words generally lack a symbolic reference and are therefore not true words. An infant does not truly acquire meaningful words until he or she understands that words are references to objects, events, and actions in the world.

Before infants learn to communicate with words, their gestures signal an understanding of language (Lock, 1978; Namy & Waxman, 1998; Woodward & Hoyne, 1999). These referential gestures imply an understanding of others' intentions, and are a nonverbal precursor of verbal reference (Golinkoff, Mervis, & Hirsh-Pasek, 1994). Truly communicative words arise when infants not only link spoken sounds with objects and events in the environment, but also understand that words reference objects and concepts. An understanding of others' intentions is essential for language acquisition. Joint attention serves as a means for referential word learning (Bloom, 2000; Tomasello, 2003). When the infant and the caregiver are jointly attending to an aspect of the environment, instigated perhaps with a communicative gesture like pointing, the caregiver labels salient objects and concepts. This joint sharing of attention allows the infant to attach the label to the object or concept in the environment. Words that are both familiar and novel to the infant thereby attain a real-world reference, and become true words.

When faced with the choice of labeling one object among a multitude of options that a caregiver is gesturing toward, infants' word learning typically follows several lexical principles. The *natural partitions hypothesis* (Gentner, 1982) suggests that infants generally choose to label objects and concepts that are easily segmented from the environment; objects are discrete and more easily conceptualized than relational words. Thus, English-speaking infants' first symbolic words are often items and concepts that can be easily partitioned from the environment including concrete nouns, performatives (e.g., *bye-bye*), and nominals (e.g., *breakfast*), but generally include words from all parts of speech (Tomasello, 2003). Additional lexical principles include a *whole-object constraint*, where the child most often assigns a novel label to a whole object rather than to a part (Golinkoff et al., 1994; MacWhinney, 1998; Saylor & Sabbagh, 2004), and an *exclusivity constraint*, where a child will most often use a novel label for a novel object, instead of acquiring a second label for a known object (Bloom, 2000; Golinkoff et al., 1994; Masur, 1997).

From 18 to 24 months, infants are continuing to add a significant number of words to their vocabulary (Tomasello, 2003); some evidence of the beginning of a "vocabulary burst" around this time has been reported (Bates & Goodman, 1997; Mervis & Bertrand, 1995; Reznick & Goldfield, 1992). Although some infants demonstrate a "spurt" or "burst," having been observed acquiring upwards of 10 new words in a 2- to 2½-week period, other infants show a more gradual increase in vocabulary (Mervis & Bertrand, 1995; Reznick & Goldfield, 1992).

Longitudinal estimates of word-learning rates vary greatly. The actual number of words known or acquired cannot feasibly be counted, so estimates of various kinds are used. The variability in reported rates of vocabulary acquisition depends to some degree on which procedures are used for calculating estimates. Biemiller and Slonim (2001) provided an estimate of 2.2 root words a day for children ages 1 through second grade. Templin (1957) provided an estimate of 5.1 new root words a day for 6-, 7-, and 8-year-olds. Carey (1978) provided an estimate of nine new words a day from 18 months to 6 years. Beck, McKeown, and Kucan (2002) conclude that the most commonly cited word-learning rate is seven new words a day, but this figure is an average of low- and high-ability word learners. Biemiller and Slonim (2001), for example, report that children in the lowest quartile for vocabulary size acquired only one word a day from age 1 to second grade, whereas children in the highest quartile acquired three new words a day. Even the most modest estimate hints at the enormous number of words that infants and young children are acquiring.

At around the time children experience a vocabulary burst, they also demonstrate the ability to acquire novel labels rapidly (Mervis & Bertrand, 1995). Carey (1978) dubbed this process of word acquisition *fast mapping*, and found that children can acquire, or *map*, lexical information about a novel label in a single encounter. Carey and Bartlett (1978) explored fast mapping in a population of 3- and 4-year-olds, finding that although a more complete understanding of a word's meaning develops over multiple exposures, children readily acquire partial knowledge about a word's meaning and its referent from a single encounter.

Researchers have continued to explore fast mapping in younger populations of children. Eighteen-month-olds can fast-map novel gestures as object labels (Namy & Waxman, 1998). Two-year-olds will map novel words in a variety of implicit situations, using intention-reading skills that allow the child to infer the meaning of a novel word from adults (Tomasello, 2003). Children as young as 2½ use familiarity and syntactical cues to map novel labels for parts of objects (Saylor & Sabbagh, 2004). Two- to 4-year-olds utilize contrast cues (presenting familiar and unfamiliar objects together) to fast-map labels to novel objects (Wilkinson, Ross, & Diamond, 2003). Two- and 3-year-olds fast-map novel adjectives to familiar nouns with strong syntactical and contrast cues (specifically cross-situational comparisons; see Mintz & Gleitman, 2002). Infants will even fast-map a novel label equally well when exposed directly (infant-directed speech) and indirectly (overhearing adult-directed speech) to a word (Akhtar, Jipson, & Callanan, 2001). In summary, young children acquire new words with and without direct instruction by utilizing various cues from the natural linguistic environment.

Around 18 months, while infants are continuing to add words to their vocabulary and gain motor control, gestures in conjunction with single words arise; this combination generally signals the onset of two-word combinations (Lock, 1978). Initial two-word combinations are concrete constructions that do not have any syntactical meaning (e.g., "bottle Mommy") (Tomasello, 2003). From 24 to 36 months, young children's syntactical awareness begins to develop; their constructions become less concrete and reflect the types of constructions that are most prevalent in their caregivers' speech (Huttenlocher, Haight, Bryk, Seltzer, & Lyons, 1991; Tomasello, 2003). A young child's earliest understanding of syntax therefore appears to be centered around verbs and constructions that are commonly heard in his or her caregiver's speech. Additional exposure to speech paired with a growing corpus of experience with language allows children to abstract general rules about grammatical speech (Tomasello, 2003). Children's ability to apply abstract syntactical rules to their speech signifies that they are able to construct grammatical phrases that are not merely reflections of the speech they have heard. In other words, an understanding of abstract rules of speech allows infants to become innovative with language.

Children's ability to be innovative with language and experiment with previously unheard words and constructions means that some innovations will contain rule overgeneralizations (e.g., "I go-ed to school"). Various environmental factors work to constrain language to conventional standards. Syntactic constraints, for example, restrict children to using commonly heard verbs in commonly heard constructions (e.g., "He made the rabbit disappear" rather than "He disappeared the rabbit"; Tomasello, 2003, p. 178). Additionally, a more complete understanding of verb subclasses (e.g., the difference between *run* and *scamper*) constrains a child's innovations by limiting the applicable contexts (Brooks, Tomasello, Dodson, & Lewis, 1999). Whereas speech perception is constrained maturationally (e.g., limited cognitive abilities), language production appears to be constrained environmentally.

LANGUAGE ACQUISITION FROM PRESCHOOL
THROUGH ELEMENTARY SCHOOL

By the age of 3, most children have acquired an almost adult-like understanding of syntactical constructions (Bates & Goodman, 1997). By the time they have entered first grade they have acquired their native language's phonological system, and can produce almost all of the sounds of their native language (Graves, 1987). The mastery of vocabulary acquisition, though, is still vastly incomplete. In school, children develop additional word-learning strategies. Direct vocabulary instruction appears to contribute to vocabulary acquisition (Graves, 1987). Biemiller (2001) suggests that at least 80% of the words children acquire by the sixth grade are learned through direct instruction; children acquire root word meanings through direct explanations from parents, educators, and peers, and within texts. Although research on the best technique of direct vocabulary instruction is mixed, several conclusions concerning its overall efficacy can be made:

> First, all instructional methods produce better word learning than no instruction. Second, no one method has been shown to be consistently superior. Third, there is advantage from methods that use a variety of techniques. Fourth, there is advantage from repeated exposures to the words to be learned. The simple version of these findings is that people tend to learn what they are taught, and more attention to what is being taught is useful. (Beck & McKeown, 1991, p. 805)

Direct instruction of words, then, needs to go beyond simply asking children to memorize a definition to providing children with repeated exposures to words, their definitions, and contextual information, and allowing the child to explore the meaning of the new words rather than simply memorizing them (Osborn & Armbruster, 2001). Three seemingly successful methods of direct vocabulary instruction include the *keyword method* (e.g., McDaniel & Pressley, 1984; Pressley, Levin, & Miller, 1982), *semantic mapping* (e.g., Johnson, Pittelman, & Heimlich, 1986), and *semantic feature analysis* (Anders & Bos, 1986). The keyword method encourages children to find a familiar word within the unfamiliar word (e.g., *car* from the novel word *carlin*, meaning old woman), and then connect the meaning of the novel word with an image associated with the familiar word (e.g., an old woman driving a car; Pressley et al., 1982). McDaniel and Pressley (1984) found significantly greater definition recall with the keyword method in comparison to a context method for acquiring word meaning. Semantic mapping and semantic feature analysis involve graphically relating novel words to a familiar thematic concept, thereby activating students' familiar experiences and concepts (Anders & Bos, 1986; Johnson et al., 1986).

In contrast with Biemiller's assertion, others suggest that incidental learning provides the primary means of vocabulary acquisition from preschool through elementary school and beyond (e.g., Leung, 1992;

Nagy, Herman, & Anderson, 1985; Osborn & Armbruster, 2001). Comparing estimates of the number of words that children acquire through their school years with estimates of the number of words they acquire through direct instruction suggests an important role for incidental learning.

Leung (1992) explored vocabulary acquisition in oral contexts, using a repeated read-aloud with children in kindergarten and first grade. She found that read-alouds influenced children's acquisition of words for familiar concepts, but did not significantly influence the acquisition of words representing unfamiliar concepts. Penno, Wilkinson and Moore (2002) assessed incidental word acquisition in children ages 5 years, 2 months to 8 years, 1 month using repeated read-alouds as the vehicle for providing an opportunity for incidental learning. Evidence of vocabulary acquisition from incidental learning was found. Adding some direct explanation of word meanings in the context of the read-alouds enhanced vocabulary acquisition. Brabham and Lynch-Brown (2002) also assessed word acquisition in repeated read-alouds, finding that first and third graders made vocabulary gains, but differentially depending on read-aloud style: students who were engaged in an interactive reading style in which word meanings were explained, or in a performance reading style where children were encouraged to ask questions before and after the story, displayed more vocabulary gains than children who simply experienced a read-aloud.

Werner and Kaplan (1950) assessed the acquisition of word meaning in oral contexts in elementary-school children (ages 8 years, 5 months–13 years, 5 months), finding that although children could make inferences about novel word meaning from oral context, older children (beginning around age 10–11) were more able to derive decontextualized meanings. McKeown (1985) also explored contextual word learning in high- and low-verbal-ability fifth graders; students were presented with read-aloud sentences that progressively constrained the possible meanings of an unknown word. She found that high-ability fifth graders were significantly better than low-ability fifth graders at choosing, evaluating, and comparing contextual constraints on novel word meaning.

When children learn to read, their ability to derive word meanings from context extends from oral to written contexts. Jenkins, Stein, and Wysocki (1984) explored fifth graders' ability to acquire word meanings incidentally, and found that students could acquire knowledge about previously unknown words in context-rich paragraphs even without explicit instruction. Nagy et al. (1985) found similar results for average and above-average eighth graders, for contextually derived word knowledge utilizing natural texts. Shore and Kempe (1999) explored student's partial knowledge of contextual words, finding that meaning-restrictive contexts allow students to limit and then infer possible word meanings.

Sternberg and Powell (1983) explored the benefits of instructing students in three strategies to better utilize context in acquiring word meaning: selective encoding, selective combination, and selective comparison (Sternberg, 1987). *Selective encoding* asks students to distinguish between relevant and irrelevant cues that will aid in defining the word. Students next use *selective combination* to decide which cues should be combined to construct the word's meaning. Then students employ *selective comparison* to relate prior knowledge to the information derived from the context, to better define the unknown word. Buikema and Graves (1993) successfully taught a small group of seventh- and eighth-grade students strategies for utilizing context in defining words, combining several cues from Sternberg and Powell (1983) with an additional strategy for assessing a word's sensual aspects (e.g., its appearance, its smell).

Fukkink and de Glopper (1998) performed a meta-analysis on studies that directly attempted to improve students' ability to derive word meanings through context. They found that direct instruction in using contextual cues is effective, with a mean instructional effect of .43 standard deviation units. It appears therefore that students learn about words in both oral and written contexts, and that direct instruction in utilizing context more effectively positively influences their vocabulary acquisition.

WHAT DO YOU KNOW IF YOU *KNOW* A WORD?

Knowledge of a word has been conceptualized in alternative ways. These alternative conceptualizations include, but are not limited to, dimensional word knowledge, stage-like word knowledge, continuum-based word knowledge, contextualized and decontextualized word knowledge, and partial and comprehensive word knowledge. Although word knowledge has traditionally been assessed in a decontextualized, dichotomous fashion, theories on what it means to know a word suggest that true knowledge cannot be measured so simplistically (Beck et al., 2002).

Dale (1965) devised one of the earliest conceptualizations of word knowledge, which addresses the extent of a person's understanding of a word:

1. Stage 1: never saw it before.
2. Stage 2: heard it, but doesn't know what it means.
3. Stage 3: recognizes it in the context as having something to do with _____.
4. Stage 4: knows it well.

These four stages of word knowledge recognize that the meaning of a word can be partial and contextually based. Beck, McKeown, and Omanson (1987) suggest that degrees of knowledge about a word can be represented on a continuum:

1. No knowledge.
2. General sense such as knowing *mendacious* has a negative connotation.
3. Narrow, context-bound knowledge, such as knowing that a "radiant bride" is beautiful and happy, but unable to describe an individual in a different context as "radiant."
4. Having knowledge of a word but not being able to recall it readily enough to use it in appropriate situations.
5. Rich, decontextualized knowledge of a word's meaning, its relationship to other words, and its extension to metaphorical uses, such as understanding what someone is doing when they are "devouring" a book.

Empirical support has been provided for the idea that a person may have a general sense of a word even if he or she does not have explicit knowledge of the word or its meaning (Shore & Durso, 1990).

Anderson and Ortony (1975) explored implications for partial word knowledge and word sense. They suggest that a single word will have many different meanings in a multitude of sentences even if the "core" meaning is the same. Take the word *piano*, for example. In a sentence context involving music, the meaning of *piano* as a musical instrument will be in the forefront. However, in a sentence context involving moving household items, the meaning of *piano* as a very heavy, bulky, but nevertheless fragile piece of furniture will be more relevant. There is a "sense" of the word that cannot be adequately defined from a dictionary meaning, one that only comes from experiences that allow for the differentiation of macro- and microdistinctions in a word's meaning. Clearly, word knowledge is not as decontextualized and dichotomous as once perceived.

Cronbach's (1942) assessment of word knowledge derived from differences in what one is asked to do to demonstrate knowledge of a word:

1. *Generalization,* or the ability to define a word.
2. *Application,* or the ability to select or recognize situations appropriate to using a word.
3. *Breadth,* or knowledge of the multiple meanings of a word.
4. *Precision,* or the ability to apply a word correctly and to recognize its inappropriate use.
5. *Availability,* or the ability to actually use a word in thinking and discourse.

Graves (1987) considered aspects of vocabulary knowledge from the perspective of tasks that represent stages of acquisition of vocabulary words:

1. Learning to read known words.
2. Learning new meanings for known words.
3. Learning new words representing known concepts.
4. Learning new words for new concepts.
5. Clarifying and enriching known words and meaning.
6. Moving words from receptive to expressive vocabulary.

Finally, Nagy and Scott (2000) argue that there are five key aspects of word knowledge:

1. *Incrementality*: the idea that words are known to varying degrees of complete knowledge.
2. *Polysemy*: words have multiple meanings, and shades of meanings, which means that context must be used to infer the intended meaning.
3. *Multidimensionality*: because word knowledge is multidimensional, it cannot be represented on a single, linear continuum.
4. *Interrelatedness*: word knowledge is represented by a configuration of relation in a semantic network of words.
5. *Heterogeneity*: different kinds of words require different kinds of word knowledge.

Two conclusions are obvious from our consideration of what you know if you know a word. First, word knowledge is not adequately represented by a dichotomous indication of whether or not you can produce an acceptable dictionary definition. Second, since what exactly "word knowledge" is beyond this is not clear, clarifying this situation is an important near-term goal for vocabulary researchers.

ACKNOWLEDGMENTS

This research was supported by Grant No. R305G030104 from the Institute for Education Sciences and by Grant No. HD23340 from the National Institute of Child Health and Human Development.

REFERENCES

Akhtar, N., Jipson, J., & Callanan, M. A. (2001). Learning words through overhearing. *Child Development, 72*(2), 416–430.

Anders, P. L., & Bos, C. S. (1986). Semantic feature analysis: An interactive strategy for vocabulary development and text comprehension. *Journal of Reading, 29*(7), 610–616.

Anderson, R. C., & Ortony, A. (1975). On putting apples into bottles: A problem of polysemy. *Cognitive Psychology, 7*, 167–180.

Bates, E., & Goodman, J. C. (1997). On the inseparability of grammar and the lexicon: Evidence from acquisition, aphasia, and real-time processing. *Language and Cognitive Processes, 12*(5–6), 507–584.

Beck, I. L., & McKeown, M. G. (1991). Conditions of vocabulary acquisition. In R. E. Barr, M. L. E. Kamil, P. Mosenthal, & P. Pearson (Eds.), *Handbook of reading research* (Vol. 2, pp. 789–814). Hillsdale, NJ: Erlbaum.

Beck, I. L., McKeown, M. G., & Kucan, L. (2002). *Bringing words to life: Robust vocabulary instruction*. New York: Guilford Press.

Beck, I. L., McKeown, M. G., & Omanson, R. C. (1987). The effects and uses of diverse vocabulary instructional techniques. In M. McKeown & M. E. Curtis (Eds.), *The nature of vocabulary acquisition* (pp. 147–163). Hillsdale, NJ: Erlbaum.

Biemiller, A. (2001). Teaching vocabulary: Early, direct, and sequential. *American Educator, 25*, 24–28, 47.

Biemiller, A., & Slonim, N. (2001). Estimating root word vocabulary growth in normative and advantaged populations: Evidence for a common sequence of vocabulary acquisition. *Journal of Educational Psychology, 93*(3), 498–520.

Bloom, P. (2000). *How children learn the meanings of words*. Cambridge, MA: MIT Press.

Brabham, E. G., & Lynch-Brown, C. (2002). Effects of teachers' reading-aloud styles on vocabulary comprehension of students in the early elementary grades. *Journal of Educational Psychology, 94*(3), 465–473.

Brooks, P. J., Tomasello, M., Dodson, K., & Lewis, L. B. (1999). Young children's overgeneralizations with fixed transitivity verbs. *Child Development, 70*(6), 1325–1399.

Buikema, J. L., & Graves, M. F. (1993). Teaching students to use context cues to infer word meanings. *Journal of Reading, 36*(6), 450–457.

Carey, S. (1978). The child as word learner. In M. Halle, J. Bresnan, & G. Miller (Eds.), *Linguistic theory and psychological reality* (pp. 264–293). Cambridge, MA: MIT Press.

Carey, S., & Bartlett, E. (1978). Acquiring a single new word. *Papers and Reports on Child Language Development, 15*, 17–29.

Cronbach, L. J. (1942). An analysis of techniques for diagnostic vocabulary testing. *Journal of Educational Research, 36*(3), 206–217.

Dale, E. (1965). Vocabulary measurement: Techniques and major findings. *Elementary English, 42*, 895–901.

Eimas, P. D., Siqueland, E. R., Jusczyk, P., & Vigorito, J. (1971). Speech perception in infants. *Science, 171*(3968), 303–306.

Fukkink, R. G., & de Glopper, K. (1998). Effects of instruction in deriving word meaning from context: A meta-analysis. *Review of Educational Research, 68*(4), 450–469.

Gentner, D. (1982). Why nouns are learned before verbs: Linguistic relativity versus natural partitioning. In S. A. Kuczaj (Ed.), *Language development: Language, thought, and culture* (Vol. 2, pp. 301–334). Hillsdale, NJ: Erlbaum.

Golinkoff, R. M., Mervis, C. B., & Hirsh-Pasek, K. (1994). Early object labels: The case for a developmental lexical principles framework. *Journal of Child Language, 21*(1), 125–155.

Graves, M. F. (1987). The roles of instruction in fostering vocabulary development. In M. E. McKeown & M. E. Curtis (Eds.), *The nature of vocabulary acquisition* (pp. 165–184). Hillsdale, NJ: Erlbaum.

Huttenlocher, J., Haight, W., Bryk, A., Seltzer, M., & Lyons, T. (1991). Early vocabulary growth: Relation to language input and gender. *Developmental Psychology, 27*(2), 236–248.

Jenkins, J. R., Stein, M. L., & Wysocki, K. (1984). Learning vocabulary through reading. *American Educational Research Journal, 21*(4), 767–787.

Johnson, D. D., Pittelman, S. D., & Heimlich, J. E. (1986). Semantic mapping. *Reading Teacher, 39*(8), 778–783.

Jusczyk, P. W., & Hohne, E. A. (1997). Infants' memory for spoken words. *Science, 277*(5334), 1984–1986.

Leung, C. B. (1992). Effects of word-related variables on vocabulary growth through CPS repeated read-aloud events. *National Reading Conference Yearbook, 41*, 491–498.

Lock, A. (1978). The emergence of language. In A. Lock (Ed.), *Action, gesture and symbol* (pp. 11–18). New York: Academic Press.

MacWhinney, B. (1998). Models of the emergence of language. *Annual Review of Psychology, 49*, 199–227.

Masur, E. F. (1997). Maternal labeling of novel and familiar objects: Implications for children's development of lexical constraints. *Journal of Child Language, 24*(2), 427–439.

McDaniel, M. A., & Pressley, M. (1984). Putting the keyword method in context. *Journal of Educational Psychology, 76*(4), 598–609.

McKeown, M. G. (1985). The acquisition of word meaning from context by children of high and low ability. *Reading Research Quarterly, 20*(4), 482–496.

Mervis, C. B., & Bertrand, J. (1995). Early lexical acquisition and the vocabulary spurt: A response to Goldfield and Reznick. *Journal of Child Language, 22*, 461–468.

Mintz, T. H., & Gleitman, L. R. (2002). Adjectives really do modify nouns: The incremental and restricted nature of early adjective acquisition. *Cognition, 84*(3), 267–293.

Moon, C., Cooper, R. P., & Fifer, W. P. (1993). Two-day-olds prefer their native language. *Infant Behavior and Development, 16*(4), 495–500.

Nagy, W. E., Herman, P. A., & Anderson, R. C. (1985). Learning words from context. *Reading Research Quarterly, 20*(2), 233–253.

Nagy, W. E., & Scott, J. A. (2000). Vocabulary processes. In M. Kamil, P. Mosenthal, P. Pearson, & R. Barr (Eds.), *Handbook of reading research* (Vol. 3, pp. 269–284). Mahwah, NJ: Erlbaum.

Namy, L. L., & Waxman, S. R. (1998). Words and gestures: Infants' interpretations of different forms of symbolic reference. *Child Development, 69*(2), 295–308.

Newport, E. L. (1990). Maturational constraints on language learning. *Cognitive Science, 14*(1), 11–28.

Newport, E. L., & Aslin, R. N. (2000). Innately constrained learning: Blending old and new approaches to language acquisition. In S. C. Howell, S. A. Fish & T. Keith-Lucas (Eds.), *Proceedings of the 24th annual Boston University Conference on Language Development* (pp. 1–21). Somerville, MA: Cascadilla Press.

Osborn, J. H., & Armbruster, B. B. (2001). Vocabulary acquisition: Direct teaching and indirect learning. *Basic Education, 46*(3), 11–15.

Penno, J. F., Wilkinson, I. A. G., & Moore, D. W. (2002). Vocabulary acquisition from teacher explanation and repeated listening to stories: Do they overcome the Matthew effect? *Journal of Educational Psychology, 94*(1), 23–33.

Pressley, M., Levin, J. R., & Miller, G. E. (1982). The keyword method compared to alternative vocabulary-learning strategies. *Contemporary Educational Psychology, 7*, 50–60.

Reznick, J. S., & Goldfield, B. A. (1992). Rapid change in lexical development in comprehension and production. *Developmental Psychology, 28*(3), 406–413.

Saylor, M. M., & Sabbagh, M. A. (2004). Different kinds of information affect word learning in the preschool years: The case of part-term learning. *Child Development, 75*(2), 395–408.

Shore, W. J., & Durso, F. T. (1990). Partial knowledge in vocabulary acquisition: General constraints and specific detail. *Journal of Educational Psychology, 82*(2), 315–318.

Shore, W. J., & Kempe, V. (1999). The role of sentence context in accessing partial knowledge of word meanings. *Journal of Psycholinguistic Research, 28*(2), 145–163.

Sternberg, R. J. (1987). Most vocabulary is learned from context. In M. McKeown & M. E. Curtis (Eds.), *The nature of vocabulary acquisition* (pp. 89–105). Hillsdale, NJ: Erlbaum.

Sternberg, R. J., & Powell, J. S. (1983). Comprehending verbal comprehension. *American Psychologist, 38*(8), 878–893.

Templin, M. C. (1957). *Certain language skills in children: Their development and interrelationships.* Minneapolis: University of Minnesota Press.

Thiessen, E. D., & Saffran, J. R. (2003). When cues collide: Use of stress and statistical cues to word boundaries by 7- to 9-month-old infants. *Developmental Psychology, 39*(4), 706–716.

Tomasello, M. (2003). *Constructing a language: A usage-based theory of language acquisition.* Cambridge, MA: Harvard University Press.

Werker, J. F., & Tees, R. C. (1999). Influences on infant speech processing: Toward a new synthesis. *Annual Review of Psychology, 50,* 509–535.

Werner, H., & Kaplan, E. (1950). Development of word meaning through verbal context: An experimental study. *Journal of Psychology, 29,* 251–257.

Wilkinson, K. M., Ross, E., & Diamond, A. (2003). Fast mapping of multiple words: Insights into when "the information provided" does and does not equal "the information perceived." *Journal of Applied Developmental Psychology, 24*(6), 739–762.

Woodward, A. L., & Hoyne, K. L. (1999). Infants' learning about words and sounds in relation to objects. *Child Development, 70*(1), 65–77.

CHAPTER 2

Vocabulary Development and the Development of Phonological Awareness Skills in Preschool Children

CHRISTOPHER J. LONIGAN

Learning to read and write is a key developmental milestone in a literate society. Children who learn to read early, without significant difficulties, and well, tend to be more avid readers than children who experience difficulties in learning to read. As a consequence, these children experience more exposure to print, thereby both solidifying and expanding their skills in reading and writing. These reading skills serve as the cornerstone to acquiring content knowledge in other domains both in school and throughout life. Significantly, a relatively large degree of children's exposure to and acquisition of vocabulary and other language skills occurs through reading. In contrast to those children who acquire reading skills early and without much difficulty, children who are poor readers tend to continue to struggle with reading and writing, read less than their peers who are more skilled in reading, and receive less exposure to content knowledge, vocabulary, and other language skills.

Whereas many children learn to read without significant difficulty, a sizable percentage of children experience at least some difficulty, and a significant number of children experience substantial difficulties. Recent results from the National Assessment of Educational Progress (National Center for Education Statistics; November, 2003) indicated that among fourth-grade children in the United States, only 32% performed at or above the proficient level in reading and 37% performed below the basic level in reading (an additional 31% scored at the basic level). Although it is tempting to conclude from these findings that schools are doing worse today in educating children, examination of results of the NAEP across years reveals that the percentage of children performing at proficient levels has remained constant. The problem is not that schools are increasingly failing to teach children to read. The problem is that societal demands for literacy are increasing.

Knowledge about the causes, correlates, and predictors of children's reading success and failure in the early elementary grades has expanded greatly over the past three decades. Much of the research that has contributed to this knowledge base has been funded by the National Institute of Child Health and Human Development (NICHD), and has been summarized in two influential documents: a report of the National Research Council, *Preventing Reading Difficulties in Young Children* (Snow, Burns, & Griffin, 1998), and the *Report of the National Reading Panel: Teaching Children to Read* (NICHD, 2000). This knowledge has been incorporated into many current reading curricula with the intent that children exposed to this pedagogy have a greater chance of learning to read successfully. Methods of identifying, monitoring, and helping struggling readers in kindergarten through grade three have been developed. This knowledge of the development of skilled reading and effective instruction has been incorporated into federal education policy as a part of the No Child Left Behind (NCLB) legislation.

PHONOLOGICAL PROCESSING SKILLS AND READING

The most common cause of early reading difficulties is a weakness in children's *phonological processing skills*, the ability to recognize, manipulate, and use the sound structure of spoken language. Children with poor phonological processing skills have difficulty cracking the alphabetic code that connects the graphemes in written alphabetic languages to the phonemes in spoken language. These children lack an effective strategy for decoding an unfamiliar word when they encounter it in print. They tend to rely too heavily on contextual cues to guess the unfamiliar word rather than using knowledge of phonics to decode it. Consequently, their attempts to decode unfamiliar words result in many word-reading errors. Reading grade-level material is difficult, and many of these children begin to develop negative attitudes about reading, resulting in reduced opportunities to practice reading (Oka & Paris, 1986).

Prior research has identified three interrelated clusters of phonological processing abilities: phonological awareness, phonological access to lexical store, and phonological memory (Wagner & Torgesen, 1987). *Phonological awareness* refers to the ability to detect or manipulate the sound structures of oral language. Research with a variety of populations, using diverse methods, has converged on the finding that phonological awareness plays a key role in the normal acquisition of reading (e.g., Adams, 1990; Byrne & Fielding-Barnsley, 1991; Stanovich, 1992; Wagner & Torgesen, 1987). Children who are better at detecting and manipulating syllables, rhymes, or phonemes are quicker to learn to read; this relation is present even after variability in reading skill due to factors such as IQ, receptive vocabulary, memory skills, and social class is partialled-out (e.g., Bryant, MacLean, Bradley, & Crossland, 1990; Wagner & Torgesen, 1987; Wagner, Torgesen, & Rashotte, 1994).

Phonological access to lexical store refers to the efficiency of retrieval of phonological codes from permanent memory (Wagner & Torgesen, 1987). In older children, lexical access typically is measured as the rate at which an array of letters, digits, or colors can be named. In younger children, lexical access may be measured as the rate at which an array of objects or colors can be named. Lexical access measures are significant predictors of growth in decoding skills in school-age children (Wagner et al., 1994, 1997), and appear to have an independent effect on growth in decoding above that of phonological sensitivity and phonological memory, consistent with the double deficit hypothesis (Bowers & Swanson, 1991; Kirby, Parrila, & Pfeiffer, 2003; Manis, Doi, & Bhadha, 2000; Schatschneider, Fletcher, Francis, Carlson, & Foorman, 2004).

Phonological memory refers to the coding of information in a sound-based representation system for temporary storage (Baddeley, 1986) and is typically measured by immediate recall of verbally presented material (e.g., repetition of nonwords or digits). Results from studies by Wagner et al. (1994, 1997) indicate that phonological memory is a significant correlate of growth in decoding skills but that it does not provide unique predictive variance to growth in decoding beyond that provided by phonological awareness for school-age children.

DEVELOPMENT OF EARLY LITERACY
SKILLS IN PREREADERS

Whereas knowledge of the development of reading in school-age children has been building over the past three decades, it is only within the past 10 years that substantial efforts have been directed toward understanding the development and contribution of reading-related skills prior to school entry. This growing body of research evidence highlights the significance of the preschool period for the development of critically important early literacy skills (e.g., see Snow et al., 1998; Whitehurst & Lonigan, 1998). This area of study is often referred to as "emergent literacy" (Sulzby, 1989; Sulzby & Teale, 1991; Teale & Sulzby, 1986; Whitehurst & Lonigan, 1998). Emergent literacy skills are the developmental precursors to conventional reading and writing skills. Whereas traditional approaches to the study of reading often take as their starting point children's entry into the formal school environment, an emergent literacy approach conceptualizes the acquisition of literacy as a developmental continuum with its origins early in the life of a child, rather than an all-or-none phenomenon that begins when children start school. The emergent literacy approach departs from other perspectives on reading acquisition in suggesting that there is no clear boundary between prereading and reading.

Whitehurst and Lonigan (1998) proposed that emergent and conventional literacy consisted of two interdependent sets of skills and processes, *outside in* and *inside out*. Outside-in skills represent children's understanding of the context in which the target text occurs (e.g., knowledge of the world, semantic knowledge, and knowledge of the written context in which a particular sentence occurs). Inside-out skills represent children's knowledge of the rules for translating the particular writing they are trying to read into meaningful sounds (e.g., letter knowledge, phonological processing skills, and perhaps vocabulary). Inside-out skills reflect code-related components of reading that are mostly specific to reading, whereas outside-in skills reflect more general abilities, like language and general knowledge that support comprehension.

Whitehurst and Lonigan (1998) hypothesized that inside-out (code-related) skills would be most important early in the sequence of learning to read, when the primary task is the development of accurate and fluent decoding skills, whereas outside-in (language) skills would become more important later in the sequence of learning to read, when the primary task in reading shifts to comprehension. Skilled reading is a complex task that requires the coordination and interaction of many skills. Although these processes may be difficult to separate in a mature, skilled reader, it is unlikely that they are well integrated in the early stages of learning to read.

Empirical Links between Early Skills and Later Reading

The National Early Literacy Panel (2005) conducted a meta-analysis of studies published in peer-reviewed English-language journals through 2004 that included data concerning the predictive relation between a skill measured in preschool or kindergarten and reading outcomes for children learning to read in an alphabetic language. A subset of the results of this meta-analysis is shown in Table 2.1. The data reported in the table includes the average zero-order correlation for decoding and reading comprehension across all retrieved studies, the number of studies contributing to each average correlation, and the number of children contributing data to the correlation across studies.

What is apparent from the results of the meta-analysis summarized in Table 2.1 is that measures of both alphabet knowledge and phonological awareness (i.e., measures of detection or manipulation of rhyme, syllables, onset rime, phonemes) have sizable relations with both decoding skills and reading comprehension. Measures of phonological access to lexical store, rapid automatic naming (RAN) tasks (both rapid naming of letters or digits and rapid naming of objects or colors), have moderate relations with both decoding and comprehension. Phonological memory (phonological STM in Table 2.1) has a relatively weak relation with decoding skills and a moderate relation with reading comprehension.

TABLE 2.1. Average Correlations between Predictor Variables Measured in Preschool or Kindergarten and Reading Outcomes Based on the Meta-Analysis of the National Early Literacy Panel

	Reading outcome					
	Decoding			Comprehension		
Predictor variable	Average r	No. of studies	No. of children	Average r	No. of studies	No. of children
Alphabet knowledge	.50	52	7,455	.48	17	2,038
RAN (letters/digits)	.40	12	2,081	.43	3	333
Phonological awareness	.39	69	7,874	.40	20	1,946
Oral language	.29	51	7,152	.26	22	2,607
RAN (objects/colors)	.29	15	2,527	.36	5	573
Phonological STM	.27	31	4,660	.39	13	1,911

Note. RAN, rapid automatized naming (lexical access); STM, short-term memory.

Oral language skills also have a relatively weak relation with both decoding skills and reading comprehension.

Additional analyses revealed that with only a few exceptions, whether these skills were measured in preschool or in kindergarten did not influence the size of the correlations. To the extent that it was possible to examine different aspects of oral language and their relations with decoding skills and reading comprehension in these studies, the results suggested that more complex aspects of oral language, such as listening comprehension, understanding syntax, and definitional vocabulary, had stronger associations with decoding and comprehension than did expressive or receptive vocabulary. Although the average correlations of oral language with both decoding and reading comprehension were only moderate, the strength of the correlation was similar for decoding skills and reading comprehension, a finding not consistent with the distinction between the relative temporal contributions of inside-out and outside-in skills proposed by Whitehurst and Lonigan (1998).

Multivariate studies, in which the longitudinal predictive influences of multiple emergent literacy skills are examined simultaneously, provide some clarification of the findings from these zero-order correlations. Lonigan, Burgess, and Anthony (2000) studied the relations between phonological awareness, letter knowledge, and oral language and decoding skills in a group of preschool children followed longitudinally for 1 year and found that only phonological awareness and letter knowledge contributed unique variance to the prediction of decoding skills. Although oral language was correlated with the code-related skills and decoding, it was not related to reading once phonological awareness and letter knowledge were in the model. Sénéchal and LeFevre (2002) also failed to show an independent relation between oral language and reading in the first and second grades. In one of the most comprehensive studies to date, Storch and Whitehurst (2002) followed 626 children from preschool through fourth grade. They measured code-related skills (print knowledge, print concepts, phonological awareness) and oral language in preschool and kindergarten, and they measured decoding skills and reading comprehension in the first through fourth grades. The results of this study revealed (1) that there was a strong connection between code-related skills and oral language during preschool, (2) that reading skill during the early elementary period was determined primarily by children's code-related skills, and (3) that reading comprehension in later elementary school was significantly influenced by children's oral language skills.

Taken together, these findings indicate that, similar to evidence concerning the development of reading skills in school-age children, phonological processing skills, particularly phonological awareness, and alphabet knowledge are important determinants of early reading acquisition for children when measured in preschool and kindergarten. Multivariate studies (Lonigan, Burgess, Anthony, & Barker, 1998; Lonigan et al., 2000; Sénéchal & LeFevre, 2002; Shatil & Share; 2003; Storch & Whitehurst, 2002) indicate that early in development, code-related skills and oral language skills are interrelated. However, these studies also reveal that the code-related skills are relatively more important for the acquisition of decoding than are oral language skills, whereas both code-related skills and oral language are important for developing good reading comprehension.

A significant finding from longitudinal studies concerns the striking continuity between the levels of reading-related skills displayed by preschool children and the levels of reading-related skills displayed by these children when they are in kindergarten (e.g., Lonigan et al., 2000; Storch & Whitehurst, 2002). This degree of consistency across time in reading-related skills is similar to what is found with grade-school children (Wagner et al., 1994). This high degree of longitudinal continuity indicates that the developmental and environmental antecedents of the skills that underlie the acquisition of reading are found early, and certainly prior to the onset of formal schooling.

Linkage between Oral Language and Phonological Awareness

A substantial body of evidence indicates that phonological awareness is a robust predictor of later reading skills. Evidence indicates that it is a skill that is acquired during the preschool period, prior to formal reading instruction (Lonigan et al., 1998, 2000). However, efforts to identify environmental causes of the development of phonological awareness have not yielded strong or consistent findings (e.g., Raz & Bryant, 1990; Sénéchal & LeFevre, 2002; Sénéchal, LeFevre, Thomas, & Daley, 1998). One possible origin for the development of phonological awareness is the development of vocabulary. As noted above, most multivariate studies do not support a direct role of oral language in the development of decoding. However, phonological awareness and oral language are significantly related during the preschool period (Chaney, 1992; Lonigan et al., 1998, 2000; Storch & Whitehurst, 2002), and studies with slightly older children have demonstrated significant concurrent and longitudinal associations between children's vocabulary skills and their phonological awareness (Bowey, 1994; Cooper, Roth, Speece, & Schatschneider, 2002; Wagner, Torgesen, Laughon, Simmons, & Rashotte, 1993; Wagner et al., 1997).

In longitudinal studies of the development of emergent literacy skills in preschool children, we have found significant concurrent and predictive linkages between preschool children's vocabulary skills and their skills on measures of phonological awareness. These studies included children from more economically advantaged homes as well as children who were from economically disadvantaged backgrounds (e.g., children attending Head Start). For instance, Burgess and Lonigan (1998), in a study of 98 4-year-old children from middle-income backgrounds, found that measures of vocabulary predicted growth in phonological awareness over a 1-year period.

In two more recent samples, we obtained results similar to those of Burgess and Lonigan (1998). The first sample consisted of 108 preschool children recruited from preschool and childcare centers serving children from middle- to upper-income families. The average age of the children was 48.8 months (SD = 7.80; range = 33–64). The majority of the sample was Caucasian (94% Caucasian, 3% African American, 3% other non-Caucasian ethnicity), and 52% of the sample were boys. The average Peabody Picture Vocabulary Test—Revised (PPVT-R) standard score was 98.4 (SD = 15.05; range = 50–138), indicating that the sample, as a whole, was not at high risk for educational difficulties.

At both an initial assessment and a 9-month follow-up assessment, these children completed tasks designed to assess variations of phonological awareness, including rhyme detection or matching, blending of parts of words to form new words, and removing parts of words to form new words (i.e., elision), as well as the PPVT-R, a measure of single-word receptive vocabulary. Table 2.2 shows partial correlations of PPVT-R scores from the initial assessment with scores on the measures of phonological awareness from both the initial and the follow-up assessment, controlling for age. Children's receptive vocabulary scores were significantly correlated with most measures of phonological awareness at both assessment periods. To examine the predictive relations between children's receptive vocabulary scores and changes in phonological awareness skills from initial to follow-up assessment, a series of hierarchical regressions were conducted in which age and initial scores were entered on the first

TABLE 2.2. Partial Correlations between Peabody Picture Vocabulary Test–Revised and Measures of Phonological Awareness at Initial and Follow-Up Assessments in Middle-Income Sample

Phonological awareness measure	Initial score controlling for age	Follow-up score controlling for age	Follow-up score controlling for age and initial score
Rhyme detection	.19†	.04	−.04
Rhyme matching	.22*	.27**	.23*
Blending words	.21*	.21*	.18†
Blending syllables/phonemes	.24*	.22*	.16†
Elision words	.24*	.22*	.18†
Elision syllables/phonemes	.15	.22*	.20*

Note. N = 110. †p < .10; *p < .05; **p < .01.

step and PPVT-R scores were entered on the second step. These regressions revealed that PPVT-R scores contributed significantly or marginally significantly to follow-up phonological awareness scores, with the exception of rhyme detection. The rightmost column of Table 2.2 includes the partial correlations of PPVT-R scores, controlling for both age and initial scores on the phonological awareness measure.

The second sample consisted of 310 children recruited from Head Start centers. The average age of the children was 49.9 months (SD = 9.01; range = 33–79). The majority of the sample was African American (94% African American, 5% Caucasian, 1% other non-Caucasian ethnicity), and 43% of the sample was boys. The average PPVT-R standard score was 76.4 (SD = 15.57; range = 25–130), indicating that the sample, as a whole, was at risk for educational difficulties. As with the middle-income sample, the children completed tasks designed to assess variations of phonological awareness as well as the PPVT-R. These measures were completed at both the beginning and the end of the Head Start year (i.e., in September and May).

Table 2.3 shows partial correlations of PPVT-R scores from the initial assessment with scores on the measures of phonological awareness from both the initial and the follow-up assessment, controlling for age. Children's receptive vocabulary scores were significantly correlated with most measures of phonological awareness at the initial assessment but were generally correlated more weakly with phonological awareness at the follow-up assessment. Again, a series of hierarchical regressions was conducted in which age and initial scores were entered on the first step

TABLE 2.3. Partial Correlations between Peabody Picture Vocabulary Test–Revised and Measures of Phonological Awareness at Initial and Follow-Up Assessments in Head Start Sample

Phonological awareness measure	Initial score controlling for age	Follow-up score controlling for age	Follow-up score controlling for age and initial score
Rhyme detection	.05	.01	.01
Rhyme matching	.02	.12*	.12*
Blending words	.19***	.01	.01
Blending syllables/phonemes	.26***	−.04	−.05
Elision words	.27***	.12*	.12*
Elision syllables/phonemes	.16**	.12*	.12*

Note. N = 350. *p < .05; **p < .01; ***p < .001.

and PPVT-R scores were entered on the second step. These regressions revealed that PPVT-R scores contributed significantly to follow-up scores on the rhyme matching and elision tasks. The rightmost column of Table 2.3 includes the partial correlations of PPVT-R scores, controlling for both age and initial scores on the phonological awareness measure.

Results from these and other studies indicate that there are concurrent and longitudinal relations between phonological awareness and vocabulary. Additionally, some data suggest that vocabulary is predictive of growth in phonological awareness. One potential explanation for the linkage between vocabulary and phonological awareness is the *lexical restructuring model* (LRM; Fowler, 1991; Metsala & Walley, 1998). According to the LRM, representations of words in the lexicon of very young children are holistic (i.e., represented as whole words) and gradually become more fine-grained and segmented during the preschool and early school-age years. Lexical restructuring is assumed to be a function of vocabulary growth that occurs in response to the learning of individual words within a spectrum of phonological similarity (i.e., neighborhood density). Evidence suggests greater segmental representation for high-frequency words and words from dense phonological neighborhoods (see Walley, Metsala, & Garlock, 2003). Stated simply, as children learn more words, they discover that it is more efficient to remember and recognize words in terms of their constituent parts rather than as wholes. Children who have small vocabularies may be limited in their phonological awareness because their memory for words has not moved from global to segmented. These findings suggest that vocabulary development may set the stage for the emergence of phonological awareness, which in this view is dependent on access to segmentally represented speech sounds.

Examining the Causal Status of Vocabulary in the Development of Phonological Awareness

Whereas there are data to suggest word frequency and neighborhood density effects on segmental representation and data to suggest that vocabulary size is related to phonological awareness skills, at present, all research in this area is correlational. This leaves open the question of whether or not vocabulary development really *causes* the development of phonological awareness. In an earlier oral language intervention study involving shared reading (Lonigan, Anthony, Bloomfield, Dyer, & Samwel, 1999), we found a small but statistically significant effect of the intervention on measures of phonological awareness. However, the design of the study did not allow us to isolate the effect as a result of an effective vocabulary intervention.

To partially address this question, a reanalysis of an early literacy intervention study (see Lonigan, 2003, 2004) was conducted. In this study, 286 preschool children (mean age = 53.8 months; *SD* = 5.66) were randomly assigned to one of five conditions. The majority of the children were African American (83% African American, 13% Caucasian, 4% other minority), and 54% were boys. The average PPVT-R standard score was 76.9 (*SD* = 15.75), indicating that the sample, as a whole, was at risk for educational difficulties. The intervention conditions consisted of partially crossed combinations of oral language intervention, phonological awareness intervention, and print knowledge intervention versus control. All children were attending preschools and the intervention programs were administered as small-group pull-out interventions lasting approximately 15 minutes a day for most of a school year. This reanalysis addressed four questions:

1. Did the vocabulary intervention have an impact on children's vocabulary?
2. Did the phonological awareness intervention have an impact on children's phonological awareness?
3. Did the phonological awareness intervention have an impact on children's vocabulary?
4. Did the vocabulary intervention have an impact on children's phonological awareness?

To address the four questions, groups were created for children who had received the oral language intervention (vs. those who had not) and for children who had received the phonological awareness intervention (vs. those who had not). Analyses examined differences between these intervention groups on two variables that reflected gains between pretest and posttest in standardized scores for either vocabulary or phonological awareness. Vocabulary was indexed by the Expressive One-Word Picture Vocabulary Test—Revised (EOWPVT-R). Phonological awareness was indexed by a composite of age-standardized scores on measures of rhyme, blending, and elision.

Results for the vocabulary measure are shown in Figure 2.1. Children who had received the oral language intervention experienced significantly more vocabulary growth on the EOWPVT-R than did children who had not received the oral language intervention, $F(1, 284) = 5.14$, $p = .02$. In contrast, the phonological awareness intervention did not have an effect on vocabulary growth, $F(1, 284) = 0.17$, $p = .68$. Results for the phonological awareness composite measure are shown in Figure 2.2. Children who had received the phonological awareness intervention experienced significantly more growth in phonological awareness skills than did children who had not received the phonological awareness intervention, $F(1, 284) = 8.76$, $p = .003$. In contrast to the lack of a crossover effect of the phonological awareness intervention on vocabulary

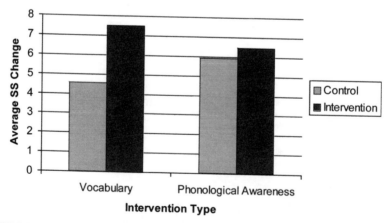

FIGURE 2.1. Effects of vocabulary or phonological awareness intervention on growth in vocabulary skills. The vocabulary intervention had a significant positive effect on children's vocabulary skills. In contrast, the phonological awareness intervention did not have an effect on children's vocabulary.

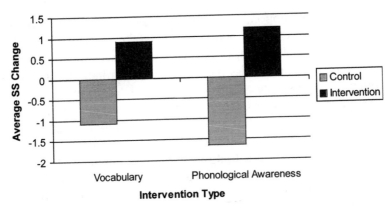

FIGURE 2.2. Effects of vocabulary or phonological awareness intervention on growth in phonological awareness skills. Both the vocabulary intervention and the phonological awareness intervention had a significant positive effect on children's phonological awareness skills.

growth, children in the oral language intervention group experienced significantly more growth in phonological awareness skills than did children who had not been exposed to the oral language intervention, $F(1, 284) = 4.31, p = .04$.

The results of this reanalysis are supportive of the hypothesis that vocabulary development is causal in the development of phonological awareness. These findings, representing a partial dissociation effect, indicate that the effects of the oral language intervention on children's phonological awareness were not simply the result of receiving an intervention (i.e., there was no impact of the phonological awareness intervention on children's vocabulary skills). Clearly, more research is needed to confirm this result, perhaps specifically manipulating vocabulary exposure in a vocabulary intervention along the dimensions of word frequency and phonological neighborhood density. However, this study is one of the first studies of preschool children to identify a potentially causal factor not involving direct training of the skill in the development of phonological awareness.

CONCLUSIONS

The evidence reviewed in this chapter indicates that the developmental origins of learning to read begin prior to the onset of formal reading instruction. Research supports a linkage between phonological processing skills, print knowledge, and oral language in the preschool period and reading in the school period, once formal reading instruction has commenced. Early reading development (i.e., decoding) appears to be most dependent on code-related skills. Later reading development (i.e., comprehension) is dependent both on code-related skills and on oral language skills. Overall, these findings indicate that these early literacy skills are relative modular with respect to their relation to later reading. However, the evidence indicates that these emergent literacy skills are also partially interdependent. Phonological awareness, a substantial predictor of later reading, is correlated both concurrently and longitudinally with oral language skills both in the preschool period and beyond. One possible explanation of this connection is a role for vocabulary development in setting the stage for the emergence of phonological awareness. According to the LRM, as children develop larger vocabularies, the lexicon is represented more segmentally, allowing access to smaller parts of words required by phonological awareness tasks. A reanalysis of data from an early literacy intervention study provided support for this hypothesis in that an effective vocabulary intervention also resulted in growth in phonological awareness, whereas an effective phonological awareness intervention had no effect on vocabulary growth. Given this correlational and experimental evidence, it appears that phonological awareness is, in part, a product of the development of vocabulary.

ACKNOWLEDGMENTS

Preparation of this work was supported, in part, by grants from the National Institute of Child Health and Human Development (Nos. HD38880, HD36067, HD36509, and HD30988), the Administration for Children and Families (No. 90YF0023), and the National Science Foundation (No. REC-0128970). Views expressed herein are solely those of the author and have not been cleared by the grantors.

REFERENCES

Adams, M. J. (1990). *Learning to read: Thinking and learning about print.* Cambridge, MA: MIT Press.
Baddeley, A. (1986). *Working memory.* New York: Oxford University Press.
Bowers, P. G., & Swanson, L. B. (1991). Naming speed deficits in reading dis-

ability: Multiple measures of a singular process. *Journal of Experimental Child Psychology, 51,* 195–219.

Bowey, J. A. (1994). Phonological sensitivity in novice readers and nonreaders. *Journal of Experimental Child Psychology, 58,* 134–159.

Bryant, P. E., MacLean, M., Bradley, L. L., & Crossland, J. (1990). Rhyme and alliteration, phoneme detection, and learning to read. *Developmental Psychology, 26,* 429–438.

Burgess, S. R., & Lonigan, C. J. (1998). Bidirectional relations of phonological sensitivity and prereading abilities: Evidence from a preschool sample. *Journal of Experimental Child Psychology, 70,* 117–141.

Byrne, B., & Fielding-Barnsley, R. F. (1991). Evaluation of a program to teach phonemic awareness to young children. *Journal of Educational Psychology, 82,* 805–812.

Chaney, C. (1992). Language development, metalinguistic skills, and print awareness in 3-year-old children. *Applied Psycholinguistics, 13,* 485–514.

Cooper, D. H., Roth, F. P., Speece, D. L., & Schatschneider, C. (2002). The contribution of oral language to the development of phonological awareness. *Applied Psycholinguistics, 23,* 399–416.

Fowler, A. E. (1991). How early phonological development might set the stage for phoneme awareness. In S. A. Brady & D. P. Shankweiler (Eds.), *Phonological processes in literacy* (pp. 97–117). Hillsdale, NJ: Erlbaum.

Kirby, J. R., Parrila, R. K., & Pfeiffer, S. L. (2003). Naming speed and phonological awareness as predictors of reading development. *Journal of Educational Psychology, 95,* 453–464.

Lonigan, C. J. (2003). Development and promotion of emergent literacy skills in preschool children at-risk of reading difficulties. In B. Foorman (Ed.), *Preventing and remediating reading difficulties: Bringing science to scale* (pp. 23–50). Timonium, MD: York Press.

Lonigan, C. J. (2004, August). *Evaluation of components of a pre-literacy intervention with children at-risk.* Paper presented at the annual convention of the American Psychological Association, Honolulu, HI.

Lonigan, C. J., Anthony, J. L., Bloomfield, B., Dyer, S. M., & Samwel, C. (1999). Effects of two preschool shared reading interventions on the emergent literacy skills of children from low-income families. *Journal of Early Intervention, 22,* 306–322.

Lonigan, C. J., Burgess, S. R., & Anthony, J. L. (2000). Development of emergent literacy and early reading skills in preschool children: Evidence from a latent variable longitudinal study. *Developmental Psychology, 36,* 596–613.

Lonigan, C. J., Burgess, S. R., Anthony, J. L., & Barker, T. A. (1998). Development of phonological sensitivity in two- to five-year-old children. *Journal of Educational Psychology, 90,* 294–311.

Manis, F. R., Doi, L. M., & Bhadha, B. (2000). Naming speed, phonological awareness, and orthographic knowledge in second graders. *Journal of Learning Disabilities, 33,* 325–333, 374.

Metsala, J. L., & Walley, A. C. (1998). Spoken vocabulary growth and the segmental restructuring of lexical representations: Precursors to phonemic awareness and early reading ability. In J. L. Metsala & L. C. Ehri (Eds.), *Word recognition in beginning literacy* (pp. 89–120). Mahwah, NJ: Erlbaum.

National Center for Education Statistics. (2003). *The nation's report card: Fourth-grade reading 2003*. Retrieved Nov. 12, 2003, from nces.ed.gov/nationsreportcard/reading/results.

National Early Literacy Panel. (2005). *Report on a synthesis of early predictors of reading*. Louisville, KY: Author.

National Institute of Child Health and Human Development. (2000). *Report of the National Reading Panel: Teaching children to read*. Washington, DC: U.S. Department of Health and Human Services.

Oka, E., & Paris, S. (1986). Patterns of motivation and reading skills in under-achieving children. In S. Ceci (Ed.), *Handbook of cognitive, social, and neuropsychological aspects of learning disabilities* (Vol. 2, pp. 116–145). Hillsdale, NJ: Erlbaum.

Raz, I. S., & Bryant, P. (1990). Social background, phonological awareness and children's reading. *British Journal of Developmental Psychology, 8*, 209–225.

Schatschneider, C., Fletcher, J. M., Francis, D. F., Carlson, C. D., & Foorman, B. R. (2004). Kindergarten prediction of reading skills: A longitudinal comparative analysis. *Journal of Educational Psychology, 96*, 265–282.

Sénéchal, M., & LeFevre, J. (2002). Parental involvement in the development of children's reading skill: A five-year longitudinal study. *Child Development, 73*, 445–460.

Sénéchal, M., LeFevre, J., Thomas, E. M., & Daley, K. E. (1998). Differential effects of home literacy experiences on the development of oral and written language. *Reading Research Quarterly, 13*, 96–116.

Shatil, E., & Share, D. L. (2003). Cognitive antecedents of early reading ability: A test of the modularity hypothesis. *Journal of Experimental Child Psychology, 86*, 1–31.

Snow, C. E., Burns, M. S., & Griffin, P. (Eds.). (1998). *Preventing reading difficulties in young children*. Washington, DC: National Academy Press.

Stanovich, K. E. (1992). Speculations on the causes and consequences of individual differences in early reading acquisition. In P. B. Gough, L. C. Ehri, & R. Treiman (Eds.), *Reading acquisition* (pp. 307–342). Hillsdale, NJ: Erlbaum.

Storch, S. A., & Whitehurst, G. J. (2002). Oral language and code-related precursors to reading: Evidence from a longitudinal structural model. *Developmental Psychology, 38*, 934–947.

Sulzby, E. (1989). Assessment of writing and of children's language while writing. In L. Morrow & J. Smith (Eds.), *The role of assessment and measurement in early literacy instruction* (pp. 83–109). Englewood Cliffs, NJ: Prentice-Hall.

Sulzby, E., & Teale, W. (1991). Emergent literacy. In R. Barr, M. Kamil, P. Mosenthal, & P. D. Pearson (Eds.), *Handbook of reading research* (Vol. 2, pp. 727–758). New York: Longman.

Teale, W. H., & Sulzby, E. (Eds.). (1986). *Emergent literacy: Writing and reading*. Norwood, NJ: Ablex.

Wagner, R. K., & Torgesen, J. K. (1987). The natural of phonological processing and its causal role in the acquisition of reading skills. *Psychological Bulletin, 101*, 192–212.

Wagner, R. K., Torgesen, J. K., Laughon, P., Simmons, K., & Rashotte, C. A. (1993). The development of young readers' phonological processing abilities. *Journal of Educational Psychology, 85*, 1–20.

Wagner, R. K., Torgesen, J. K., & Rashotte, C. A. (1994). Development of reading-related phonological processing abilities: New evidence of bidirectional causality from a latent variable longitudinal study. *Developmental Psychology, 30*, 73–87.

Wagner, R. K., Torgesen, J. K., Rashotte, C. A., Hecht, S. A., Barker, T. A., Burgess, S. R., et al. (1997). Changing relations between phonological processing abilities and word-level reading as children develop from beginning to skilled readers: A 5-year longitudinal study. *Developmental Psychology, 33*, 468–479.

Walley, A. C., Metsala, J. L., & Garlock, V. M. (2003). Spoken vocabulary growth: Its role in the development of phoneme awareness and early reading ability. *Reading and Writing: An Interdisciplinary Journal, 16*, 5–20.

Whitehurst, G. J., & Lonigan, C. J. (1998). Child development and emergent literacy. *Child Development, 68*, 848–872.

CHAPTER 3

Parents' Support of Children's Language Provides Support for Later Reading Competence

SUSAN H. LANDRY
KAREN E. SMITH

Basic science research and studies examining influences on children's development reaffirms that brain development in the early years is influenced by experience that affects learning (DiPietro, 2000; Dawson, Klinger, Panagiotides, Hill, & Spieker, 1992; Elman et al., 1996). So much of the brain is devoted to processing language that it appears to be socially inclined and develops most effectively from interactions with other people. Language is a critically important emergent literacy skill that is known to predict later reading competence (Butler, Marsh, Sheppard, & Sheppard, 1985). This is particularly true for reading comprehension because language lays the foundation for understanding concepts that are important for comprehending meaning in print (Whitehurst & Lonigan, 1998). For example, language development includes understanding a broad range of vocabulary, comprehending grammatically appropriate phrases and sentences (i.e., grammar, syntax), and using words together to convey meaning (i.e., semantics) (e.g., Dore, 1979). As these are all significant for the process of comprehending text, it is important to understand how the early environment best supports more optimal language development. Such information should provide insight into the process of enhancing language, a critical foundation skill for later reading competence.

In the early years, input from parents is a major means by which children learn about the natural links between objects and actions and how to understand and talk about past and current experiences (Bridges, 1979; Smith, Landry, & Swank, 2000). Children have exposure to this form of rich language input during everyday conversations with parents and other caregivers, as well as during shared book reading and play activities. At these times, children are exposed to a range of vocabulary, have the opportunity to ask and answer questions, and express their own ideas. Research demonstrates that this process enhances children's vocabulary as well as their cognitive and memory skills (Landry, Miller-Loncar, Smith, & Swank, 2002). Recently, links were identified between parental use of rich language input at 3 years of age with higher language development at 4 years of age that, in turn, predicted higher reading comprehension skills at 10 years of age (Dietrich, Assel, Swank, Smith, & Landry, 2006).

WHAT IS KNOWN ABOUT PARENTAL LANGUAGE INPUT ACROSS EARLY CHILDHOOD

Characteristics of parent–child interactions that are important for children's language development include features of the parents' language input (e.g., word expansion, questioning) (Snow, 1977), language input in different social contexts (e.g., book reading, games) (Whitehurst & Lonigan, 1998), and parents' speech content (Hart & Risley, 1995; Huttenlocher, Haight, Bryk, Seltzer, & Lyons, 1991). The processing of speech sounds begins in early infancy. Indeed, experiments have demonstrated that by 4 months of age infants no longer attend to sounds that are not part of the primary language to which they are exposed (Gopnick, Meltzoff, & Kuhl, 1999; Kuhl et al., 1997). This work, combined with that of others (e.g., Bruner, 1977), highlights the importance of conversations between parents and their young infants.

Other work highlights the importance of parental responsiveness during these interactions. Parents' sensitive responsiveness to early communication, including infant distress signals, is thought to promote future signaling and the beginning of parent–infant "conversation" (Anderson, 1977; Bornstein & Tamis-LeMonda, 1989). When conversing with their infants and young children to support language learning, parents adjust their speech by simplifying and repeating utterances, as well as by using interrogatives and questions at surprisingly high levels (Snow, 1977). Parents also adjust the quality of their voice—for example, by using a higher voice pitch and greater prosody (Fernald, 1992). In these early conversations, contingent vocal responsivity and imitation of vocalizations are two additional important features of parent–infant conversation (Hardy-Brown & Plomin, 1985). Researchers such as Bruner (1977) highlight the importance of the reciprocal nature of parent–infant conversations where parents attempt to communicate specific information to the infant and wait for information from the infant to guide their further input.

Parental adjustment of language input to match children's language-processing ability continues into the toddler/preschool period. During this time, a decrease in parental imitation of young children's language as well as an expansion of their utterances has been documented (Slobin, 1968). Now, in contrast to the infancy period, a parent's conversation involves a greater frequency of description of objects, events, and actions (Nelson, 1973); asking questions (Moerk, 1975); and discussing past and future experiences (Moerk, 1975). It is important for children to receive language input that, for example, assists them in understanding what objects are called and how objects and actions go together in order for them to develop vocabulary and semantic knowledge (Weizman & Snow, 2001). Although parental language input that assists children in knowing what is expected of them (i.e., high levels of directiveness) appears important for very young children, parental shifting to a greater reliance on comments and questions beginning in the toddler period appears to facilitate the child's language development and problem-solving ability (Landry, Smith, Swank, & Miller-Loncar, 2000). Verbalizations that are low in directing children's actions also have been related to more initiative and verbal input in shared writing activities between parents and preschoolers (Burns & Casbergue, 1992).

OTHER PARENTAL BEHAVIORS THAT SUPPORT LANGUAGE DEVELOPMENT

In addition to the type of language input that children receive, characteristics of the way in which children receive this input are important in language development, particularly their exposure to a highly responsive and reciprocal caregiving style (Bornstein & Tamis-LeMonda, 1989; Londerville & Main, 1981; Olson, Bates, & Bayles, 1984). This style includes a constellation of behaviors that provide emotional support, reciprocal communication, acceptance of the need for growing independence, and cognitive stimulation that scaffolds the young child's early learning. While these behaviors cut across different theoretical frameworks (e.g., attachment, sociocultural), there is evidence that together they provide the most optimum support for development (Bornstein & Tamis-LeMonda, 1989). Vygotsky (1978) emphasizes the importance of the social context for understanding the origins of children's independent functioning and provides a strong conceptual basis for understanding the type of support young children need in social interactions.

Initially, in order to learn from interactions, young children need to develop a set of behaviors known as *joint attention skills* that include coordinating eye gaze between caregivers and objects of interest as well as the combined use of gestures, verbalizations, and expression of affect to respond to and direct another's attention (Adamson & Bakeman, 1991). Vygotsky proposes that children have a "zone of proximal development" where adult support is critical for elevating a child's ability to accomplish goals beyond his or her autonomous performance. Within this social context the parent provides "other regulation" through specific interactive behaviors that are necessary for the very young child to accomplish tasks. Shared engagement with objects and others is a complex attentional process given that young children must shift attention from person to object and back to person, as well as coordinate gestures, vocalizations, and affect to communicate their interest and respond appropriately (Bakeman & Adamson, 1984). One example of parental scaffolding is to maintain rather than to redirect young children's focus of attention, which supports increased levels of learning in an object-centered activity by not placing high demands on their immature attentional and cognitive capacity (Landry, Garner, Swank, & Baldwin, 1996). In our longitudinal study, we found that when provided across early childhood, parenting behaviors such as maintaining and building on interests that can be considered other regulation predicted faster rates of language growth through age 8 years (Landry, Smith, & Swank, 2003). Thus, there is evidence supporting the need for consistency and intensity in the use of a style that is responsive to children's interests and abilities and provides them with rich stimulation within a context of nurturance and emotional support.

The importance of different learning experiences in supporting the distinct domains of emerging literacy skills has been described by Whitehurst and Lonigan (1998). In their model, children's language competence is highly influenced in the early years by exposure to language in the home environment. In contrast, phonological awareness and alphabet knowledge are particularly sensitive to experiences that explicitly teach these skills such as those that might occur in pre-K classroom experiences. The results of this study highlight the critical nature of parental language input and the importance of understanding its impact for later reading.

CHILDREN LESS LIKELY TO RECEIVE RICH LANGUAGE INPUT AT HOME

Although research clearly defines the type of parental input that is critical for optimal early language development, there are striking differences in whether this occurs across families that vary in economic and educational backgrounds. Dramatic differences have been documented for the language children from lower socioeconomic families heard from their parents as compared to those from middle and more affluent levels. Children from lower income families heard a paucity of vocabulary that included rich content (Hart & Risley, 1995). The use of rich and varied vocabulary is one of the most important types of parental input for understanding differences in children's later language, and potentially reading, competence.

Parents of lower socioeconomic status also are at highest risk for difficulty in providing children with responsive interactions because of life stresses, psychological distress, and poor parental role models (Conger, McCarty, Yang, Lahey, & Kropp, 1984; McLoyd, 1990). Poverty has been associated with low levels of affective expression, sensitivity, and responsiveness and more frequent use of power-assertive control techniques. Thus children with parents demonstrating these risk factors are the least likely to receive the type of responsive parenting known to predict more optimal outcomes. Given the importance of early experiences for establishing positive trajectories of children's development, models are needed that demonstrate how to enhance responsive caregiving.

ENHANCING RESPONSIVE CAREGIVING

In light of the large number of families that are at risk for difficulties in providing appropriate levels and types of stimulation known to promote children's language development, historically there have been programs to facilitate more optimal parent–child interactions. The emphasis of these programs often has been placed on supporting parents' ability to (1) carefully observe their children and respond sensitively to their signals

(Resnick, Armstrong, & Carter, 1988; Scarr-Salapatek & Williams, 1973), (2) engage children in specific developmental activities (Brooks-Gunn, Klebanov, Liaw, & Spiker, 1993; Erickson, 1989), and (3) encourage children's use of language at increased levels through shared play and book-reading interactions (Royce, Darlington, & Murray, 1983). Outcomes from intervention studies show at least short-term increases in children's language and cognitive abilities. However, in light of the large body of research examining effects of parent interventions, results often are not impressive (e.g., St. Pierre & Layzer, 1998). Less-than-impressive results may be due to the lack of a clearly defined focus that links intervention goals to theoretical models and incorporates aspects of the family's social context as well as the insufficient intensity of some programs (Drummond, Weir, & Kysela, 2002; Gomby, Culross, & Behrmann, 1999; Hebbeler & Gerlach-Downie, 2002).

A factor critical to facilitating change in parent behaviors, but less often specifically addressed, is the ability of the facilitator to assume the role of "change agent" (Hebbeler & Gerlach-Downie, 2002). In addition, interventions rarely incorporate adult learning approaches into facilitating change in caregiver behavior (Bransford, Brown, & Cocking, 2000). Using an adult learning model, facilitators outline what new knowledge and skills will be learned through their participation, how this knowledge and these new skills can be used in daily practice, and what specific activities will lead to this learning. Better outcomes should occur when adults actively construct knowledge from an organized approach that allows them to use a set of behaviors in real-life contexts. Thus adult learners need to be supported within a scaffolding framework similar to that described for children's learning. In this process, a facilitator helps the caregiver move to a higher level of understanding and action in ways that build on previously learned experiences.

DEVELOPMENT OF A RESPONSIVE PARENTING INTERVENTION

In response to some of the limitations identified in previous interventions, in a project funded by the National Institutes of Health (NIH; Grant No. HD 36099), we developed and examined the efficacy of an intervention across early childhood to enhance parents' use of a broad constellation of responsive behaviors including rich language input when interacting with their children. The model was informed by several theoretical and research frameworks: attachment (Ainsworth, Blehar, Waters, & Wall, 1978; Sroufe, 1983), sociocultural (Rogoff, 1990; Vygotsky, 1978), and socialization of young children (Grusec & Goodnow, 1994; Maccoby & Martin, 1983). For example, the work of a number of investigators including Rovee-Collier (1996) describes a theory of "time windows," where children's repeated successful experiences in learning activities help them develop networks of associations that ultimately develop into memories. Children build networks of associations through their learn- ing experiences by assimilating new information into memories from a previous related experience. Children develop more efficient memories (i.e., learned skills) if they have successful learning experiences that occur while previous memories are still retained.

The maternal behaviors targeted in the intervention also were em- phasized due to findings from our longitudinal study (funded by the NIH) of parenting and children's long-term cognitive and social outcomes (Grant No. HD24128) (e.g., Landry, Smith, Swank, Assel, & Vellet, 2001). In 1990 and 1991 a cohort of 360 families were recruited. The children in these families have been evaluated eight times beginning at 6 months through 10 years of age, with continued participation by 72% of the sample. The primary caregiver has been the biological mother for the majority of the study children (98%), although about 4% of the children have had changes in the primary caregiver over time. Because of our interest in examining both parenting and biological influences on children's development, the cohort included children born at term (n = 134) and at very low birth weight (n = 236). However, in this chap- ter we emphasize results that were comparable across all children.

All children were from economically disadvantaged families. At each time point, a broad range of information was collected through home visits including standardized assessment of language and cognitive development. In addition, parent–child interactions were observed in two contexts: toy- centered play and daily routines. In both contexts, observers coded a range of parent responsiveness behaviors. The focus on these interactive be- haviors was informed by our previous research and that of others indicat- ing the importance of these behaviors for children's development.

The mothers observed in this study provided verbal associations with their children during situations such as meals, hair brushing, or card games. During these activities mothers were observed to facilitate their children's concept development in a number of ways. Examples included helping them understand how objects were grouped together in the home and how an activity in which they were involved related to a previous experience. However, an important finding was the low incidence of this type of observed verbal input. On average, it occurred in only about 18% of the interactions in this sample of families from lower economic backgrounds, with as few as 10% and as many as 30% of the interactions containing this type of rich input. These results are consistent with that of other researchers and further confirm the relatively low levels of rich verbal input to which children from poverty are exposed in the home environment (e.g., Hart & Risley, 1995).

There was considerable variability in other interactive behaviors that related, in part, to mother's level of education, social support, and parenting belief systems (Landry et al., 2001; Smith, Landry, Miller-Loncar, & Swank, 1997; Smith et al., 2000). Within this cohort, four subgroups of mothers were identified who varied in the level and consistency of their use of responsive behaviors across early childhood (Landry et al., 2001). While mothers were grouped on their use of contingent responsiveness, cluster membership showed strong correlations with the use of a broad range of responsive interactive behaviors including rich language input, maintaining attentional focus, and restrictiveness. One group of mothers demonstrated high levels and consistent use of responsiveness across infancy and the preschool period while a second group showed minimal use of this behavior in both developmental periods. Two inconsistent groups were found, with one demonstrating high levels of responsiveness that were comparable to that of the first group of mothers during infancy. However, their responsiveness declined significantly in the preschool period. The final group showed low levels of responsiveness across infancy with some increases evident in the preschool period.

When examining the association of mothers' group membership with children's cognitive and social outcomes through 4 years of age, only children parented by mothers with high levels of responsiveness that were consistent across time showed development at expected rates by entry into kindergarten. The importance of the consistency in this behavior in early childhood was documented by similar findings through 8 years of age even when controlling for parenting at 6 and 8 years of age (Landry, Smith, Swank, Assel, & Vellet, 2001; Landry, Smith, & Swank, 2003).

Parents' consistent use of specialized support (e.g., maintaining, provision of information, contingent responsiveness) is thought to be the process by which infants and young children can have a series of successful experiences upon which to build networks of associations.

When mothers do not require their young children to shift their attention, but rather maintain their focus of attention and assist their learning through verbal and physical demonstrations, they are more likely to learn from the experience. If this specialized support is consistently provided, children are more likely to build language concepts to establish a more optimal foundation upon which later, more complex behaviors are built.

TESTING A MODEL TO ENHANCE PARENT RESPONSIVENESS: PLAYING AND LEARNING STRATEGIES

In the Playing and Learning Strategies (PALS) intervention, we targeted a responsive caregiving style that was comprised of three components. Each component included a group of behaviors selected because of the consistent research support for their predictive role in development and their importance in our NIH-funded, 12-year longitudinal study: (1) support of signals and interests, (2) quality of cognitive and language input, and (3) emotional support.

Behaviors chosen to operationalize each of the components were expected to be discrete but to complement each other and together provide a more complete picture of responsive parenting. We included an affective emotional component, as this support has been demonstrated to be critically important in early childhood by researchers of attachment theory (Ainsworth et al., 1978). Our responsive style was expanded to include the contingently responsive and cognitively stimulating components because recent work has included these behaviors in responsiveness constructs (Darling & Steinberg, 1993; Maccoby & Martin, 1983). The components and their behaviors and rationale for their importance are as follows:

Component I: Support of Signals and Interests

Contingent responsiveness is a behavior consistent with attachment theory that posits a special role for the early caregiving environment for providing a foundation that allows children to feel secure and develop trust in their caregivers (Ainsworth et al., 1978). This is described as a three-term chain of events in which (1) the child signals, (2) the caregiver responds promptly and sensitively to that signal, and (3) the child experiences a positive outcome (Bornstein & Tamis-LeMonda, 1989). Another behavior, maintaining rather than redirecting, attends to child signals and supports interests and is posited by sociocultural theories as important for development because it is responsive to children's capacities and levels of learning (Darling & Steinberg, 1993; Maccoby & Martin, 1983; Tomasello & Farrar, 1986; Vygotsky, 1978). While both behaviors support infants' more active participation in interactions, the mechanism that explains this support is different. Contingent responsiveness provides the infant with a predictable, positive response that encourages greater trust in the caregiving environment. This trust, in turn, promotes a willingness to continue to signal and, ultimately, to cooperate with caregiver requests (Ainsworth et al., 1978; Maccoby & Martin, 1983). In contrast, maintaining, as opposed to redirecting, supports the infant's immature attentional and cognitive capacities by not requiring a shift in attentional focus. A decreased demand on attention allows greater ability to sustain focus, understand and build knowledge about aspects of the interaction, and organize a more competent response (Akhtar, Dunham, & Dunham, 1991). Descriptive studies have shown that contingent responsiveness and maintaining predict more extensive vocabulary (e.g., Akhtar et al., 1991; Tomasello & Farrar, 1986) and faster rates of growth in language (Landry et al., 2002).

Component II: Quality of Cognitive and Language Input

In support of the young child's immature language, the caregiver's role includes helping with the development of vocabulary and understanding of simple relations (Bridges, 1979; LeMonda, Bornstein, & Baumwell, 2001). This includes provision of labels and verbal causal information, often done in combination with gestural and physical demonstrations that facilitate focused attention. Quality of cognitive and language input, the second component, is comprised not only of rich information, but also includes requests for child engagement (e.g., verbalizations, following requests) and affirmation of actions. This might occur through a mother's support in specific learning activities like constructing puzzles or reading books together, as well as during daily activities like dressing where concepts and vocabulary can be highlighted. Thus children receive information that advances an understanding of their world in a way that encourages active learning. When rich language input is combined with caregiver behaviors that are attentive and responsive to the child's interests, language and cognitive outcomes are enhanced (Landry et al., 2001; LeMonda et al., 2001).

Component III: Supportive Emotional Climate

The supportive emotional behaviors established by high degrees of warmth and the absence of highly negative behaviors (e.g., harsh voice tone, physical intrusiveness) are thought to communicate affectively the caregiver's interest and acceptance (Darling & Steinberg, 1993). The mutual accommodation of a warm responsive style facilitates children's understanding of cause and effect, alters openness to parental socialization practices, and facilitates learning how to make appropriate choices (Grusec & Goodnow, 1994; Maccoby & Martin, 1983; Weiss, Dodge, Bates, & Pettit, 1992). Maternal affective expressions also have been linked to children's cognitive processes by eliciting attention and increasing the ability to process parental input and engage in independent play (Cohn & Tronick, 1983; Hoffman, 1983; Termine & Izard, 1988). In contrast, a highly intrusive style interferes with children experiencing a supportive "give-and-take" relationship (Grusec & Goodnow, 1994; Maccoby & Martin, 1983), contributes to behavioral disorganization (Landry et al., 2000), and disrupts normal social and cognitive developmental trajectories (Landry et al., 2001; Landry, Smith, Miller-Loncar, & Swank, 1997; Smith et al., 2000).

As with the quality of language input, parents from lower economic and educational backgrounds are less likely to use these types of responsive behaviors when interacting with their children. Parents living in poverty display low levels of affective expression and sensitivity and more frequently use power-assertive control techniques, based in part on putting greater value on compliance than on child autonomy (e.g., Conger et al., 1984; McLoyd, 1990). Such parents are more likely to believe that they have less impact on their children's outcomes (McLoyd, 1990). Such attitudes are associated with lower levels of sensitive and responsive parenting (Landry et al., 1997). Other parenting factors associated with lower economic circumstances include high levels of social stress without adequate social support (Landry & Chapieski, 1989). Social support can have a direct impact on parent beliefs (e.g., reasons for children's behavior) that, in turn, affect parents' ability to effectively deal with children's behaviors (Bridges, 1979; Landry et al., 1997; LeMonda et al., 2001).

Although these risk factors may negatively impact parenting in infancy, their impact may be even greater in the toddler and preschool period. As toddlers seek greater independence, these risk factors associated with lower SES may be detrimental to parents learning how to

adapt to their children's changing needs. As the toddler/preschool period requires an acceptance of children's need for autonomy, parents
with more restricted reasons for why children make increased demands
are more likely to respond with inflexibility and rejection of children's
needs.

Study Design

The intervention included two phases, infancy and toddler/preschool,
and was conducted with mother–infant pairs randomly assigned to one
of two conditions during each phase: parent facilitation using the Play
and Learning Strategies (PALS) program or receiving developmental
assessment sessions (DAS) with feedback. This allowed for examination
of four groups of mothers and the impact of duration of intervention on
children's outcomes. One group of mothers received the PALS in both
infancy and the preschool period, while a second group received DAS
in both developmental periods. A third group received PALS during infancy and DAS in the preschool period, while the fourth group received
PALS in the preschool period and DAS in infancy. Thus the study was
uniquely designed to address the question of whether mothers required
the parenting intervention with coaching across both infancy and the
preschool period in order to use greater amounts of rich language input
and responsive techniques. The effect of the intervention at different
developmental periods on children's language development also was
examined.

Both conditions in the two developmental periods were conducted
using a home visitation model with the targeted PALS concepts presented
in each session for each developmental period summarized in Table 3.1.
The infants included in this study varied in their biological risk at birth
(e.g., very low birthweight, term-born), and groups were comparable
on child gender and birth status. Table 3.2 summarizes the demographic
characteristics of the mothers for the four groups of families included in
both phases of the intervention study. Results of the infancy intervention (Phase 1) have been previously published (Landry, Smith, & Swank,
in press; Smith, Swank, & Landry, 2005). This chapter describes the outcome of mothers who participated in both the infancy and toddler/pre-
school phases with an emphasis on changes in maternal scaffolding and
children's language development.

For PALS, a facilitator/coach worked with mothers through a combination of viewing and discussing educational videotapes developed

TABLE 3.1. Description of Targeted Concepts for PALS Infancy and Toddler/ Preschool Sessions

	PALS–Infancy (10 sessions)	PALS–Toddler/Preschool (12 sessions)
Session 1	Learning the child and family routine (e.g., sleep, feeding patterns, demands on mother's time) and the maternal expectations and beliefs regarding her role in promoting development	
Session 2	Recognizing and understanding the intent of positive and negative signals as a means of child communication and, for PALS toddler, how this changes from infancy to the toddler/preschool period	
Session 3	Contingently responding to infant and child signals in warm and responsive ways and, for PALS toddler, how to use these behaviors even when requests need to be denied	
Session 4	Review with alternative caregiver	Behavioral guidance, with an emphasis on helping children learn to cooperate through sharing control when possible, providing choices, and other specific strategies (e.g., praising, ignoring, transitions)
Session 5	How to attend to attentional focus and maintain and build interest rather than redirect	Review with alternative caregiver
Session 6	Continue to develop maintaining skills, become aware of good times to introduce a new activity or conversation when infant is ready	How to attend to attentional focus and maintain and build interest rather than redirect interest
Session 7	Using rich language while maintaining attention and introducing activities	Using rich language, with an emphasis on using labels of objects and actions when maintaining attention
Session 8	Review with alternative caregiver	Using rich language, with an emphasis on linking objects and actions by using language to provide clues that will assist children to become more independent in solving problems
Session 9	Integrating use of responsive interactive behaviors together in everyday situations	

TABLE 3.1. (continued)

	PALS–Infancy (10 sessions)	PALS–Toddler/Preschool (12 sessions)
Session 10	Continued practice in integrating use of responsive interactive behaviors	Review with alternative caregiver
Session 11		Integrating use of responsive interactive behaviors in everyday situations
Session 12		Continued practice in integrating use of responsive interactive behaviors

specifically for the intervention. Each tape highlighted each session's interactive behavior by defining and demonstrating mothers using this with their children. Mothers then were coached to practice the behaviors with their children in various situations such as book reading, puzzle play, and conversation around meals. The practice was videotaped and mothers reviewed these tapes with their coach and critiqued their own behavior with a particular emphasis on their children's responses to mothers' behaviors.

The strong changes for the constellation of maternal behaviors across a relatively short-term intervention were thought to be due to the engagement of mothers in a trusting, respectful relationship with the coach. Responsive parenting is a construct with an implicit requirement that a caregiver notice and appreciate the child as an individual with unique interests and needs, independent of the caregiver. Thus the coaching relationship was critical to guiding mothers to this level of respect for their infants. This was accomplished, in part, by the coach establishing a social context for the mother's learning that acknowledged and respected her opinions and ability.

Impact of the PALS Intervention on Change in Maternal Responsiveness and Child Language Outcomes

An important outcome of this study was that changes in mothers' use of rich language input was greater for mothers receiving the PALS intervention than for those in the DAS condition. This finding demonstrated that receiving the PALS program and coaching in the preschool period

TABLE 3.2. Comparison of Infant, Maternal, and Program Characteristics by Intervention Condition

	PALS/PALS	PALS/DAS	DAS/PALS	DAS/DAS
Infant				
Gender: (% male/female)	52/48	52/48	52/48	52/48
Maternal				
Age (years)	28.5 (6.4)	27.7 (5.6)	26.6 (6.9)	25.8 (5.8)
Education (years)	11.8 (3.2)	12.9 (2.6)	12.2 (2.3)	12.7 (2.4)
Socioeconomic status[a]	28.9 (13.8)	30.3 (12.0)	31.1 (11.6)	32.2 (11.9)
Ethnicity (%)				
African American	22	41	36	35
Caucasian	28	18	26	23
Hispanic	50	41	32	38
Other	0	0	6	4
One parent (%)	66	62	51	52
Two parent (%)	34	38	49	48
N	34	27	50	48

Note. Data are M (SD) unless otherwise indicated as percentages (%). Study condition assignment in infancy and toddler/preschool periods indicated as infancy (PALS vs. DAS)/toddler–preschool (PALS vs. DAS).

[a]Based on Hollingshead four-factor scale.

was particularly important as PALS mothers, irrespective of whether they received PALS during the infancy period, displayed greater changes in their use of verbal scaffolding. In addition, by the end of the intervention they had fewer requests that did not include language input as compared to the mothers who received DAS. Another positive change in the mothers receiving PALS during the preschool period was their increased use of responsiveness that was contingent on the child's signals when compared to those in the DAS condition. In contrast to changes in rich language input, the greatest increases in contingent responsiveness were found only for mothers who received the PALS program in both developmental periods. Together, these findings show that PALS mothers understand how to support their children's development such that they make their input responsive in contingent ways to the child's signals and interests rather than ignoring this interest, and they do this in ways that are prompt and sensitive.

When examining the impact of the program on children's language development, a different picture emerged. Although mothers' language input appeared to benefit from receiving the program specifically in the preschool period, the greatest gains in children's language skills, as measured by standardized assessment (i.e., the Preschool Language Scale), were seen for children whose mothers participated in PALS in both in-fancy and the toddler/preschool period. However, children whose mothers received PALS during either period showed significantly stronger language gains than those whose mothers never received this program.

There is limited information from experimental studies regarding the most optimal time for responsive parenting interventions and whether timing varies depending upon the type of responsive behavior being targeted. These results indicate that timing is important and varies across maternal behaviors. It seems that mothers can be supported to enhance their use of rich language content in shorter periods of time while responsiveness behaviors that are more linked to attachment frameworks require longer interventions. As both aspects of parenting are important for children's language development, it is not surprising that language growth was most optimal for children whose mothers received PALS across infancy and early childhood.

FUTURE DIRECTIONS

Recently, there has been considerable focus on the importance of supporting young children's school readiness. This focus has resulted in new approaches to promote early literacy skills including language. However, these approaches are often classroom-based with less emphasis on the role of the home environment. While studies are demonstrating how to promote emergent literacy effectively in classroom-based settings, there is much less evidence concerning how to accomplish this for parents. Thus more research is needed that demonstrates effective models for enhancing parenting practices specific to supporting school readiness.

ACKNOWLEDGMENTS

The work described here was supported by Grant Nos. HD24128 and 36099 from the National Institutes of Health. We are grateful to the research staff for their assistance in data collection.

REFERENCES

Adamson, L. B., & Bakeman, R. (1991). The development of shared attention during infancy. *Annals of Child Development, 8,* 1–41.

Ainsworth, M., Blehar, M., Waters, E., & Wall, S. (1978). *Patterns of attachment: A psychological study of the Strange Situation.* Hillsdale, NJ: Erlbaum.

Akhtar, N., Dunham, F., & Dunham, P. J. (1991). Directive interactions and early vocabulary development: The role of joint attention focus. *Journal of Child Language, 18,* 41–49.

Anderson, B. J. (1977). The emergence of conversational behavior. *Journal of Communication, 27,* 85–91.

Bakeman, R., & Adamson, L. B. (1984). Coordinating attention to people and objects in mother–infant and peer–infant interactions. *Child Development, 55,* 1278–1289.

Bornstein, M., & Tamis-LeMonda, C. S. (1989). Maternal responsiveness and cognitive development in children. In M. H. Bornstein (Ed.), *Maternal responsiveness: Characteristics and consequences* (pp. 49–61). San Francisco: Jossey-Bass.

Bransford, J., Brown, A., & Cocking, R. R. (Eds.). (2000). *How people learn: Brain, mind, experience, and school.* Washington, DC: Academic Press.

Bridges, A. (1979). Directing two-year-olds' attention: Some clues to understanding. *Journal of Child Language, 6,* 211–226.

Brooks-Gunn, J., Klebanov, P. K., Liaw, F., & Spiker, D. (1993). Enhancing development of low-birthweight, premature infants: Changes in cognition and behavior over the first three years. *Child Development, 64,* 736–753.

Bruner, J. (1977). Early social interaction and language acquisition. In H. R. Schaffer (Ed.), *Studies in mother–infant interaction* (pp. 271–289). New York: Academic Press.

Burns, M. S., & Casbergue, R. (1992). Parent–child interaction in a letter-writing context. *Journal of Reading Behavior, 24,* 289–331.

Butler, S. R., Marsh, H. W., Sheppard, M. J., & Sheppard, J. L. (1985). Seven-year longitudinal study of the early prediction of reading achievement. *Journal of Educational Psychology, 77,* 349–361.

Cohn, J. F., & Tronick, E. Z. (1983). Three-month-old infants' reactions to simulated maternal depression. *Child Development, 54,* 185–193.

Conger, R., McCarty, J., Yang, R., Lahey, B., & Kropp, J. (1984). Perception of child, childrearing values, and emotional distress as mediating links between environmental stress and observed maternal behaviors. *Child Development, 54,* 2234–2247.

Darling, N., & Steinberg, L. (1993). Parenting style as context: An integrative model. *Psychological Bulletin, 113,* 487–496.

Dawson, G., Klinger, L. F., Panagiotides, H., Hill, D., & Spieker, S. (1992). Frontal lobe activity and affective behavior of infants of mothers with depressive symptoms. *Child Development, 63,* 725–737.

Dieterich, S., Assel, M., Swank, P., Smith, K. E., & Landry, S. H. (2006). The impact of early maternal verbal scaffolding and child language abilities on later decoding and reading comprehension. *Journal of School Psychology, 43,* 481–494.

DiPietro, J. A. (2000). Baby and the brain: Advances in child development. *Annual Review of Public Health, 21,* 455–471.

Dore, J. (1979). Conversational acts and the acquisition of language. In E. Ochs

& B. B. Schieffelin (Eds.), *Developmental pragmatics* (pp. 339–361). New York: Academic Press.

Drummond, J. E., Weir, A. E., & Kysela, G. M. (2002). Home visitation programs for at-risk young families: A systematic literature review. *Canadian Journal of Public Health, 93*, 153–158.

Elman, J. L., Bates, E. A., Johnson, M. H., Karmiloff-Smith, A., Parisi, D., & Plunkett, K. (Eds.). (1996). *Rethinking innateness: A connectionist perspective on development.* Cambridge, MA: MIT Press.

Erickson, M. F. (1989). The STEEP program: Helping young families rise above "at-risk." *Family Resource Coalition Report, 8*, 14–15.

Fernald, A. (1992). Human maternal vocalizations to infants as biologically relevant signals: An evolutionary perspective. In J. Barkow, L. Cosmides, & J. Tooby (Eds.), *The adapted mind: Evolutionary psychology and the generation of culture* (pp. 391–428). New York: Oxford University Press.

Gomby, D. S., Culross, P. L., & Behrmann, R. E. (1999). Home visiting: Recent program evaluations: Analysis and recommendations. *The Future of Children, 9*, 4–26.

Gopnik, A., Meltzoff, A. N., & Kuhl, P. K. (1999). *The scientist in the crib: What early learning tells us about the mind.* New York: HarperCollins.

Grusec, J. E., & Goodnow, J. J. (1994). Impact of parental discipline methods on the child's internalization of values: A reconceptualization of current points of view. *Developmental Psychology, 30*, 1–19.

Hardy-Brown, K., & Plomin, R. (1985). Infant communicative development: Evidence from adoptive and biological families with genetic and environmental influence on rate differences. *Developmental Psychology, 21*, 378–385.

Hart, B., & Risley, T. R. (1995). *Meaningful differences in the everyday experiences of young American children.* Baltimore: Brookes.

Hebbeler, K. M., & Gerlach-Downie, S. G. (2002). Inside the black box of home visiting: A qualitative analysis of why intended outcomes were not achieved. *Early Childhood Research Quarterly, 17*, 28–51.

Hoffman, M. L. (1983). Affective and cognitive processes in moral internalization. In E. T. Higgins, D. N. Ruble, & W. W. Hartup (Eds.), *Social cognition and social development: A social–cultural perspective* (pp. 236–274). Cambridge, UK: Cambridge University Press.

Huttonlocher, J., Haight, W., Bryk, A., Seltzer, M., & Lyons, T. (1991). Early vocabulary growth: Relation to language input and gender. *Developmental Psychology, 27*, 236–248.

Kuhl, P. K., Andruski, J. E., Chistovich, I. A., Chistovich, L. A., Kozhevnikova, E. V., Ryskina, V. L., et al. (1997). Cross-language analysis of phonetic units in language addressed to infants. *Science, 277*, 684–686.

Landry, S. H., & Chapieski, M. L. (1989). Joint attention and infant toy exploration: Effects of Down syndrome and prematurity. *Child Development, 60*, 103–118.

Landry, S. H., Garner, P. W., Swank, P. R., & Baldwin, C. D. (1996). Effects of maternal scaffolding during joint toy play with preterm and full-term infants. *Merrill Palmer Quarterly, 42*, 1–23.

Landry, S. H., Miller-Loncar, C. L., Smith, K. E., & Swank, P. R. (2002). The role of early parenting in children's development of executive processes. *Developmental Neuropsychology, 21,* 15–41.

Landry, S. H., Smith, K. E., Miller-Loncar, C. L., & Swank, P. R. (1997). Predicting cognitive-linguistic and social growth curves from early maternal behaviors in children at varying degrees of biologic risk. *Developmental Psychology, 33,* 1040–1053.

Landry, S. H., Smith, K. E., & Swank, P. R. (2002). Environmental effects of language development in normal and high-risk child populations. *Seminars in Pediatric Neurology, 9,* 192–200.

Landry, S. H., Smith, K. E., & Swank, P. R. (2003). The importance of parenting in early childhood for school age development. *Developmental Neuropsychology, 24,* 559–592.

Landry, S. H., Smith, K. E., & Swank, P. R. (2006). Responsive parenting: Establishing early foundations for social, communication, and independent problem solving. *Developmental Psychology, 42*(4), 508–516.

Landry, S. H., Smith, K. E., Swank, P. R., Assel, M. A., & Vellet, S. (2001). Does early responsive parenting have a special importance for children's development or is consistency across early childhood necessary? *Developmental Psychology, 37,* 387–403.

Landry, S. H., Smith, K. E., Swank, P. R., & Miller-Loncar, C. (2000). Early maternal and child influences on children's later independent cognitive and social functioning. *Child Development, 71,* 358–375.

LeMonda, C. S., Bornstein, M. H., & Baumwell, L. (2001). Maternal responsiveness and children's achievement of language milestones. *Child Development, 72,* 748–767.

Londerville, S., & Main, M. (1981). Security of attachment, compliance, and maternal training methods in the second year of life. *Developmental Psychology, 17,* 289–299.

Maccoby, E., & Martin, J. A. (1983). Socialization in the context of the family: Parent–child interactions. In P. H. Mussen (Series Ed.) & E. M. Hetherington (Vol. Ed.), *Handbook of child psychology: Vol. 4. Socialization, personality, and social development* (4th ed., pp. 1–102). New York: Wiley.

McLoyd, V. C. (1990). The impact of economic hardship on black families and children: Psychological distress, parenting, and socioemotional development. *Child Development, 61,* 311–346.

Moerk, E. L. (1975). Verbal interactions between children and their mothers during the preschool years. *Developmental Psychology, 11,* 788–794.

Nelson, K. (1973). Structure and strategy in learning to talk. *Monographs of the Society for Research in Child Development, 38*(1–2, Serial No. 149).

Olson, S. L., Bates, J. E., & Bayles, K. (1984). Mother–infant interaction and the development of individual differences in children's cognitive competence. *Developmental Psychology, 20,* 166–179.

Resnick, M. B., Armstrong, S., & Carter, R. L. (1988). Developmental intervention program for high-risk premature infants: Effects on development and parent–infant interactions. *Developmental and Behavioral Pediatrics, 9,* 73–78.

Rogoff, B. (1990). *Apprenticeship in thinking.* New York: Oxford University Press.

Rovee-Collier, C. (1996). Time windows in cognitive development. *Developmental Psychology, 31,* 147–169.

Royce, J. M., Darlington, R. B., & Murray, H. W. (1983). Pooled analyses: Findings across studies. In Consortium for Longitudinal Studies (Eds.), *As the twig is bent: Lasting effects of preschool programs* (pp. 411–459). Hillsdale, NJ: Erlbaum.

Scarr-Salapatek, S., & Williams, M. L. (1973). The effects of early stimulation on low-birth-weight infants. *Child Development, 44,* 94–101.

Slobin, D. I. (1968). Imitation and grammatical development in children. In N. S. Endler, L. R. Boulter, & H. Osser (Eds.), *Contemporary issues in developmental psychology* (pp. 437–443). New York: Holt, Rinehart, & Winston.

Smith, K. E., Landry, S. H., Miller-Loncar, C. L., & Swank, P. R. (1997). Characteristics that help mothers maintain their infants' focus of attention. *Journal of Applied Developmental Psychology, 18,* 587–601.

Smith, K. E., Landry, S. H., & Swank, P. R. (2000). The influence of early patterns of positive parenting on children's preschool outcomes. *Early Education and Development, 11,* 147–169.

Smith, K. E., Landry, S. H., & Swank, P. R. (2005). The influence of decreased parental resources on the efficacy of a responsive parenting intervention. *Journal of Consulting and Clinical Psychology, 73,* 711–720.

Snow, C. E. (1977). The development of conversation between mothers and babies. *Journal of Child Language, 4,* 1–22.

Sroufe, L. A. (1983). Infant–caregiver attachment and patterns of adaptation in preschool: The roots of maladaptation and competence. In M. Perlmutter (Ed.), *Minnesota Symposium in Child Psychology* (Vol. 16, pp. 41–81). Hillsdale, NJ: Erlbaum.

St. Pierre, R. G., & Layzer, J. I. (1998). Improving the life chances of children in poverty: Assumptions and what we have learned. *Social Policy Report, Society for Research in Child Development, 7,* 1–25.

Termine, N. T., & Izard, C. E. (1988). Infants' responses to their mothers' expressions of joy and sadness. *Developmental Psychology, 24,* 223–229.

Tomasello, M., & Farrar, M. (1986). Joint attention and early language. *Child Development, 57,* 1454–1463.

Vygotsky, L. S. (1978). *Mind in society: The development of higher psychological processes.* Cambridge, MA: Harvard University Press.

Weiss, B., Dodge, K. A., Bates, J. E., & Pettit, G. S. (1992). Some consequences of early harsh discipline: Child aggression and a maladaptive social information processing style. *Child Development, 63,* 1321–1335.

Weizman, Z. O., & Snow, C. E. (2001). Lexical input as related to children's vocabulary acquisition: Effects of sophisticated exposure and support for meaning. *Developmental Psychology, 37,* 265–279.

Whitehurst, G. C., & Lonigan, C. J. (1998). Child development and emergent literacy. *Child Development, 69,* 848–872.

CHAPTER 4

Metalinguistic Awareness and the Vocabulary–Comprehension Connection

WILLIAM NAGY

To a great extent, our interest in vocabulary growth is motivated by the correlation between vocabulary knowledge and reading comprehension: people with bigger vocabularies also tend to be better readers. However, before we can draw any implications for instruction from that correlation, we need to understand what sorts of causal relationships lie behind it. It turns out that these relationship are rather complex (Anderson & Freebody, 1981; RAND Reading Study Group, 2002). In this chapter, I explore one particular aspect of the relationship between vocabulary knowledge and comprehension: the hypothesis that a significant portion of the variance underlying the correlation between tests of vocabulary knowledge and tests of reading comprehension can be accounted for by metalinguistic awareness. At the end of the chapter, I discuss some implications of this hypothesis for literacy instruction.

Anderson and Freebody (1981) suggested three possible types of causal links between vocabulary knowledge and reading comprehension. The first they labeled the *instrumentalist hypothesis*. This is the common-sense idea that knowing more words per se makes you a better reader. A second hypothesis is the *knowledge hypothesis*: that it is one's store of concepts and the relationships among them that drives comprehension, with vocabulary knowledge simply being the visible tip of the conceptual iceberg. Their third hypothesis is the *aptitude hypothesis*. According to this hypothesis, vocabulary knowledge and reading comprehension are correlated with each other because both are impacted by a common set of aptitudes or abilities. What makes a person a good comprehender also makes a person a good word learner. This could be true even if knowing more words did not have a direct impact on reading comprehension.

The implications of the aptitude hypothesis depend on which aptitudes or abilities one has in mind. If the primary factor contributing to both word learning and reading comprehension is simply general intelligence, for example, there might be little that could be done in terms of instruction. On the other hand, the abilities that are hypothesized to underlie the correlation between vocabulary knowledge and reading comprehension might be amenable to instruction. Sternberg and Powell (1983) suggested that the abilities linking word learning and reading comprehension had to do with making inferences, and that instruction could improve students' abilities to make inferences about the meanings of unfamiliar words (Fukkink & de Glopper, 1998; Sternberg, 1987). In this chapter, I explore the hypothesis that the abilities shared by word learning and reading comprehension are primarily metalinguistic in nature. Like Sternberg and Powell's (1983) version of the aptitude hypothesis, mine is an optimistic one, given that metalinguistic abilities are demonstrably teachable (e.g., National Reading Panel, 2000). For convenience, I refer to this as the *metalinguistic hypothesis.*

METALINGUISTIC AWARENESS

Tunmer, Herriman, and Nesdale (1988) define *metalinguistic awareness* as the ability to "reflect on and manipulate the structural features of spoken language" (p. 136). In some respects, limiting the definition to spoken language is useful—for example, by forcing one to make a distinction between phonemic awareness and phonics. However, I would prefer to remove the word "spoken" from the definition, since this word narrows the scope of the construct "metalinguistic awareness" too much. For example, I would want to consider reflecting on or manipulating the order of words in a sentence (i.e., syntactic awareness) to be a kind of metalinguistic awareness whether the sentence was written or spoken.

In the field of reading, the ubiquity of the term *phonemic awareness* has made many aware of at least one type of metalinguistic awareness. However, there are a variety of subcategories of metalinguistic awareness, each defined in terms of the particular units of linguistic structure that one is reflecting on or manipulating—for example, phonemes, in the case of phonemic awareness, or morphemes, in the case of morphological awareness. Gombert (1992) divides metalinguistic awareness into six categories: metaphonological, metasyntactic, metalexical, metasemantic, metapragmatic, and metatextual. My purpose here, though, is not to provide an exhaustive account of the different types of metalinguistic awareness, but to give some examples of the ways that both vocabulary acquisition and reading comprehension are dependent on metalinguistic abilities.

To recap, the metalinguistic hypothesis I am arguing for is a particular version of the aptitude hypothesis: that some of the correlation between vocabulary knowledge and reading comprehension can be accounted for by appealing to the relationship of each of these with a third construct, metalinguistic awareness. To support this claim, I try to show, first, that there are strong connections, in some cases arguably causal, between metalinguistic awareness and vocabulary growth; and, second, that there are strong connections, again some causal, between metalinguistic awareness and reading comprehension.

Understanding the role of metalinguistic awareness in the vocabulary–comprehension relationship has implications for how we approach vocabulary instruction. One main implication is that more attention should be given to the metalinguistic demands of vocabulary learning, which may be a source of difficulty for some students (Nagy & Scott, 2000). Another is that vocabulary instruction needs to be more explicitly metalinguistic—that is, that "word consciousness" is an obligatory, not an optional, component. Finally, the metalinguistic hypothesis suggests that there are ways to integrate vocabulary instruction and comprehension that make both more effective.

METALINGUISTIC AWARENESS AND INDIVIDUAL DIFFERENCES IN VOCABULARY LEARNING

Children enter school with large differences in vocabulary size, differences that are correlated with socioeconomic status (SES) and other risk factors, and which to a large extent may be attributable to differences in exposure to vocabulary-rich language (Hart & Risley, 1995). The early years of schooling do not necessarily reduce these differences (Cantalini, 1987). Persisting differences in vocabulary size have been suggested as a cause of the "fourth-grade slump" that many students experience even after having received effective beginning reading instruction (Biemiller, 1999).

Given the importance of vocabulary knowledge, it would make sense to intervene in some way that would narrow the vocabulary gap. More exposure to rich language is certainly essential. However, simply providing a linguistically richer environment might exacerbate rather than reduce preexisting differences in vocabulary size because children differ in their ability to learn words from context (McKeown, 1985; Shefelbine, 1990). Therefore, it has been suggested that more explicit instruction concerning the meanings of words is necessary to help children who enter school with smaller vocabularies (Biemiller, 1999).

However, explaining word meanings to children does not necessarily solve the problem. Penno, Wilkinson, and Moore (2002) found that the more able children benefited more from explanations of word meanings than did the less able children. In this case, an intervention that might be hoped to reduce the vocabulary gap separating less able from more able students actually widened it.

My point is not that closing the vocabulary gap is impossible, but that to do so we need to take differences in word-learning ability into account. If we want to make instruction maximally beneficial, we need to understand what types of knowledge and abilities contribute to word learning.

Sources of Individual Differences in Word-Learning Ability

Individuals differ substantially in their ability to make use of information about the meanings of new words, whether this information if provided by context, by explanations, or by definitions. What are some possible sources of these differences?

One essential step in learning a word is getting the phonological form established in memory. Presumably this has to take place before learners can start collating the information that they gain through repeated encounters with a word. Therefore, it is not surprising that measures of phonological short-term memory have been found to predict vocabulary-learning ability (e.g., Gathercole & Baddeley, 1989, 1990). Some studies suggest that this effect may be strongest for young children (Gathercole, Willis, Emslie, & Baddeley, 1992), for second-language acquisition (Service, 1992), or when the words to be learned differ from the normal phonological structure of words in one's native language (Papagno, Valentine, & Baddeley, 1991). However, a significant relationship between phonological short-term memory and first-language vocabulary has also been found for 11- to 12-year-olds (Henry & MacLean, 2003) and for 13-year-olds (e.g., Gathercole, Service, Hitch, Adams, & Martin, 1999).

Another factor that may influence word-learning ability is the number of words that the individual already knows. Shefelbine (1990) concluded from his study of individual differences in the use of context to learn new words that one of the main obstacles confronting the less able students in figuring out the meaning of a new word was that they didn't know the meanings of the other words in the context either. Likewise, not knowing some of the words used to explain a new word renders the explanation useless.

Word-learning ability also depends on the variety and depth of the child's experiences. It is much easier to learn a new label for an existing concept than to learn a completely new concept as well as its label (Graves, 1986; Nagy, Anderson, & Herman, 1987).

Phonological short-term memory and existing knowledge of words and concepts may be important factors in word-learning ability, but they give us only limited help in figuring out how to make children better word learners—they simply put the source of the problem back further, and underscore the fact that the task of building children's vocabularies should start as soon as possible. However, there are also metacognitive and metalinguistic factors that are likely to make an important contribution to word learning.

Metalinguistic Aspects of Word Learning

To the extent that one is aware of the process at all, learning a new word is a metalinguistic activity. As such, it requires a variety of metalinguistic abilities, many of which are still in the process of developing during the elementary school years (Gombert, 1992). Because of the substantial developmental differences that exist, and because of the diversity of individual children's experiences relating to language and literacy, teachers cannot simply assume that vocabulary-learning activities are within the grasp of all their students.

Even simple, straightforward explanations of word meanings may require metalinguistic abilities on the part of students that should not be taken for granted. One is the child's grasp of the metalinguistic term *word*. Roberts (1992) found that this concept was still in the process of development through third grade. Even seemingly simple tasks involving this concept are not necessarily within the grasp of primary-grade children. For example, if a child is not able to tell you how many words there are in a spoken sentence, this inability might raise concerns about how well prepared this child is to understand explanations of word meanings. According to Berthoud-Papandropoulou (1980; cited in Gombert, 1992), the ability to accurately count the number of words in a spoken sentence is rare in children under age 7. A typical response by a 5-year-old to the question "How many words are there in the sentence *The pig ate a lot?*" is "Nineteen—because he eats lots and lots" (Gombert, 1992, p. 66). Although performance on this task improves by age 7, it is not till age 11 or 12 that children become completely accurate.

Gombert's (1992) extensive review of research on metalinguistic development identifies a number of other basic metalinguistic abilities—for example, the ability to distinguish between a linguistic form and its referent—that are not reliably present before age 7, and not always completely developed even then. Given that knowledge of many metalinguistic constructs is the result of being part of a literate culture (Olson, 1999), teachers may find even some upper-elementary children who lack foundational metalinguistic concepts and terminology.

In the primary grades, then, differences in metalinguistic foundations such as the concept of word may have an impact on children's vocabulary growth. With higher grade levels, the metalinguistic demands of word learning continue to increase, giving us all the more reason to expect a relationship between metalinguistic awareness and word learning. As children get older, they take on an increasing share of the responsibility for learning new words. They need to learn to use definitions, context, and word parts. Each of these three sources of information about words demands a high level of metalinguistic sophistication (Nagy & Scott, 2000).

Definitions

Definitions are by nature metalinguistic statements. Understanding definitions is metalinguistically demanding in a number of ways. Several studies have documented the problems that children have using dictionary definitions (McKeown, 1993; Miller & Gildea, 1987; Scott & Nagy, 1997). No studies that I know of directly test the link between metalinguistic awareness and the understanding of definitions. However, an examination of the kind of errors that children make when they use definitions strongly suggests that metalinguistic awareness plays an important role. For example, Scott and Nagy (1997) found that upper-elementary students were very likely to mistake the meaning of a salient word in a definition for the meaning of the whole definition—for example, to think that a word defined as "to make a strong request for help" simply meant "strong." Such errors show a disregard for the syntax of the definition, and may be analogous to the errors children make in using context.

Problems with using definitions do not end with elementary school, as is evidenced by the following quote (from one of my students, in a class e-mail discussion):

> I tutored a young woman who was taking an honors English class as a freshman and she was supposed to write sentences for her vocabulary words every week. She rarely wrote a sentence that made sense on the first try; in fact, she would sometimes use an adjective as a noun or make some similar mistake because, even though she knew the definition, the word didn't mean anything to her. (C. Strawn, personal communication, 2004)

It seems unlikely, then, that the impact of metalinguistic awareness on word learning would be confined to any particular age or grade level. Rather, as the complexity of the language students encounter increases, so do the metalinguistic demands.

Context

There are a variety of reasons why children may fail to make effective use of context in figuring out the meaning of a new word. One is that they may not know the meanings of the other words in the context (Shefelbine, 1990). Another problem, and one that is likely to involve metalinguistic ability, is failure to use information provided by the syntactic structure of the sentence.

The syntax of a sentence provides important clues to the meaning of a word and also to what information in the context is most relevant to its meaning (Nagy & Gentner, 1990). Sometimes use of context requires sensitivity to subtle syntactic clues that may be missed even by advanced second-language learners (Nagy, McClure, & Mir, 1997).

Examination of children's use of context reveals that many of their difficulties stem from a failure to reflect on the information provided by the structure of the sentence—that is, from lack of syntactic awareness.

For example, in Werner and Kaplan's (1952) seminal study of use of context, the first problem they identify is that the younger child often "lacks the distinctiveness in the relation of the word to context that characterizes . . . mature verbal activity" (p. 14). They illustrate this point with the example of a child trying to infer the meaning of the nonsense word *bordick* in the sentence "People talk about the bordicks of others and don't like to talk about their own." The child's explanation of the word is "People talk about other people and don't talk about themselves. That's what *bordick* means" (Werner & Kaplan, 1952, p. 15). Similarly, Goerss, Beck, and McKeown (1999) identify one of the main categories of misuse of context as being that "students confounded the meaning of the target word with that of the sentence as a whole, endowing the word with the meaning of the entire context" (p. 162). Another problem noted by Goerss et al. is "limited use of context, in which the student simply did not consider all aspects of the context that were needed to derive the meaning of a target word" (p. 161).

It might be argued that the problems identified by Werner and Kaplan and by Goerss et al. are not exclusively syntactic. For example, a third major misuse of context identified by Goerss et al. (1999) is "going beyond the limits of meaning set by the context in order to hypothesize a situation or 'scenario' into which a meaning might fit" (p. 162). This would perhaps best be understood as a failure in the area of pragmatic awareness, and, more specifically, as an inability to understand the pragmatics of decontextualized language (Snow, 1994). Tunmer et al. (1988) define *pragmatic awareness* as "an awareness of the relationships that obtain between a given sentence and the context in which it is embedded, where context is defined broadly (prior text, prior knowledge, situational context, etc.)" (p. 136). Thus more than one type of metalinguistic ability contributes to successful use of context, and it may be difficult to distinguish completely between the roles of syntactic, semantic, and pragmatic awareness. In any case, sensitivity to sentence structure is essential.

I am not aware of any studies that have directly examined the link between syntactic awareness and learning from context. However, a recent meta-analysis (Fukkink & de Glopper, 1998) examined the effects of instruction on the ability to infer word meanings from context. As it turns out, this ability can be increased through relatively short-term interventions. A few of the effective interventions in Fukkink and de Glopper's (1998) meta-analysis were as short as 90 minutes, only a few involved more than 8 hours of instruction, and there was no relationship between the length of the intervention and its effectiveness. The success of such brief interventions constitutes evidence that learning from context is dependent in part on metacognitive and metalinguistic abilities, and not completely on traits such as overall vocabulary size and phonological short-term memory that are less amenable to such sudden changes.

Kuhn and Stahl (1998) have a slightly less optimistic interpretation of the studies analyzed by Fukkink and de Glopper (1998), suggesting that the effects of instruction in using context are not greater than the effects of simple practice. However, this concern does not weaken the force of the argument that metalinguistic awareness contributes to word learning, since increased metalinguistic awareness is one of the mechanisms by which practice in using context would increase performance on word-learning tasks.

Word Parts

Anglin's (1993) study of vocabulary development showed that between the first and the fifth grade, children learned new derived (prefixed and suffixed) words at more than three times the rate at which they learned new root words. One reason for this striking difference in the rate of growth for these two categories of words is the kind of language to which children are exposed. As children get older, and their reading takes them into increasingly lower ranges of word frequency, the proportion of derived words they encounter increases (Nagy & Anderson, 1984). However, there is also development in their morphological awareness, that is, awareness of the internal structure of complex words, as has been demonstrated in a variety of studies (e.g., Carlisle, 2000; Tyler & Nagy, 1989; Wysocki & Jenkins, 1987). There are also substantial individual differences in morphological awareness, which are correlated with vocabulary size and reading ability (Singson, Mahony, & Mann, 2000; Carlisle & Fleming, 2003; Freyd & Baron, 1982). Nagy, Berninger, Abbott, Vaughn, and Vermeulen (2003) found a strong correlation ($r = .78$ for fourth-grade students) between morphological awareness and vocabulary knowledge that remained significant even when orthographic and phonological abilities were taken into account. Nagy, Berninger, and Abbott (2006) found a similarly strong correlation between morphological awareness and vocabulary knowledge for fourth- and fifth-grade students ($r = .83$). Interestingly, Nagy et al. (2006) found that the correlations between morphological awareness and vocabulary decreased slightly for older students. The especially high correlation between vocabulary knowledge and morphological awareness around fourth grade could be associated with the striking jumps in students' knowledge of derived words and their use of morphological problem solving between first and fifth grade, as reported by Anglin (1993).

The high correlations between morphological awareness and vocabulary are consistent with the plausible hypothesis that there is a causal link from morphological awareness to vocabulary, but obviously they do not constitute proof of such a link. Some of the shared variance probably reflects a causal link *in the other direction*: the larger one's vocabulary, the more examples of morphologically related words one has in one's lexicon, and hence the more opportunities one has to become aware of morphological relationships. In fact, it seems likely that this relationship is reciprocal. In any case, the fact that teaching students to use word parts can increase their ability to learn suffixed or prefixed words (e.g., Baumann, Edwards, Boland, Olejnik, & Kame'enui, 2003; Baumann, Edwards, Font, Tereshinski, Kame'enui, & Olejnik, 2002) indicates that at least part of the relationship is due to a causal link from morphological awareness to word learning.

There are yet other possible explanations of the variance shared by measures of vocabulary and morphological awareness. One is that the morphological tasks used are also in part measures of students' vocabulary knowledge. Although the words in the morphological tasks used by Nagy et al. (2003, 2006) were intended to be common words familiar to all students (and the items were read aloud to students to avoid an impact of decoding ability on the morphological awareness tasks), this possibility cannot be ruled out. Another possibility, however, is that the vocabulary task had a metalinguistic component. In fact, the oral vocabulary measure used by Nagy et al. (2003), the Vocabulary subtest of the WISC-III, requires children to explain the meanings of words, many of them familiar, so it is in fact a task with a strong metalinguistic component. The measure of vocabulary used by Nagy et al. (2006) was the Vocabulary subtest of the Stanford Diagnostic Reading Test. This task too requires students to reflect on the meaning of words, and is hence in part a test of metalinguistic ability. The fact that vocabulary tests generally have some metalinguistic demands, though it does not imply a causal relationship between metalinguistic awareness and word learning, is still consistent with the metalinguistic hypothesis.

METALINGUISTIC AWARENESS
AND READING COMPREHENSION

My purpose in this chapter is to present evidence for the metalinguistic hypothesis, that is, to argue that some of the variance shared by measures of vocabulary knowledge and reading comprehension can be attributed to the contribution of metalinguistic awareness to each of these variables. So far, I have argued that some of the variance shared by vocabulary knowledge and metalinguistic awareness can be attributed to causal links between the two, and also to the metalinguistic demands of vocabulary measures. In this next section, I try to make the case that metalinguistic awareness also makes a direct contribution to reading comprehension, above and beyond any contribution to comprehension it might make through its impact on vocabulary growth.

Metalinguistic awareness can be thought of as a subset of metacognition, that is, it is metacognition that involves language structure in some way. Metacognition is acknowledged as being essential to reading comprehension; what may not be as widely recognized is how much of the metacognition that goes on during reading has a metalinguistic component.

Comprehension monitoring is fundamental to metacognition in reading. Much comprehension monitoring takes place at the level of individual words. Readers often become aware of a breakdown in comprehension when they encounter a word they do not know. But comprehension monitoring can involve other levels of linguistic structure as well—for example, recognizing that one hasn't understood the structure of a sentence, or that one doesn't know to what or to whom some pronoun is supposed to refer.

Reading comprehension depends on metalinguistic awareness because understanding text requires attention to its linguistic form. I want to emphasize, though, that "linguistic" doesn't necessarily imply "literal." All kinds of subtleties of meaning—style, sarcasm, metaphor, and mood—are signaled by details of form. Poetry demands even closer attention to the language than prose. So metalinguistic aspects of reading comprehension are not limited to the word level, or to literal meaning.

Metalinguistic Awareness and Decontextualized Language

The more difficult the language, the greater the role that metalinguistic awareness is likely to play in comprehension. However, it is not just older students reading sophisticated texts, or English language learners, who encounter language that is difficult to understand. Snow (1994) argues that one of the major hurdles facing children learning to read is the fact that the language of texts is so different from the language of conversation.

The difference between text and conversation is not simply a matter of unfamiliar vocabulary or syntactic structures, but also of the way language is used and processed. Compared to conversation, the language of text can be called *decontextualized*. In a face-to-face conversation, contextual factors such as the physical surroundings, assumptions about knowledge shared by the participants, and nonverbal channels of communication play an important role in constructing meaning. In reading, the task of constructing meaning is far more dependent upon the language itself, and less dependent on such contextual factors.

The decontextualized nature of most written language thus affects the kind of strategies that can be used to repair gaps in comprehension. In a conversation, if you fail to understand what someone just said, you can ask for clarification. You can also attempt to infer what was meant on the basis of intonation, facial expression, or body language. When comprehension breaks down during reading, on the other hand, you are much more dependent on the language of the text per se. As Olson (1994) has pointed out, written language makes it possible to reflect on language in a way that spoken language typically does not allow. However, written language also often makes it *necessary* to reflect on language in a way that spoken language does not normally require.

Bilingualism, Metalinguistic Awareness, and Comprehension

It has also been suggested that metalinguistic awareness contributes to comprehension for bilingual readers. Jiménez, García, and Pearson (1996) found that a striking difference between successful and less successful bilingual readers was that the former were more aware of the relationships between their two languages. Similarly, Nagy, García, Durgunoglu, and Hancin-Bhatt (1993) found that the relationship between first-language vocabulary and second-language comprehension of texts containing cognates was positive for those students who recognized the most cognate relationships, and negative for those who recognized the least cognate relationships.

Morphological Awareness and Comprehension

Earlier I used morphological awareness as an example of a kind of metalinguistic awareness that contributes to vocabulary growth. Morphological awareness may also contribute directly to reading comprehension. Several studies have shown that morphological awareness has a significant relationship with reading comprehension, even when vocabulary knowledge and other variables have been statistically controlled for (Carlisle, 1995; Ku & Anderson, 2003; Nagy et al., 2003). Singson et al. (2000) found that the contribution of morphological awareness to reading comprehension increased between third and sixth grades, while the contribution of phonological awareness decreased.

One way that morphological awareness may contribute to comprehension is by facilitating the interpretation of novel morphologically complex words the student encounters while reading—in effect, on-the-spot vocabulary learning. Another way that morphological awareness may contribute to comprehension is through the use of syntactic signals provided by suffixes to parse complex sentences. For example, the difference between *Observant investigators proceed carefully* and *Observe investigators' procedures carefully* is signaled completely by suffixes. Poorer readers are more likely to miss such signals (Tyler & Nagy, 1990). Morphological awareness also may contribute to comprehension via its effect on reading fluency. Nagy et al. (2006) found that morphological awareness made a unique significant contribution to eighth- and ninth-grade students' rate of decoding morphologically complex words, when decoding ability had been controlled for.

Syntactic Awareness and Comprehension

Syntactic awareness should also contribute to reading comprehension in several ways. For example, since most common words have a number of meanings, the one intended by the writer must be determined on the basis of context. Though the selection of contextually appropriate meanings of ambiguous words may depend in part on automatic spreading-activation processes, the use of context must at least in some cases depend on more conscious, and hence metalinguistic, processes.

Schreiber's (1987) work on the role of intonation in sentence processing suggests another mechanism by which syntactic awareness may contribute to comprehension. He argues that young children are dependent on intonation rather than word order to process the syntactic structure of spoken sentences. They therefore face a problem when confronted with written language, which represents intonation only very minimally, and indirectly, through punctuation. To become fluent readers, children must be able to use word order and punctuation to assign syntactic structures to sentences. This transition from reliance on intonation to reliance on word order and punctuation necessarily involves reflecting on sentence structure. Hence syntactic awareness should be on the causal path to fluency, which in turn is necessary for comprehension.

A variety of correlational evidence relates syntactic awareness to comprehension. Good readers have higher levels of syntactic awareness than poor readers (Bentin, Deutsch, & Liberman, 1990; Bowey, 1986). Though some studies have found that syntactic awareness fails to discriminate between normal and disabled readers when other variables (especially phonological awareness and phonological short-term memory) have been controlled for (Shankweiler et al., 1995), others have found measures of syntactic awareness to be related to the ability to understand text, even when decoding ability has been taken into account (Nation & Snowling, 2000). Demont and Gombert (1996) found that when other variables had been controlled for, phonological awareness predicted decoding ability, but syntactic awareness predicted comprehension.

Metalinguistic Interventions to Increase Reading Comprehension

Although I am not aware of any intervention studies that set out to test the effects of metalinguistic awareness per se on reading comprehension, some interventions could accurately be described as being primarily metalinguistic in content. For example, Kennedy and Weener (1974) found that training with the cloze procedure—which is arguably training primarily in syntactic awareness—produced gains in both listening and reading comprehension. More recently, Cartwright (2002) tested the effects of reading-specific multiple classification skill (i.e., the ability to sort words by sound and meaning at the same time) on reading comprehension. Not only did reading-specific classification skill make a significant contribution to reading comprehension after a number of other factors were controlled for, but training in this skill was found to produce a significant increase in comprehension. Given the short duration of the training (five sessions of 15 minutes within 1 week), it is most plausible to interpret the training as training in metalinguistic awareness. This interpretation is further supported by the fact that no effect on comprehension was found for multiple-classification skill training that did not have a metalinguistic component.

It should also be noted that comprehension strategy instruction, which has a documented impact on reading comprehension (National Reading Panel, 2000), often has a metalinguistic component. Klingner and Vaughn's (1999) collaborative strategic reading intervention, for example, incorporates strategies for dealing with unfamiliar words. Many other comprehension strategies are at the very least in part implicitly metalinguistic. Most of the queries in Beck, McKeown, Hamilton, and Kucan's (1997) Questioning the Author intervention (e.g., *What is the author trying to say here? Does the author explain this clearly? Does the author tell us why?*) are metalinguistic in content. Not surprisingly, one of the documented effects of the intervention was an increase in students' comprehension monitoring (Beck, McKeown, Sandora, Kucan, & Worthy, 1996). Flood, Lapp, and Fisher (2002) propose a comprehension intervention ("parsing, questioning, and rephrasing") that is even more explicitly metalinguistic.

SOME IMPLICATIONS OF THE METALINGUISTIC HYPOTHESIS

In this chapter, I have reviewed a variety of evidence for what I have called the "metalinguistic hypothesis": that some of the correlation between vocabulary knowledge and reading comprehension is due to variance that each shares with metalinguistic awareness. In one sense, the metalinguistic hypothesis is speculative, in that no studies have specifically set out to test it, and the empirical evidence for it is largely (though not exclusively) correlational. On the other hand, the individual pieces are hardly in question—for example, whether or not instruction in morphological awareness can increase students' learning of morphologically complex words, or whether awareness of language plays a role in comprehension monitoring. So, just as is the case for Anderson and Freebody's (1981) three hypotheses about the relationship between vocabulary knowledge and comprehension, the question for the metalinguistic hypothesis is not *whether* it is true, but *how* true—that is, how much of the connection between vocabulary knowledge and comprehension does it account for?

The National Reading Panel (2000) has identified vocabulary as one of five areas crucial to literacy, with the motivation for this emphasis on vocabulary being because of its relationship with reading comprehension. Though we know a little about what sort of vocabulary instruction is most effective at improving reading comprehension (Stahl & Fairbanks, 1986), the National Reading Panel concluded that there was not yet enough rigorous research on the vocabulary–comprehension relationship to allow for a meta-analysis. However, we need more than just more research comparing different methods of vocabulary instruction; we need a more complete model of the complex causal links that underlie the correlation between vocabulary knowledge and comprehension. The metalinguistic hypothesis is one plausible component of such a model. In the remainder of this chapter, I outline some of the instructional implications of this hypothesis.

Giving More Attention to the Metalinguistic Demands of Vocabulary Instruction

Earlier in this chapter, I reviewed a variety of evidence that vocabulary learning is metalinguistically demanding, that the metalinguistic abilities necessary to get the most out of instruction are still developing during the school years, and that there is substantial individual variation in these abilities. One of the implications of the metalinguistic hypothesis I would emphasize most, then, is that we need to be more aware of possible mismatches between the metalinguistic *demands* of vocabulary instruction and the metalinguistic *abilities* of our students. Recognizing the metalinguistic demands of vocabulary learning can help us make vocabulary instruction more effective, and especially can help us know what modifications may be necessary when we try to address the vocabulary needs of younger children. There are good arguments for paying attention to developing students' vocabularies as early as possible (Biemiller, 1999), but we cannot simply take instruction designed for upper-elementary students and use it for students in the primary grades.

Just as the concept of phonemic awareness has given us a better understanding of why some children fail to learn phonics, recognizing some of the metalinguistic abilities involved in word learning can give us a better understanding of why some children have difficulty benefiting from vocabulary instruction. Excellent teachers of phonics may have always been able to help children with limited phonemic awareness, but for many teachers the concept of phonemic awareness has provided important new insights into the difficulties some children face. Likewise, excellent teachers of vocabulary may always have been able to help children who are in need of more metalinguistic support in word learning, but other teachers may be helped by having the pitfalls children face made more explicit.

Research on phonological awareness has provided a richer and more finely differentiated understanding of some of the metalinguistic abilities that support decoding. Likewise, research on other aspects of metalinguistic awareness such as that reviewed by Gombert (1992) can provide deeper insight into some of the hurdles that may face younger or less experienced word learners.

Recognizing potential metalinguistic pitfalls can help us devise vocabulary instruction that is more accessible to more students. Providing more user-friendly explanations of word meanings in place of dictionary definitions in the traditional format is one step. Providing more examples of words to be learned, and more processing of these examples, is another. The benefits of the rich vocabulary instruction described by Beck, McKeown, and their colleagues (e.g., Beck, McKeown, & Kucan, 2002; Beck, Perfetti, & McKeown, 1982) may in part be due to the way that it helps students bridge the metalinguistic gap between definitions and functional word knowledge. Likewise, discussion among students about word meanings may help translate dictionary definitions or teacher explanations into terms more accessible to less metalinguistically sophisticated students.

Increasing Metalinguistic Awareness as an Instructional Goal

If the metalinguistic demands of word learning are a problem for some students, then we not only want to reduce some of the metalinguistic hurdles in vocabulary instruction, we also want to increase the metalinguistic capabilities of our students. A number of vocabulary interventions do in fact incorporate elements that should increase metalinguistic awareness. For example, Foorman, Seals, Anthony, and Pollard-Durodola's (2003) Vocabulary Enrichment Program involves not just teaching word meanings, but use of context and word parts, synonyms and antonyms, multiple meanings, dictionary skills, word games, and figurative language— a smorgasbord of metalinguistic activities. Likewise, the "Text Talk" approach to early vocabulary learning (Beck & McKeown, 2001; McKeown & Beck, 2003) can be seen in part as a metalinguistic awareness intervention. A chief purpose of Text Talk, according to the title of the McKeown and Beck (2003) chapter, is "to help children make sense of decontextualized language." The way they help students make sense of decontextualized language is to scaffold the children's participation in talk about text. And by "talk about text," they mean talk that focuses on the language of the text itself, rather than simply on the content in general, the pictures, or children's experiences that are related in some way to the text. Thus the prompts suggested for following up on student responses include explicitly metalinguistic questions such as "What does that mean . . . ?," "Why does the story say . . . ?," and "So we know . . . , but why does it say . . . ?" (p. 169).

Discussion can be a powerful tool for promoting metalinguistic awareness. It is known that discussion that includes talk about words is associated with increased vocabulary growth (De Temple & Snow, 2003; Dickinson & Smith, 1994). One of the reasons is that talk about words includes explanations of specific word meanings. However, talk about words is, by definition, also a form of metalinguistic awareness. Acknowledging discussion as a forum for promoting metalinguistic awareness should shape how we conceptualize and promote effective discussions around vocabulary. Getting children to talk about words is not just a means for them learning the meanings of specific words; it is a way to help them think in more powerful ways about their language.

Integrating Vocabulary Instruction and Comprehension Instruction

According to the metalinguistic hypothesis I have presented here, one of the reasons that vocabulary knowledge and reading comprehension share variance is that they both depend on a common set of metalinguistic abilities. This is quite a different picture of the vocabulary–comprehension connection than is presented by the instrumentalist hypothesis, which treats the link between the two solely in terms of knowledge of individual words. The picture presented by the metalinguistic hypothesis suggests the possibility of more integration between vocabulary instruction and comprehension instruction.

One example of such integration is teaching word-learning strategies as part of a package of comprehension strategies. Use of context clues and word parts, for example, would be taught not just as word-learning skills, but as comprehension repair strategies, as in Klingner and Vaughn's (1999) collaborative strategic reading. However, the metalinguistic abilities that word learning and comprehension share go beyond commonly recognized word-learning skills. Dealing with multiple meanings and figurative language, for example, both part of Foorman et al.'s (2003) vocabulary intervention, are elements of both vocabulary and text comprehension.

Curtis and Longo (2001) give further examples of activities I see as simultaneously addressing both vocabulary and comprehension. They describe a 16-week vocabulary intervention that aimed at improving the reading comprehension of adolescents reading 2–3 years below their grade level. The instruction was based in part on the rich vocabulary instruction developed by Beck and her colleagues (e.g., Beck et al., 2002). At the end of Curtis and Longo's (2001) intervention, the students had gained about 1 year (i.e., one grade level) in their scores on the Vocabulary and Comprehension subtests of the Stanford Diagnostic Reading Test, a result they report as typical in many replications of this intervention.

I am reluctant to attribute the benefits of this intervention solely to gains in word knowledge. The intervention covered 10 words a week, or a total of 160 words. According to the most conservative estimates of vocabulary growth (e.g., D'Anna, Zechmeister, & Hall, 1991; Goulden, Nation, & Read, 1990; Zechmeister, Chronis, Cull, D'Anna, & Healy, 1995), average students add about 1,000 words per year to their reading vocabularies. In 16 weeks—30% of the calendar year, less than 40% of the school year—average students would therefore be expected to learn 300–400 words; so a gain of 160 words during this interval does not constitute a dramatic increase in absolute vocabulary size. (Since some of the words are known by the students before the intervention, the number of words actually learned from instruction is still smaller.) Furthermore, the odds are reasonably low that very many of the words covered in the intervention would actually occur in a standardized measure of vocabulary or reading comprehension.

Where do the gains in vocabulary and reading comprehension scores come from, then, if not primarily from learning specific words? I would argue that many if not most of the activities that Curtis and Longo (2001) describe as part of their intervention can be seen as ways to increase the metalinguistic abilities that contribute to both vocabulary learning and to reading comprehension.

Among the activities, for example, are tasks in which students use instructed words to fill in the blanks in cloze sentences and paragraphs. In keeping with what is known about effective strategy instruction, teachers model the activities and use think-alouds to explain the strategies necessary for this task. The strategies are further developed and practiced in small-group and whole-class discussion.

Other activities used in the intervention that are obviously meta-linguistic are the analogies task, questions about possible relationships among instructed words ("Is something *astounding* always *spectacular?*"), and the improving sentences activity, in which students are given examples of incorrect uses of the instructed words reflecting common student errors and discuss ways to revise them. Other activities in the intervention may not be as explicitly metalinguistic, but all in some way involve reflecting on, and discussing, the meaning and uses of the words that are being learned. I therefore see the metalinguistic hypothesis as explaining some of the success of Curtis and Longo's (2001) intervention, and the activities they use as illustrating some of the ways that vocabulary instruction can be integrated more with comprehension instruction.

CONCLUSION

The metalinguistic hypothesis—that some of the variance shared by vocabulary knowledge and reading comprehension can be attributed to metalinguistic abilities that impact both—is one part of a model of the complex relationship between vocabulary and reading comprehension. According to this hypothesis, both vocabulary learning and reading comprehension are more pervasively metalinguistic than is commonly recognized. Vocabulary instructions is more than teaching words, it is teaching *about* words: how they are put together, how they are learned, and how they are used. If students are to take charge of their own learning in the area of vocabulary, they need to be able to reflect on word meanings, on the sources of information about word meanings, and on the process of vocabulary learning. Likewise, for students to construct meaning effectively, they need to be able to reflect on authors' use of language forms and structures.

The instructional implications of this hypothesis are not novel. Graves (2000) has argued that word consciousness should be one component of a vocabulary curriculum. Moreover, recommendations for rich vocabulary instruction (e.g., Beck et al., 2002; Curtis & Longo, 2001; Foorman et al., 2003; McKeown, Beck, Omanson, & Pople, 1985) have a strong metalinguistic dimension. The point of this chapter has been to articulate a theoretical rationale—and to make a call for more research—that supports this kind of rich instruction. I also hope to have shown that the "word consciousness" component of vocabulary instruction is not simply a matter of word histories and word games, but rather encompasses a variety of metalinguistic abilities that contribute to both word learning and comprehension (Nagy & Scott, 2000; Scott & Nagy, 2004). Finally, given the important role I see metalinguistic awareness playing in both vocabulary instruction and comprehension instruction, I suggest that it is important to support teachers in attaining the level of metalinguistic sophistication needed to carry out vocabulary and comprehension instruction flexibly, and to integrate them effectively.

REFERENCES

Anderson, R. C., & Freebody, P. (1981). Vocabulary knowledge. In J. Guthrie (Ed.), *Comprehension and teaching: Research reviews* (pp. 77–117). Newark, DE: International Reading Association.

Anglin, J. M. (1993). Vocabulary development: A morphological analysis. *Monographs of the Society of Research in Child Development, 58*(10, Serial No. 238).

Baumann, J. F., Edwards, E. C., Boland, E. M., Olejnik, S., & Kame'enui, E. (2003). Vocabulary tricks: Effects of instruction in morphology and context on fifth-grade students' ability to derive and infer word meanings. *American Educational Research Journal, 40*(2), 447–494.

Baumann, J. F., Edwards, E. C., Font, G., Tereshinksi, C. A., Kame'enui, E. J., & Olejnik, S. (2002). Teaching morphemic and contextual analysis to fifth-grade students. *Reading Research Quarterly, 37*, 150–176.

Beck, I., & McKeown, M. (2001). Text talk: Capturing the benefits of read-aloud experiences for young children. *The Reading Teacher, 55*(1), 10–20.

Beck, I., McKeown, M., Hamilton, R., & Kucan, L. (1997). *Questioning the author: An approach for enhancing student engagement with text.* Newark, DE: International Reading Association.

Beck, I., McKeown, M., & Kucan, L. (2002). *Bringing words to life.* New York: Guilford Press.

Beck, I., McKeown, M., Sandora, C., Kucan, L., & Worthy, J. (1996). Questioning the author: A yearlong classroom implementation to engage students with text. *The Elementary School Journal, 96*, 385–414.

Beck, I., Perfetti, C., & McKeown, M. (1982). Effects of long-term vocabulary instruction on lexical access and reading comprehension. *Journal of Educational Psychology, 74*(4), 506–521.

Bentin, S., Deutsch, A., & Liberman, I. (1990). Syntactic competence and reading ability in children. *Journal of Experimental Child Psychology, 48*, 147–172.

Berthoud-Papandropoulou, I. (1980). *La réflexion métalinguistique chez l'enfant.* Geneva, Switzerland: Imprimerie Nationale.

Biemiller, A. (1999). *Language and reading success.* Cambridge, MA: Brookline Books.

Bowey, J. (1986). Syntactic awareness in relation to reading skill and ongoing reading comprehension monitoring. *Journal of Experimental Child Psychology, 41*, 282–299.

Cantalini, M. (1987). *The effects of age and gender on school readiness and school success.* Unpublished doctoral dissertation, Ontario Institute for Studies in Education, Toronto, Canada.

Carlisle, J. F. (1995). Morphological awareness and early reading achievement. In L. Feldman (Ed.), *Morphological aspects of language processing* (pp. 189–209). Hillsdale, NJ: Erlbaum.

Carlisle, J. F. (2000). Awareness of the structure and meaning of morphologically complex words: Impact on reading. *Reading and Writing, An Interdisciplinary Journal, 12*, 169–190.

Carlisle, J. F., & Fleming, J. (2003). Lexical processing of morphologically complex words in the elementary years. *Scientific Studies of Reading, 7*, 239–253.

Cartwright, K. (2002). Cognitive development and reading: The relation of reading-specific multiple classification skill to reading comprehension in elementary school children. *Journal of Educational Psychology, 94*, 79–87.

Curtis, M. E., & Longo, A. M. (2001, November). Teaching vocabulary to adolescents to improve comprehension. *Reading Online, 5*(4). Available: http://www.readingonline.org/articles/art_index.asp?HREF=curtis/index.html.

D'Anna, C. A., Zechmeister, E. B., & Hall, J. W. (1991). Toward a meaningful definition of vocabulary size. *Journal of Reading Behavior, 23*, 109–122.

Demont, E., & Gombert, J. (1996). Phonological awareness as a predictor of recoding skills and syntactic awareness as a predictor of comprehension skills. *British Journal of Educational Psychology, 66*, 315–332.

De Temple, J., & Snow, C. (2003). Learning words from books. In A. van Kleeck, S. Stahl, & E. Bauer (Eds.), *On reading books to children* (pp. 16–36). Mahwah, NJ: Erlbaum.

Dickinson, D., & Smith, M. (1994). Long-term effects of preschool teachers' book readings on low-income children's vocabulary and story comprehension. *Reading Research Quarterly, 29*(2), 104–122.

Flood, J., Lapp, D., & Fisher, D. (2002). Parsing, questioning, and rephrasing (PQR): Building syntactic knowledge to improve reading comprehension. In C. Block, L. Gambrell, & M. Pressley (Eds.), *Improving comprehension instruction: Rethinking research, theory, and classroom practice* (pp. 181–198). San Francisco: Jossey-Bass.

Foorman, B., Seals, L., Anthony, J., & Pollard-Durodola, S. (2003). A vocabulary enrichment program for third and fourth grade African-American students: Description, implementation and impact. In B. Foorman (Ed.), *Preventing and treating reading disabilities: Bringing science to scale* (pp. 419–441). Timonium, MD: York Press.

Freyd, P., & Baron, J. (1982). Individual differences in acquisition of derivational morphology. *Journal of Verbal Learning and Verbal Behavior, 21*, 282–295.

Fukkink, R. G., & de Glopper, K. (1998). Effects of instruction in deriving word meaning from context: A meta-analysis. *Review of Educational Research, 68*(4), 450–469.

Gathercole, S., & Baddeley, A. (1989). Evaluation of the role of phonological STM in the development of vocabulary in children: A longitudinal study. *Journal of Memory and Language, 28,* 200–213.

Gathercole, S., & Baddeley, A. (1990). The role of phonological memory in vocabulary acquisition: A study of young children learning new names. *British Journal of Psychology, 81,* 439–454.

Gathercole, S., Service, E., Hitch, G., Adams, A., & Martin, A. (1999). Phonological short-term memory and vocabulary development: Further evidence of the relationship. *Applied Cognitive Psychology, 13,* 65–77.

Gathercole, S., Willis, C., Emslie, H., & Baddeley, A. (1992). Phonological memory and vocabulary development during the early school years: A longitudinal study. *Developmental Psychology, 28,* 887–898.

Gaux, C., & Gombert, J. (1999). Implicit and explicit syntactic knowledge and reading in preadolescents. *British Journal of Developmental Psychology, 17,* 169–188.

Goerss, B., Beck, I., & McKeown, M. (1999). Increasing remedial students' ability to derive word meaning from context. *Reading Psychology, 20,* 151–175.

Gombert, J. E. (1992). *Metalinguistic development.* Chicago: University of Chicago Press.

Goulden, R., Nation, P., & Read, J. (1990). How large can a receptive vocabulary be? *Applied Linguistics, 11,* 341–363.

Graves, M. F. (1986). Vocabulary learning and instruction. In E. Z. Rothkopf & L. C. Ehri (Eds.), *Review of research in education* (Vol. 13, pp. 49–89). Washington, DC: American Educational Research Association.

Graves, M. F. (2000). A vocabulary program to complement and bolster a middle-grade comprehension program. In B. Taylor, M. Graves, & P. van den Broek (Eds.), *Reading for meaning: Fostering comprehension in the middle grades* (pp. 116–135). Newark, DE: International Reading Association.

Hart, B., & Risley, T. (1995). *Meaningful differences in the everyday lives of young American children.* Baltimore: Brookes.

Henry, L., & MacLean, M. (2003). Relationships between working memory, expressive vocabulary and arithmetical reasoning in children with and without intellectual disabilities. *Educational and Child Psychology, 20,* 51–64.

Jiménez, R., García, G., & Pearson, P. D. (1996). The reading strategies of bilingual Latina/o students who are successful English readers: Opportunities and obstacles. *Reading Research Quarterly, 31,* 90–112.

Kennedy, D., & Weener, P. (1974). Visual and auditory training with cloze procedure to improve reading and listening comprehension. *Reading Research Quarterly, 8,* 524–541.

Klingner, J., & Vaughn, S. (1999). Promoting reading comprehension, content learning, and English acquisition through collaborative strategic reading (CSR). *The Reading Teacher, 52*(7), 738–747.

Ku, Y., & Anderson, R. C. (2003). Development of morphological awareness in

Chinese and English. *Reading and Writing: An Interdisciplinary Journal, 16*, 399–422.

Kuhn, M. R., & Stahl, S. (1998). Teaching children to learn word meanings from context: A synthesis and some questions. *Journal of Literacy Research, 30*, 119–138.

McKeown, M. (1985). The acquisition of word meaning from context by children of high and low ability. *Reading Research Quarterly, 20*, 482–496.

McKeown, M. (1993). Creating definitions for young word learners. *Reading Research Quarterly, 28*, 16–33.

McKeown, M., & Beck, I. (2003). Taking advantage of read-alouds to help children make sense of decontextualized language. In A. van Kleeck, S. Stahl, & E. Bauer (Eds.), *On reading books to children* (pp. 159–176). Mahwah, NJ: Erlbaum.

McKeown, M. G., Beck, I. L., Omanson, R. C., & Pople, M. T. (1985). Some effects of the nature and frequency of vocabulary instruction on the knowledge and use of words. *Reading Research Quarterly, 20*, 522–535.

Miller, G., & Gildea, P. (1987). How children learn words. *Scientific American, 257*(3), 94–99.

Nagy, W. E., & Anderson, R. C. (1984). The number of words in printed school English. *Reading Research Quarterly, 19*, 304–330.

Nagy, W., Anderson, R. C., & Herman, P. A. (1987). Learning word meanings from context during normal reading. *American Educational Research Journal, 24*, 237–270.

Nagy, W., Berninger, V., & Abbott, R. (2006). Contributions of morphology beyond phonology to literacy outcomes of upper elementary and middle school students. *Journal of Educational Psychology, 98*, 134–147.

Nagy, W., Berninger, V., Abbott, R., Vaughan, K., & Vermeulen, K. (2003). Relationship of morphology and other language skills to literacy skills in at-risk second grade readers and at-risk fourth grade writers. *Journal of Educational Psychology, 95*, 730–742.

Nagy, W., García, G. E., Durgunoglu, A., & Hancin-Bhatt, B. (1993). Spanish–English bilingual students' use of cognates in English reading. *Journal of Reading Behavior, 25*, 241–259.

Nagy, W., & Gentner, D. (1990). Semantic constraints on lexical categories. *Language and Cognitive Processes, 5*, 169–201.

Nagy, W., McClure, E., & Mir, M. (1997). Linguistic transfer and the use of context by Spanish–English bilinguals. *Applied Psycholinguistics, 18*, 431–452.

Nagy, W. E., & Scott, J. A. (1990). Word schemas: Expectations about the form and meaning of new words. *Cognition and Instruction, 7*, 105–127.

Nagy, W. E., & Scott, J. A. (2000). Vocabulary processes. In M. L. Kamil, P. B. Mosenthal, P. D. Pearson, & R. Barr (Eds.), *Handbook of reading research* (Vol. 3, pp. 269–284). Mahwah, NJ: Erlbaum.

Nation, K., & Snowling, M. (2000). Factors influencing syntactic awareness skills in normal readers and poor comprehenders. *Applied Psycholinguistics, 21*, 229–241.

National Reading Panel. (2000). *Teaching children to read: An evidence-based assessment of the scientific research literature on reading and its implications for reading instruction.* Washington, DC: National Institute of Child Health and Human Development.

Olson, D. R. (1994). *The world on paper: The conceptual and cognitive implications of writing and reading.* Cambridge, UK: Cambridge University Press.

Olson, D. R. (1999). Literacy and language development. In D. Wagner, B. Street, & R. Venezky (Eds.), *Literacy: An international handbook* (pp. 132–136). New York: Garland.

Papagno, C., Valentine, T., & Baddeley, A. (1991). Phonological short-term memory and foreign-language vocabulary learning. *Journal of Memory and Language, 30,* 331–347.

Penno, J. F., Wilkinson, I. A. G., & Moore, D. W. (2002). Vocabulary acquisition from teacher explanation and repeated listening to stories: Do they overcome the Matthew effect? *Journal of Educational Psychology, 94*(1), 23–33.

RAND Reading Study Group. (2002). *Reading for understanding: Toward an R&D program in reading comprehension.* Santa Monica, CA: RAND Education.

Roberts, B. (1992). The evolution of the young child's concept of word as a unit of spoken and written language. *Reading Research Quarterly, 27,* 124–138.

Schreiber, J. (1987). Prosody and structure in children's syntactic processing. In R. Horowitz & S. J. Samuels (Eds.), *Comprehending oral and written language* (pp. 243–270). New York: Academic Press.

Scott, J. A., & Nagy, W. (1997). Understanding the definitions of unfamiliar verbs. *Reading Research Quarterly, 32,* 184–200.

Scott, J. A., & Nagy, W. (2004). Developing word consciousness. In J. Baumann & E. Kame'enui (Eds.), *Vocabulary instruction: Research to practice* (pp. 201–217). New York: Guilford Press.

Service, E. (1992). Phonology, working memory, and foreign-language learning. *Quarterly Journal of Experimental Psychology, 45A,* 21–50.

Shankweiler, D., Crain, S., Katz, L., Fowler, A. E., Liberman, A. E., Brady, S. A., et al. (1995). Cognitive profiles of reading disabled children: Comparisons of language skills in phonology, morphology, and syntax. *Psychological Science, 6,* 149–156.

Shefelbine, J. (1990). Student factors related to variability in learning word meanings from context. *Journal of Reading Behavior, 22,* 71–97.

Singson, M., Mahony, D., & Mann, V. (2000). The relation between reading ability and morphological skills: Evidence from derivational suffixes. *Reading and Writing: An Interdisciplinary Journal, 12,* 219–252.

Snow, C. (1994). What is so hard about learning to read?: A pragmatic analysis. In J. Duchan, L. Hewitt, & R. Sonnenmeier (Eds.), *Pragmatics: From theory to practice* (pp. 164–184). Englewood Cliffs, NJ: Prentice-Hall.

Stahl, S., & Fairbanks, M. (1986). The effects of vocabulary instruction: A model-based meta-analysis. *Review of Educational Research, 56,* 72–110.

Sternberg, R. (1987). Most vocabulary is learned from context. In M. McKeown

& M. Curtis (Eds.), *The nature of vocabulary acquisition* (pp. 89–105). Hillsdale, NJ: Erlbaum.

Sternberg, R., & Powell, J. (1983). Comprehending verbal comprehension. *American Psychologist, 38*, 878–893.

Tunmer, W., Herriman, M., & Nesdale, A. (1988). Metalinguistic abilities and beginning reading. *Reading Research Quarterly, 23*, 134–158.

Tunmer, W., Nesdale, A., & Wright, A. (1987). Syntactic awareness and reading acquisition. *British Journal of Developmental Psychology, 5*, 25–34.

Tyler, A., & Nagy, W. (1989). The acquisition of English derivational morphology. *Journal of Memory and Language, 28*, 649–667.

Tyler, A., & Nagy, W. (1990). Use of derivational morphology during reading. *Cognition, 36*, 17–34.

Werner, H., & Kaplan, E. (1952). The acquisition of word meanings: A developmental study. *Monographs of the Society for Research in Child Development, 15*(Serial No. 51, No. 1).

Wysocki, K., & Jenkins, J. (1987). Deriving word meanings through morphological generalization. *Reading Research Quarterly, 22*, 66–81.

Yelland, G., Pollard, J., & Mercuri, A. (1993). The metalinguistic benefits of limited contact with a second language. *Applied Psycholinguistics, 14*, 423–444.

Zechmeister, E., Chronis, A., Cull, W., D'Anna, C., & Healy, N. (1995). Growth of a functionally important lexicon. *Journal of Reading Behavior, 27*(2), 201–212.

CHAPTER 5

Fostering Morphological Processing, Vocabulary Development, and Reading Comprehension

JOANNE F. CARLISLE

Breadth and depth of word knowledge is a key factor in reading comprehension. Not surprisingly, therefore, students' difficulties comprehending school texts are attributable in part to their word knowledge. Such comprehension problems, in turn, hinder students' learning in content-area courses throughout the school years. How, then, can we address the educational needs of students whose vocabulary is limited relative to grade-level expectations? To answer this question, it seems that we first need to understand how children (indeed, adults) learn words.

My approach to answering this question is circumscribed by an interest in morphological processing as one component in vocabulary learning and comprehension of texts. Thus, in the initial section of this chapter, I discuss the nature of morphological processing and its role in vocabulary learning. I then frame an argument for the importance of incidental word learning, looking in particular at analysis of word structure as one source of information individuals use to infer the meaning of unfamiliar words from context. The final section of the chapter focuses on programs that provide instruction in morphological knowledge designed to improve vocabulary and reading skills. I argue that such programs need to engage students in analysis of texts so that they internalize the inferential processes that will, over time, foster vocabulary growth and text comprehension.

The rationale for the focus on the role of morphology in students' learning of words from context stems from evidence that about 90% of the approximately 3,000 words children learn each year in school are learned through exposure to words in discourse contexts that are relevant to the learner (Baumann & Kame'enui, 1991). By contrast, only about 10% of the words students learn in a given year come from intentional word study (i.e., vocabulary lessons or activities). Students learn words from oral and written contexts, including listening to discussions in science class and reading textbooks or works of literature (Carlisle, Fleming, & Gudbrandsen, 2000; Jenkins, Stein, & Wysocki, 1984; Nagy, Herman, & Anderson, 1985). A large percentage of the new words students learn after about the third grade are *derived words* (Anglin, 1993)—words like *discontinuous* that have a base word with one or more affixes that change the meaning and grammatical role. It has been estimated that 60% of the unfamiliar words students encounter in texts they read are derived words whose meaning could be figured out by analysis of word structure and their use in the passage (Nagy & Anderson, 1984). Put together, these findings suggest the importance of understanding how morphological processing affects vocabulary development and reading comprehension, and how under-standing this relation informs teachers about methods they might use to foster students' engagement in analytic reading of texts.

MORPHOLOGICAL PROCESSING

Morphemes are the basic units of language learning. When children first learn names for objects and actions, such as *fly* or *brush*, they are learning words, but importantly each of these is also a morpheme. This is because morphemes are the smallest units of meaning. It isn't long before children learn combinations of morphemes that refer to objects or actions they know (e.g., *toothbrush*) and learn to combine morphemes to refer to objects or actions for which they do not already have a name (e.g., they might refer to a broom as a *floorbrush*). By 2 or 3 years of age, knowing the words *brush* and *toothbrush*, children will infer the meaning of a word like *dogbrush*, even though they have never heard it before. Furthermore, gradual exposure to words in different contexts builds their grasp of com-plex form–meaning relations. Thus, *snowbrush* refers to a brush used to remove snow from a car in winter, whereas *toothbrush* refers to a brush used for cleaning teeth, not to removal of the teeth with the brush.

The productive aspects of word formation enable children to invent words by combining morphemes to refer to things, actions, or characteristics for which they do not have an available verbal label. Clark (2003,

p. 276) gave the following example of spontaneous analysis of word parts, which makes clear the child's sensitivity to the word parts:

> D (*age 2 years, 10 months, offering a pretend present to father*): I brought you a tooth-brush and a finger-brush.
> FATHER: What's a finger-brush?
> D: It's for cleaning your nails.

As these principles and examples suggest, morphological analysis helps children acquire new words, including derived words, as well as inflected words and compounds. *Free morphemes* (i.e., base words that can stand alone) and *bound morphemes* (i.e., affixes that cannot stand alone) serve as building blocks (e.g., *lovenest, lovely, lover,* and *lovable* build on *love*). As they encounter new words, children gradually develop a mental representation of not only the base word (e.g., *love*) but also the bound morphemes that are attached to base words (e.g., *-ly* on *lovely*) (Schreuder & Baayan, 1995). Children generally learn most of the suffixes that make inflected forms (e.g., plural forms, verb tense markers) before they start school, but they also know some productive suffixes that create derived forms, such as *-er* (e.g., *runner, teacher*) and the *-y* adjective (e.g., *smelly*) (Berko, 1958; Clark, 1982).

The process of learning morphologically complex words, then, entails developing mental representations of both bound and free morphemes. In a study of young children's understanding of morphologically complex words, Carlisle and Fleming (2003) asked first and third graders to define words, using Anglin's (1993) task of asking for definitions of words and their use in a sentence. Analysis of responses to morphologically complex words was carried out to examine children's awareness of the morphemic composition. This awareness was apparent when children mentioned the base word or the suffix. By this measure, children were likely to decompose words with familiar base forms, such as *still* in *stillness*. Specifically, about half the first and third graders mentioned the base form in their efforts to define *knotless* and *stillness*. In contrast, unfamiliarity with the suffix *-let* on *treelet* appeared to have prevented them from recognizing the familiar base word *tree*. Asked "What does treelet mean?," only 10.8% of the first graders mentioned the word *tree*; in fact, most commented that they "did not know" the word *treelet* or that they "had never heard that word before."

Models of morphological processing (Schreuder & Baayan, 1995; Taft, 2003) indicate that available linguistic information at the level of morphemic and submorphemic elements is used to identify words in oral and written contexts. In his activation interactive model, Taft (2003) proposed that morphemic information is used to bridge form and meaning. When a person encounters a morphologically complex word in speech or in written text, activation of its constituent morphemes might or might not occur, depending first on whether there are representations of the whole word and its constituent morphemes in the individual's lexical memory. If there are, access to the morphemes is likely to facilitate identification and therefore access to meaning. In Figure 5.1, a simplified version of Taft's (Taft & Zhu, 1995) interactive-activation model is shown, with the example of an uncommon derived word (*sunless*). We could imagine that an underlying concept is available for school-age children. Because of the familiarity of the morphemes in the word (*sun* and *–less*), both morphemic and submorphemic elements would probably be activated and play a role in word identification.

According to Reichle and Perfetti (2003), mental representations differ with regard to their lexical quality, which they define as "the degree to which orthographic, phonological and semantic features that collectively

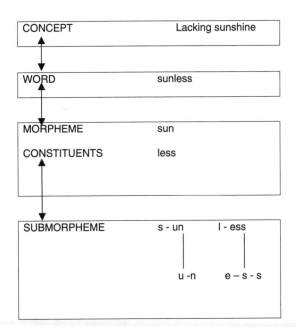

FIGURE 5.1. A version of Taft and Zhu's (1995) interactive-activation model applied to an unfamiliar written word.

define a given word are both well represented and well interlocked in the reader's memory" (p. 231). To the extent that constituent morphemes in a word are represented in memory, they contribute to the collective processing. The quality of a representation affects the ease with which the spelling, meaning, or pronunciation can be retrieved from memory. Central to the development of lexical quality of words held in memory is the extent of an individual's experience with language, oral and written. The more words an individual knows, the more likely he or she can effectively use this word knowledge to infer the meanings of unfamiliar words in oral or written language texts (Nelson, 1996).

Along with familiarity with the whole word and its individual morphemes, transparency of word's form and meaning affect morphological processing. When the phonological representation of the base form is not intact in the derived word, as is the case with *decide* as it appears in *decisive* and *decision*, the sound shift is likely to impede awareness of the morphological structure. The same is true when the spelling of the base word does not appear intact in the derived form (e.g., *solve*, *solution*). Semantic transparency is also important. For example, the word *appliance* does not have an obvious link to the meaning of *apply*—that is, it does not mean a condition in which one is applying something. The results of a number of studies have demonstrated that phonological transparency has a particularly noticeable effect on tasks of morphological awareness and reading derived words (e.g., Carlisle, Stone, & Katz, 2001; Mann & Singson, 2003; Tyler & Nagy, 1989).

This discussion of the complexities of morphological processing might make one think that processing the word parts of unfamiliar words is quite conscious and deliberate. This is not the case. Most processing is automatic and fast moving, proceeding without control or awareness on the part of the listener or reader. Individuals who are curious about words and attuned to strange forms or uses of words might have a heightened level of awareness of word forms and their relation to meanings. However, as a general rule, processing of familiar and unfamiliar words (morphologically complex or not) proceeds quite automatically.

INCIDENTAL WORD LEARNING

For children, as well as adults, learning an unfamiliar word begins when it is encountered in an oral or written language context *and* when understanding of that word matters to the listener or reader. If a word is encoded phonologically (and, in written contexts, orthographically) but no lexical representation is available, an inferential process is initiated such that cues from the immediate context of the new word are used to assign some sort of meaning, if only a vague association with the topic (Carlisle et al., 2000). This process is called *incidental word learning*. It is the primary way that people, regardless of age, learn new words.

Nelson (1996) has argued that one essential condition for word learning is the relevance of the word in the discourse situation in which it is encountered. Perceived relevance determines whether the child will seek to understand the meaning of an unfamiliar word or not. Inferences about meaning are also likely to be influenced by the discourse context. For example, hearing the sentence "Mother told you not to eat that *wormy* apple," a child might make one or more of the following inferences: *wormy* is a kind of apple or a characteristic of an apple; *wormy* must be something harmful or unpleasant, something mother does not approve of. With the apple in hand, the child might look at it to see if there was something about the apple that could further explain *wormy*. Along with clues from the discourse and the situation at hand, familiarity with the word parts, *worm* and -*y*, would play a role as well. The base form might lead the child to infer that the "unpleasant" characteristic had to do with the presence of a worm (possibly in the apple). Thus, where morphemes are represented in the mental lexicon, they are likely to work interactively with context clues in the process of inferring meaning. Such initial inferences, referred to as *fast mapping* (e.g., Carey, 1978; Nelson, 1996), might result in only a primitive or vague formulation of the meaning of a word. Further encounters with the word *wormy*, or even with its constituent morphemes, will lead to increased depth of knowledge about the meaning(s) and uses of the word and word parts. Incidental word learning, drawing on both structural analysis and context analysis, is an incremental process.

The example of a child's first encounter with the word *wormy* might be misleading because discourse context does't always yield helpful clues to the meaning of the word (Funking & deGlopper, 1998). As Baumann and Kame'enui (1991) pointed out, "Contexts can be generous or parsimonious, helpful or hostile in the amount of assistance they provide the reader or listener" (p. 609). Still, as Nagy and Scott (2000) argued, "context and morphology (word parts) are the two major sources of information immediately available to a reader who comes across a new word" (p. 275). Whether in oral language or in reading, the relative importance of the roles played by context clues and morphological structure depends on several factors. One is the extent to which context clues converge to suggest a clear meaning. If they do, morphological analysis might play a relatively small role. A second factor is the transparency of word structure and familiarity of its parts. These affect the activation of morphemic units in the initial phase of word identification. A third factor is the extent to which morphemes reinforce a known concept.

Incidental word learning, which depends on both contextual clues and morphological analysis, is the primary means through which students acquire new vocabulary. While estimates of the number of words children know at different age levels vary considerably, researchers tend to agree that school-age children learn about 3,000 words a year, on average (e.g., Beck & McKeown, 1991). Of these, we can account for relatively few words learned through instruction in school. Students who learn 10 words a week in vocabulary lessons might recall about 300 of these by the end of the school year. Thus development of inferential processes plays a crucial role in the development of a child's vocabulary.

Morphology, Vocabulary Growth, and Reading

"It is hard to overstate the importance of morphology in vocabulary growth," according to Nagy and Scott (2000, p. 275). Support for this assertion comes from a study of the vocabulary knowledge of students in first, third, and fifth grade carried out by Anglin (1993). Using an interview protocol devised from sampling words in an unabridged dictionary, Anglin compared students' learning of psychologically basic words (base or root words), inflections, derivations, compounds, and idioms. A major finding was that students learned about 4,000 base words and about 14,000 derived words between grades one and five. A dramatic increase in knowledge of derived words between first and fifth grade highlights the important contribution of morphological processing to vocabulary growth.

This growth spurt in knowledge of derived words reflects the increase in the presence of derived words in written texts from the later elementary years on (White, Power, & White, 1989). Nagy and Anderson (1984) estimated that over half of the new words students encounter in the texts they read for school are derived forms whose meaning is accessible through analysis of word parts. They estimated that in texts read by children in grades three through nine, there are 139,020 semantically transparent derived words (e.g., *redness*). In contrast, there are only 49,080 derived words that are semantically opaque (e.g., *emerge* and *emergency*). Among these, there are about 27,000 words whose component parts contribute to the meaning of the derived word. These researchers pointed out that awareness of morphological structure would help school-age readers figure out the meanings of numerous morphologically complex words in the texts they encounter.

The ability to use reasoning or problem solving to infer meanings from word structure and context seems to develops dramatically as children move through the elementary- and middle-school years. Anglin (1993) found that fifth graders were often adept at using what he called "morphological problem solving" to work out the meaning of unfamiliar derivatives. His qualitative analyses of students' explanations of their reasoning demonstrate vividly their use of a morphological strategy to analyze unfamiliar words presented out of context. Two examples are as follows:

Example 1 (p. 100)

Fifth-grade student, defining *foundationless*:

I. The next word is *foundationless*. What does the word *foundationless* mean?

C. I know what a foundation is. Like when you build a house, you have a foundation, but if you don't have it, you're foundationless because you don't have it. Most houses have a foundation because they have to start it in the ground and they gradually build up. But if you don't have one, you just kind of like have some smooth ground and start the house by there.

I. Can you tell me anything more about the word *foundationless*?

C. Like maybe just a foundation is all the dirt and like the bottom kind of. If you didn't have dirt in the foundation, it would be like . . . it's -*less* . . . it's not there anymore. Like it never was probably, it's just foundationless.

Example 2 (p. 101)

Fifth-grade child: defining *priesthood*:

I. What does the word *priesthood* mean?

C: I know what a priest is.

I. Mmm.

C. It's like a pastor or somebody like that. And -*hood*, a childhood.

I. Mmm.

C. Maybe when you grow up you have a good childhood. Oh, priesthood. Um. Like you might grow up when you're a child with a priest, and you'll have a good prie-, priesthood. And you'll know lots of stuff from the Bible and everything. Like you know verses and chapters, and you'll know all the days, and you'll go to church, and stuff like that.

I. OK. I'm not sure I understand what you're saying. Are you saying like if you're a child and you grow up with a priest, that's priesthood?

C. [*nods yes*]

In the first example, the student explains *foundation* and then defines the bound morpheme (-*less*), successfully explaining how a house might be built without a foundation. In the second example, the fifth grader clearly knows the base word (*priest*) and relies on another known word that has –*hood* as a suffix to try to figure out the meaning of the whole. While not very successful, this response is a good example of the kind of reasoning that is used in morphological analysis of unfamiliar words. Younger students also make use of analogical reasoning, although only with words that contain familiar morphemes—and even then with less success. Using Anglin's definition task, Carlisle and Fleming (2003) found that third graders were better than first graders at using analogy to infer the meaning of *treelet* (e.g., "Piglet is a little pig, so treelet must be a little tree"); however, third graders would not be likely to do so with words like *priesthood* because the base morpheme and suffix are probably not in their lexical store.

Morphological problem solving undoubtedly contributes to the experiences with words that Reichle and Perfetti (2003) find to be so central to the development of high-quality lexical representations. As reusable building blocks, base words and affixes (such as *priest* and -*hood*) facilitate learning new words (e.g., *priestly* or *brotherhood*) in a way that cannot happen for morphologically simple words (e.g., *prolific, promontory*). Support for this role of morphology in word learning comes from a study carried out by Freyd and Baron (1982). These researchers gave fifth and eighth graders a vocabulary test on which they were to define simple words (e.g., *bachelor*) and derived words (e.g., *oceanic*). The fifth graders had above average verbal abilities, whereas the eighth graders were average in their verbal abilities. The able fifth graders showed an advantage over the eighth graders in defining the derived words. On a later task that involved learning pseudowords, the fifth graders did better on words that appeared to be morphologically related (e.g., *skaff* = steal; *skaffist* = thief), whereas the eighth graders performed similarly on the related and the unrelated words. The researchers concluded that students at these grade levels use morphological relations to learn new words but that students with larger funds of word knowledge made greater use of known morphemes in learning unfamiliar words.

Characteristics of Children Affect Morphological Aspects of Word Learning

While characteristics of words and the richness of learning contexts influence students' use of morphological processing in vocabulary acquisition, so, too, do the language-learning capabilities of the children. Beck and McKeown (1991) stressed the wide range of individual differences in the number of words students learn. They remarked that "even if some students are learning as many as seven new words a day, many others may be learning only one or two" (p. 795). Aspects of cognitive and linguistic development are likely to affect both the development of morphological knowledge and the quality of inferential reasoning that is crucial for learning morphologically simple and complex words from oral and written contexts.

Delayed word learning may stem from deficits in cognitive or linguistic processes, including problems related to perception and memory. Children with speech–language impairment learn fewer words than their peers (McGregor, 2004). They are also less able to learn new words by inferring meanings from context (Oetting, Rice, & Swank, 1995). Similarly, poor readers are less adept at identifying and manipulating morphemes within words (e.g., Fowler & Liberman, 1995). Children with language disorders or language-learning disabilities perform significantly less well than their peers on tasks that assess morphological awareness, such as the production of derived words to complete sentences accurately (e.g., Carlisle, 1987; Fowler & Liberman, 1995; Leong, 1989; Windsor, 2000).

Reading disabilities may contribute to deficits in word learning because of Matthew effects (Stanovich, 1986)—that is, the likelihood is that poor readers read less, and they read easier books. As a result, they have less exposure to words that are not in their spoken vocabularies and thus less opportunity to expand their word knowledge. As Reichle and Perfetti (2003) put it, "Individual differences in reading skill arise from differences in word knowledge, which in turn arise from differences in word experiences" (p. 231). Compared to less skilled readers, skilled readers have more words represented in memory, and these representations are high quality, such that they lead to ready retrieval of the spelling, pronunciation, or meaning of words and word parts that are needed for fluent and meaningful reading.

Given the importance of inferential processes in assigning meaning to unfamiliar words in context, students' cognitive and reasoning capabilities are of paramount importance. Students with low levels of vocabulary knowledge are less sensitive to context clues that would be helpful in inferring the meaning of an unfamiliar word and are less likely than their peers to make reasonable inferences about meanings of words from context (McKeown, 1985; Shefelbine, 1990).

Role of Morphological Awareness in Reading Comprehension

Morphological awareness, which implies explicit knowledge of the morphemic structure of words, has been found to be related to both word reading and reading comprehension (Carlisle, 2002), but is this because of its influence on vocabulary knowledge? Katz (2004) investigated the effects of different aspects of morphological awareness on reading comprehension. She found that morphological awareness and the ability to read morphologically complex words significantly contributed to reading comprehension capabilities in fourth and sixth graders, after controlling for the effects of other language and reading variables (e.g., vocabulary, word attack). Specifically, students' ability to define derived words and to produce a correct derived word for a particular sentence context directly influenced reading comprehension. Morphological awareness contributed to reading comprehension, independent of its relation to vocabulary.

An important point about the process of word learning during reading is that knowledge of derived words and analysis of written context (sentences or passages) work together in the process of constructing meaning. Wysocki and Jenkins (1987) taught fourth, sixth, and eighth graders the meaning of derived words (e.g., *gratuity*) and then tested their knowledge of other words in the same word family (e.g., *gratuitous*). The students showed that they were able to make use of knowledge of word structure to infer the meaning of the new (transfer) words (here, *gratuitous*). They also compared the effect of sentence contexts on the students' ability to provide appropriate definitions for transfer and control words. When the words were semantically transparent, the students did not need the sentence context to provide clues of the meaning of the word. In contrast, for words whose definitions were less evident from their morphological components, the sentence contexts were helpful. They also found that eighth graders made greater use of the combined morphological and sentence clues than did the fourth graders.

Tyler and Nagy (1990) designed a study to determine how older students (9th and 11th graders) interpreted sentences that contained derived words. They asked the students to select the version of a target sentence that best paraphrased that sentence. The sentences were constructed in such a way that understanding of the suffix was critical. For example, one item focused on students' reading and interpretation of the word *indecision*; it read as follows: "Mary was afraid that a general indecision about the use of nuclear weapons might be a threat to national security." Two of the four options that followed were these:

1. Mary feared that, if most people couldn't make up their minds about using atomic bombs, the country could be put in danger. (correct)
2. Mary feared that a military officer who couldn't make up his mind about using atomic bombs might put the country in danger. (syntactic error)

Note that the second choice (2) would be selected if the reader processed "indecision" as "indecisive."

The results of this study showed that students made fewer errors on suffixed target words than nonsuffixed target words that were similar in word frequency. This finding indicates that morphological processing influences word identification and meaning in the reading and interpretation of sentences. A second finding was that there were more syntactic errors on the suffixed than on the nonsuffixed words. This suggests that students had difficulty processing suffixes for syntactic (and perhaps semantic) features. The poorer readers made more syntactic errors than the good readers.

The results of this study, as well as the those of Wysocki and Jenkins (1987), provide evidence of the interactive use of the two inferential processes discussed earlier: context analysis and structural analysis. They also illustrate the point made by Nagy and Anderson (1984) that awareness of morphemic structure is beneficial for decoding and analyzing the meaning of unfamiliar words during reading.

INSTRUCTION IN WORD LEARNING

There are potential benefits to word study programs that provide students with knowledge about word structure and strategies to infer the meanings of words. One reason is that not all students come to this understanding with ease. As was mentioned earlier, students with language learning and reading disabilities are likely to be delayed, relative to their peers, in vocabulary development, including morphological knowledge and awareness (Fowler & Liberman, 1995; Windsor, 2000). Furthermore, students who are English language learners (ELLs) face particular challenges learning English vocabulary and benefit from instruction in word-learning strategies including morphological analysis (Carlo, August, Snow, Lively, & White, 2004). Leaving morphological analysis to be discovered by students on their own means that those who are in some way challenged by language learning are likely to be left behind their peers in the development of vocabulary, word reading, and reading comprehension.

Word study programs that focus on morphology tend to do so for the primary purpose of either improving word reading and spelling or improving vocabulary. Most programs also include some amount of reading of natural texts. However, what is missing is assistance for students in learning how to use decoding and meaning-making strategies while reading. Unfortunately, poor readers are unlikely to use decoding strategies and comprehension strategies without considerable scaffolding to learn to apply these strategies during reading (Baker & Brown, 1984; Paris, Lipson, & Wixson, 1983). They also need sufficient guided practice so that they see the value of the new strategies and use them relatively automatically as they encounter glitches in their understanding of texts they read on their own (Westby, 2004). In short, struggling readers seem to need help improving the inferential processes that will jointly support their learning of vocabulary during reading and their comprehension of texts.

Word Study Programs

Word study programs often include morphological awareness (particularly instruction in derived words) with the goal of improving word-reading and spelling skills; in such programs, vocabulary development may also be a goal (Templeton, 1989). Berninger and her colleagues developed one such program for students with reading disabilities

(Berninger et al., 2003). These researchers investigated the effectiveness of interventions that focused on either phonological or morphological awareness. In the morphological awareness condition, students were provided with instruction that emphasized morphological analysis for purposes of word reading. This included activities designed to help students gain insights into the writing system and build their sensitivity to the morphological composition of words, such as word building (producing written words by combining base words and affixes) and unit finding (identifying base words and affixes in written words). Students also received instruction in the meanings of prefixes and suffixes, opportunities to highlight and discuss unfamiliar words, and practice in oral reading fluency and text comprehension. The program for students in the phonological awareness condition had the same goals, but activities focused at the level of phonemes and graphemes, not the level of morphemes.

Results showed that phonological and morphological treatments, embedded in a balanced reading program, were effective in increasing accuracy of phonological decoding for students with reading disabilities. One intriguing finding was that students in the morphological condition made greater improvements than their peers in the phonology condition on efficiency of nonsense word reading. Measures of comprehension and vocabulary were not used in this study, as the focus was on improvement of word recognition and decoding skills.

Another program intended to improve the word-reading skills of students with reading disabilities is Lovett's PHAST program (Lovett, Lacerenza, & Borden, 2000). This program combined direct instruction in phonics (called PHAB) and strategy instruction in decoding (called WIST). Of the four strategies students learned, one involved morphological analysis. This strategy, called "peeling off," provided extensive training for students in the recognition of prefixes and suffixes in morphologically complex words. In one study Lovett et al. (2000) used the PHAST program with 7- to 13-year-olds with severe reading disabilities. After systematic instruction and practice, the students demonstrated significant gains in word identification skills.

Yet another program, developed by Henry (1988, 1989), entails instruction in word structure and word etymology with the goal of improving students' reading, spelling, and vocabulary. The program is based on the principle that understanding word etymology is important for learning different linguistic units (e.g., phonemes/graphemes, syllables, morphemic units). Henry's program orchestrates instruction by linguistic unit and word origins. Young students are taught sound and letter correspondences in the Anglo-Saxon layer; later lessons involve the transparent morphological units of Anglo-Saxon (e.g., *helpful*). Older students receive instruction in the Latinate and then Greek layers of language, learning relations of word structure and meaning (e.g., *script* means "write," as in *manuscript* and *scripture*, or *micro* means "small," as in *microscope* and *microcosm*). Students learn the meanings of affixes as well as word roots. In one study, third- and fifth-grade normally achieving students and students with learning disabilities who were taught to analyze word structure made significant gains in decoding as well as in deriving meaning from unfamiliar words. Henry also found that the students were able to use these strategies in their content-area reading and writing activities.

The second general type of word study program has the central goal of improving students' vocabulary. Baumann and his colleagues (2002) studied the effectiveness of teaching prefixes and a process of morphemic analysis to fifth graders. In a 12-week program, students in the morphology condition were taught the meanings of prefixes (e.g., *sub-* meaning "under") and then worked on words containing that prefix (e.g., *subzero, subsoil*). A second group of students was taught a context analysis strategy, and a third group received a combination of the two strategies. The results showed positive effects for the two types of strategy instruction, alone and combined, on words the students had worked on in their instructional sessions, as well as on other, untaught words. The strategies did not improve the students' reading comprehension significantly, but perhaps this outcome would be more likely with a longer program of instruction and practice with the strategies.

Along with programs that focus specifically on decoding or word meaning, some programs include instruction in a variety of literacy areas, including decoding, word meaning, vocabulary-learning strategies, and comprehension. An example is Wolf's RAVE-O program, which stands for retrieval, automaticity, vocabulary elaboration, enrichment with language, and orthography (Wolf et al., 2003). In one study, interventions using two versions of Lovett's PHAB program were compared to an intervention that combined PHAB and RAVE-O. The goal of RAVE-O is to develop accuracy and automaticity of word reading at lexical and sublexical levels and to help the students see connections among linguistic systems. Preliminary results indicated that students with low vocabulary scores who received RAVE-O and PHAB made greater progress on a combined measure of oral reading and comprehension (Gray Oral Reading Quotient) than students who received either of the PHAB programs

(PHAB or WIST). These results suggest that emphasis on vocabulary and language learning, combined with an intensive, structured program in phonics, might provide the kind of integration of language processing that is needed to facilitate improvements in vocabulary and reading comprehension for struggling readers.

Learning to Use Morphological Analysis While Reading

All of the above approaches focus on the improvement of decoding and vocabulary knowledge, but they appear not to provide specific instruction in application of newly acquired knowledge during reading of natural texts. A very different goal is to improve students' ability to infer meanings of words in texts when they are reading independently. Some researchers have explored different ways to reach this goal. One such method is teaching students how to derive word meanings from context (e.g., Goerss, Beck, & McKeown, 1999). A second method is called Reciprocal Teaching, in which students learn to generate as well as answer questions about text, ideally developing sensitivity to the ways of thinking about texts as they read (Palincsar & Brown, 1987). A third method focuses on teacher-led discussions of texts, such as Text Talk and Questioning the Author (Beck & McKeown, 2001b; McKeown & Beck, 2004). In each of these programs, teachers discuss the book with the students, including (for example) discussion of unfamiliar words that appear in the text. With sufficient experience with guided discussion of books, students ideally internalize the process of analyzing texts and unfamiliar words in texts.

Common goals of all of these methods are (1) providing students with the cognitive and linguistic tools to understand texts and (2) fostering engagement with texts that will lead to effective comprehension monitoring while reading (Paris et al., 1983). However, given the importance of vocabulary and word analysis strategies for successful comprehension, a crucial component that might be added to these methods is instruction in word analysis strategies and scaffolded experiences applying these strategies in the act of reading.

With this goal in mind, Katz and Carlisle (2002) developed a program they called Close Reading. The program was designed to help upper-elementary students learn to analyze morphologically complex words in context and in doing so to become more engaged in the process of understanding the texts they were reading. From the outset, the program was considered to be most appropriate for poor readers who typically have had few positive experiences reading difficult texts on their own. Because the program would be effective only if students became invested in using analytic strategies for word analysis while reading independently, a major focus was understanding the role of the teacher, who needed to scaffold the student's learning and use of word analysis strategies during reading, gradually relinquishing control as the student took on more and more responsibility for his or her meaning making.

We explored the effectiveness of this program in a series of case studies of students with different types of language-learning difficulties. Students who have a history of reading problems tend to skip over difficult words or to read for a general sense of the meaning of a text; they lack the ability to read and work out the meanings of unfamiliar words and to use the inferences so generated to construct meaning from sentences and longer portions of the text (Westby, 2004). The emphasis on shared reading of texts was important because of the need to replace students' ineffective reading habits and attitudes with a set of analytic tools that they knew they could use effectively. It was our premise that poor comprehension monitoring cannot be corrected by instruction in decoding and/or vocabulary strategies unless that instruction is primarily geared to application of strategies in text reading.

The instructional program was implemented in a tutorial setting over the course of a 12-week intervention. The strategies taught in the program were presented in two modules: morphological analysis followed by context analysis. The format of every 30-minute lesson was the same. For the first 15 minutes, the teacher and the student worked on new material and practice exercises. During this time in the first module, the focus was on morphological analysis. Instruction focused on building morphological awareness, increasing understanding of common suffixes and prefixes, and learning how to use the dictionary. Practice exercises included identifying affixes and base words in speeded drills (e.g., underlining the prefixes and suffixes on words), word sorts (sorting words into categories based on structure and meaning), and word building (constructing morphologically complex words from prefixes, suffixes, and base words).

During the first 15 minutes of the second module, the focus was on context analysis. One goal was to heighten the students' awareness of unfamiliar words in text. Another was to make the students aware that context could be helpful for recognizing and deriving meanings from unfamiliar words. Students received instruction and practice in identifying clues in passages useful in analyzing words in text. They worked with a procedure for using context to read and/or derive meaning from unfamiliar words called the SLAP strategy. The steps include the following: SAY the unknown word to yourself; LOOK for passage clues to the meaning of the word; ASK yourself what the word might mean and find a word or phrase that shows the meaning; PUT the definition in the passage to see if it makes sense. This strategy was practiced using sentence-level and paragraph-level exercises in the first half of the sessions. Then, during shared reading, the SLAP strategy was modeled by the teacher until the students began to use it independently.

In the second half of each session, the student and the teacher read an African folk tale together. A technique of shared reading allowed the teacher as well as the student to have some control over what each person would read. The teacher could stop reading at any point (even mid-sentence), indicating that it was the student's turn. This immediate switch could be used to give the student the opportunity to practice reading a particular word. When it was the student's turn to read, he or she could also decide to stop reading at any point, at which time the teacher took over the reading.

While reading the story, the teacher modeled strategic behaviors. The amount of support the teacher provided decreased over time. Early on, the teacher might say, "That's an interesting word . . . *satiny* . . . hmmm . . . I wonder what that might mean? Do you see a base word in that word?" After several weeks of shared reading, the teacher might say, "I noticed an unfamiliar word in that sentence—did you?" In addition, the teacher periodically stopped to summarize and question what had been read and to ensure that the student was following the meaning of the passage. The goal was for the students to come to use the strategies independently— that is, with less and less support from the teacher over time.

The teacher modeled the two word analysis strategies to demonstrate their value. For example, the teacher might say, "You just read the word *countless*. What do you think it means here? Do you see clues in the sentence that can help you?" Students were encouraged to integrate the morphological analysis and the context analysis strategies. For example, the teacher pointed out instances where using one of the strategies alone would not be sufficient for recognizing and/or deriving meaning from an unknown word.

The findings from three case studies of fourth-grade students suggest that instruction in word analysis and context analysis strategies and extensive practice using these strategies hold promise as a way to improve word reading and comprehension for struggling readers in the upper-elementary years. All three fourth graders made significant gains in reading and listening comprehension, with moderate to large effect sizes, based on comparison of pretest and posttest scores on the Woodcock–Johnson Psychoeducational Battery subtests (Woodcock & Johnson, 1989), as Table 5.1 shows. They also showed significant improvement in oral vocabulary and word-reading skills. The effect sizes varied across students, reflecting the nature of their reading difficulties. Similarly, experimental measures of word reading and word meaning administered at regular intervals through the intervention showed different levels of gains for the three students, largely in keeping with the severity of their difficulties with reading. For example, the student with the most severe word-reading problem at the outset also made the most modest gains on both the experimental and the standardized measures in this area. One implication is that the more severe the reading difficulty, the more likely that a program such as Close Reading needs to be extended through the school year, providing lots of time for practice and integration of learning into familiar routines while working with natural texts.

Because our expectation was that students with language-learning disabilities needed considerable adult support in learning to apply word analysis and text analysis strategies, we carried out a separate study to examine features of one of the students' and the teacher's dialogue while engaged in shared reading (Stone, Carlisle, & Katz, 2002). Of particular interest was the degree of student engagement in, and control of, instructional discourse, as this would represent an index of ownership of the process of engaging in close reading. The guidelines for the teachers

TABLE 5.1. Pretest and Posttest Scores for Three Students from Subtests of the Woodcock–Johnson Psychoeducational Battery–Revised

Subtest	Student 1		Student 2		Student 3	
	Pretest	Posttest	Pretest	Posttest	Pretest	Posttest
Picture Vocab	82 (2.0)	96 (4.2)***	119 (7.2)	115 (7.2)**	91 (2.9)	88 (2.9)*
Oral Vocab	91 (3.3)	99 (4.7)***	103 (4.7)	114 (6.7)***	83 (2.5)	91 (3.7)***
Listening Comp	97 (3.9)	109 (6.4)***	103 (4.9)	116 (8.6)***	75 (1.0)	90 (3.1)***
Letter–Word Id	95 (3.8)	102 (5.1)***	88 (3.1)	90 (3.6)*	93 (3.6)	87 (3.3)***
Passage Comp	99 (4.2)	117 (7.6)***	99 (4.2)	106 (5.6)**	85 (2.8)	89 (3.3)**
Word Attack	91 (3.0)	97 (4.1)**	82 (2.0)	90 (3.0)***	79 (1.9)	78 (2.0)

Note. Standard deviations given in parentheses. Vocab, Vocabulary; Comp, Comprehension; Id, Identification.

*Small effect (.1); ** moderate effect (.3); *** large effect (.5).

in the Close Reading program were relatively unspecified, but they adhered to two general principles: (1) provide only the help the student needs to make successful interpretations of words and texts; and (2) help the student appreciate his or her own progress in using strategies effectively to work out the meanings of unfamiliar words and sentences. At regular intervals during the instructional program, the teachers' interactions with the student were recorded on videotape; analysis of the videotaped shared reading component focused on teacher–student interactions, which were coded for the frequency and context of occurrence of key features of instructional dynamics.

Our analyses focused particularly on student 1 in Table 5.1. The results showed that the coding system was useful in documenting the growth of her interest in paying attention to and working on word meanings, as well as the benefit she derived from the teacher's indirect guidance. The analyses of transcripts complement the standardized measures by indicating changes in the students' engagement and reading behaviors. The following excerpts from student–teacher discourse demonstrate the changes in the teacher's scaffolding of this student's analysis of text, in response to her increasing ability to be aware of and analyze unfamiliar words during reading.

Excerpt 1

TEACHER: Oh, okay (*starts reading*). "Of course, Najeeri didn't know if he'd forgotten anything . . . and hadn't it been set as *cunningly* as any trap that had ever been laid?" Do you know that word, *cunningly*?

STUDENT: I think *cunningly* means, like, the best trap or something?

TEACHER: You're on the right track, yeah.

STUDENT: I know.

TEACHER: Highlight it (*points to text*) and see, you know, um, *cunning* is "clever."

Excerpt 2

STUDENT: (*reading from text*) "Time to get up," he muttered with a yawn. Time to get up (*repeated with a sleepy intonation*). (*Both student and teacher laugh.*) Not there, not that there is anything to get *up* for. Or is there? He frowned *thoughtfully.*"

TEACHER: That's a good word: *thoughtfully.*

STUDENT: I know what *thoughtfully* is.

TEACHER: (*Nods expectantly.*)

STUDENT: Like you're thinking of someone, like, ahh (*smiles.*)

TEACHER: You're full of thought?

STUDENT: Yeah.

In the first excerpt, the teacher raised the question about the word *cunningly*, asked the student to "highlight it" in the text, and initiated discussion of the meaning. In the second excerpt, the teacher merely remarked that *thoughtfully* is a "good word." The student, now accustomed to having conversations about words, volunteered that she knew the meaning and took it upon herself to attempt a definition. The teacher's scaffolding here involves nodding expectantly. These examples show a transition that might have been important in the transfer of the strategy instruction to the student's reading of texts. The study yielded some discourse-based evidence of the student's growing mastery of meaning-making strategies at the level of word and text. For example, the student initiated 43% of the word discussions in session 3, as compared to 67% in session 16. In addition, she made more inferences about word meanings over time. She was successful at inferring meaning from indirect teacher cues in 15% of the opportunities in session 3 and 100% of the opportunities in session 16. Missing here is a way to assess the student's "close reading" when she is working entirely on her own. Trustworthy information on this goal of the Close Reading program would require another study, one presumably of longer duration and requiring the use of a methodology that would suggest students' independent analysis of unfamiliar words (e.g., think aloud).

While our study of teacher–student discussion of texts and words in texts is a work in progress, we note that other researchers, too, hold the conviction that teachers' scaffolding of students' analysis of text is crucial if we hope to see significant changes in their engagement and skill at reading and interpreting words and texts (see Biemiller & Meichenbaum, 1998). If this method is to find a place in the array of evidence-based comprehension-building techniques, one particular challenge is understanding the process of preparing teachers so that they are effective at carrying out analytic discussions of words and texts. Beck and McKeown have led the way in studying ways to train teachers to engage their students in detailed discussion of texts through programs such as Text Talk and Questioning the Author (Beck & McKeown, 2001b; Beck, McKeown,

Hamilton, & Kucan, 1999; McKeown & Buck, 2004). These authors have articulated both the inherent difficulties and the promise of these methods. The promise is so great that continued efforts are warranted.

SUMMARY

If our goal is to help reticent and less skilled readers get more from their reading, researchers and educators need to find ways for the students to become more adept at decoding and understanding unfamiliar words and at using this understanding in the process of interpreting texts that they read on their own. Understanding unfamiliar words in texts, which is critical for reading content-area texts in school, requires inferences about word meanings. Inferences about word meaning are made on the basis of analysis of morphological structure of words and analysis of the use of the words in context. This being the case, it appears that some combination of direct instruction in morphology, decoding strategies, and context analysis strategies should be provided, along with considerable assistance in the process of text analysis. It is only when students believe they know how to analyze unfamiliar words in texts that they will expend the energy to become close readers. Engagement in analytic reading is contingent on their motivation to work at understanding a text, which in turn is contingent on their perception of their ability to address the challenges that inevitably arise when reading texts in school.

Of considerable importance is further study of methods to prepare teachers so that they understand the importance of word analysis for text comprehension, are effective at teaching word and text comprehension strategies, and can lead discussions of texts that help students internalize methods of thinking about the meanings of words and texts.

REFERENCES

Anglin, J. M. (1993). Vocabulary development: A morphological analysis. *Monographs of the Society for Research in Child Development, 58*(10, Serial No. 238).

Baker, L., & Brown, A. C. (1984). Metacognitive skills and reading. In P. D. Pearson, M. Kamil, R. Barr, & P. Mosenthal (Eds.), *Handbook of reading research* (Vol. 1, pp. 353–394). White Plains, NY: Longman.

Baumann, J. F., Edwards, E. C., Font, G., Tereshinski, C. A., Kame'enui, E. J., & Olejnik, S. F. (2002). Teaching morphemic and contextual analysis to fifth-grade students. *Reading Research Quarterly, 37*, 150–176.

Baumann, J. F., & Kame'enui, E. J. (1991). Research on vocabulary instruction: Ode to Voltaire. In J. Flood, J. M. Jensen, D. Lapp, & J. R. Squire (Eds.), *Handbook on research on the teaching of English language arts* (pp. 604–632). New York: Macmillan.

Beck, I., & McKeown, M. (1991). Conditions of vocabulary acquisition. In R. Barr, M. L. Kamil, P. Mosenthal, & P. D. Pearson (Eds.), *Handbook of reading research* (Vol. 2, pp. 789–814). New York: Longman.

Beck, I. L., & McKeown, M. G. (2001a). Inviting students into the pursuit of meaning. *Educational Psychology Review, 13,* 225–241.

Beck, I. L., & McKeown, M. G. (2001b). Text talk: Capturing the benefits of reading aloud experiences for young children. *The Reading Teacher, 55,* 10–20.

Beck, I. L., McKeown, M. G., Hamilton, R. L., & Kucan, L. (1999). *Questioning the author: An approach for enhancing student engagement with text.* Newark, DE: International Reading Association.

Berko, J. (1958). The child's learning of English morphology. *Word, 14,* 150–177.

Berninger, V. B., Nagy, W. E., Carlisle, J. F., Thomson, J., Hoffer, D., Abbott, S., et al. (2003). Effective treatment for children with dyslexia in grades 4–6: Behavioral and brain evidence. In B. Foorman (Ed.), *Preventing and remediating reading difficulties: Bringing science to scale* (pp. 381–347). Baltimore: York Press.

Biemiller, A., & Meichenbaum, D. (1998). The consequences of negative scaffolding for students who learn slowly: A commentary on C. Addison Stone's "The metaphor of scaffolding: Its utility for the field of learning disabilities." *Journal of Learning Disabilities, 31,* 365–369.

Carey, S. (1978). The child as word learner. In M. Halle, J. Bresnan, & G. Miller (Eds.), *Linguistic theory and psychological reality* (pp. 177–194). Cambridge, MA: MIT Press.

Carlisle, J. F. (1987). The use of morphological knowledge in spelling derived forms by learning-disabled and normal students. *Annals of Dyslexia, 37,* 90–108.

Carlisle, J. F. (2002). Awareness of the structure and meaning of morphologically complex words: Impact on reading. *Reading and Writing: An Interdisciplinary Journal, 12,* 169–190.

Carlisle, J. F., & Fleming, J. (2003). Lexical processing of morphologically complex words in the elementary years. *Scientific Studies of Reading, 7,* 239–253.

Carlisle, J. F., Fleming, J., & Gudbrandsen, B. (2000). Incidental word learning in science classes. *Contemporary Educational Psychology, 25,* 184–211.

Carlisle, J. F., Stone, C. A., & Katz, L. A. (2001). The effects of phonological transparency on reading derived words. *Annals of Dyslexia, 51,* 249–276.

Carlo, M. S., August, D., Snow, C. E., Lively, T. J., & White, C. E. (2004). Closing the gap: Addressing the vocabulary needs of English-language learners in bilingual and mainstream classrooms. *Reading Research Quarterly, 39,* 188–215.

Clark, E. V. (1982). The young word maker: A case study of innovation in the child's lexicon. In E. Wanner & L. Gleitman (Eds.), *Language acquisition: The state of the art* (pp. 390–425). Cambridge, UK: Cambridge University Press.

Clark, E. V. (2003). *First language acquisition.* Cambridge, UK: Cambridge University Press.

Fowler, A., & Liberman, I. Y. (1995). The role of phonology and orthography in morphological awareness. In L. Feldman (Ed.), *Morphological aspects of language processing* (pp. 157–188). Hillsdale, NJ: Erlbaum.

Freyd, P., & Baron, J. (1982). Individual differences in acquisition of derivational morphology. *Journal of Verbal Learning and Verbal Behavior, 21,* 282–295.

Fukkink, R. G., & deGlopper, K. (1998). Effects of instruction in deriving word meaning from context: A meta-analysis. *Review of Educational Research, 68*(4), 450–469.

Goerss, B. L., Beck, I. L., & McKeown, M. G. (1999). Increasing remedial students' ability to derive word meaning from context. *Reading Psychology, 20,* 151–175.

Henry, M. K. (1988). Beyond phonics: Integrated decoding and spelling instruction based on word origin and structure. *Annals of Dyslexia, 38,* 258–275.

Henry, M. K. (1989). Children's word structure and knowledge: Implications for decoding and spelling instruction. *Reading and Writing, 1,* 135–152.

Jenkins, J. R., Stein, M. L., & Wysocki, K. (1984). Learning vocabulary through reading. *American Educational Research Journal, 21,* 767–787.

Katz, L. A. (2004). *An investigation of the relationship of morphological awareness to reading comprehension in fourth and sixth grades.* Unpublished doctoral dissertation, University of Michigan.

Katz, L. A., & Carlisle, J. F. (2002, November). *Teaching word-level comprehension to promote literacy.* Invited presentation for the annual meeting of the American Speech–Language–Hearing Association, Atlanta, GA.

Leong, C. K. (1989). Productive knowledge of derivational rules in poor readers. *Annals of Dyslexia, 39,* 94–115.

Lovett, M. W., Lacerenza, L., & Borden, S. L. (2000). Putting struggling readers on the PHAST track: A program to integrate phonological and strategy-based remedial reading instruction and maximize outcomes. *Journal of Learning Disabilities, 33*(5), 458–476.

Mann, V., & Singson, M. (2003). Linking morphological knowledge to English decoding ability: Large effects of little suffixes. In E. M. H. Assink & D. Sandra (Eds.), *Reading complex words: Cross-linguistic studies* (pp. 1–25). New York: Kluwer Academic.

McGregor, K. K. (2004). Developmental dependencies between lexical semantics and reading. In C. A. Stone, E. R. Silliman, B. J. Ehren, & K. Appel (Eds.), *Handbook of language and literacy: Development and disorders* (pp. 302–317). New York: Guilford Press.

McKeown, M. G. (1985). The acquisition of word meaning from context by children of high and low ability. *Reading Research Quarterly, 20*(4), 482–496.

McKeown, M. G., & Beck, I. L. (2004). Transforming knowledge into professional development resources: Six teachers implement a model of teaching for understanding text. *Elementary School Journal, 104,* 391–408.

Nagy, W. E., & Anderson, R. C. (1984). The number of words in printed school English. *Reading Research Quarterly, 19,* 304–330.

Nagy, W. E., Herman, P. A., & Anderson, R. (1985). Learning words from context. *Reading Research Quarterly, 20,* 233–253.

Nagy, W. E., & Scott, J. A. (2000). Vocabulary processes. In M. L. Kamil, P. Mosenthal, P. D. Pearson, & R. Barr (Eds.), *Handbook of reading research* (Vol. 3, pp. 269–284). Mahwah, NJ: Erlbaum.

Nelson, K. (1996). *Language in cognitive development: The emergence of the mediated mind.* Cambridge, UK: Cambridge University Press.

Oetting, J. B., Rice, M. L., & Swank, L. K. (1995). Quick incidental learning (QUIL) of words by school-age children with and without specific language impairment. *Journal of Speech and Hearing Research, 38,* 434–445.

Palincsar, A. S., & Brown, D. A. (1987). Enhancing instructional time through attention to metacognition. *Journal of Learning Disabilities, 20*(2), 66–75.

Paris, S. G., Lipson, M. Y., & Wixson, K. K. (1983). Becoming a strategic reader. *Contemporary Educational Psychology, 8,* 293–316.

Reichle, E. D., & Perfetti, C. A. (2003). Morphology in word identification: A word-experience model that accounts for morpheme frequency effects. *Scientific Studies of Reading, 7,* 219–237.

Schreuder, R., & Baayan, R. H. (1995). Modeling morphological processing. In L. Feldman (Ed.), *Morphological aspects of language processing* (pp. 131–154). Hillsdale, NJ: Erlbaum.

Shefelbine, J. L. (1990). Student factors related to variability in learning word meanings from context. *Journal of Reading Behavior, 22,* 71–97.

Stanovich, K. E. (1986). Matthew effects in reading: Some consequences of individual differences in the acquisition of literacy. *Reading Research Quarterly, 21,* 360–407.

Stone, C. A., Carlisle, J. F., & Katz, L. A. (2002). *Tracking variations in instructional discourse across teachers, students, and time.* La Jolla, CA: Pacific Coast Research Conference.

Taft, M. (2003). Morphological representation as a correlation between form and meaning. In E. M. H. Assink & D. Sandra (Eds.), *Reading complex words: Cross-language studies* (pp. 113–137). New York: Kluwer Academic.

Taft, M., & Zhu, X. (1995). The representation of bound morphemes in the lexicon: A Chinese study. In L. B. Feldman (Ed.), *Morphological aspects of language processing* (pp. 293–316). Hillsdale, NJ: Erlbaum.

Templeton, S. (1989). Tacit and explicit knowledge of derivational morphology: Foundations for a unified approach to spelling and vocabulary development in the intermediate grades and beyond. *Reading Psychology, 10,* 233–253.

Tyler, A., & Nagy, W. (1989). The acquisition of English derivational morphology. *Journal of Memory and Language, 28,* 649–667.

Tyler, A., & Nagy, W. E. (1990). Use of derivational morphology during reading. *Cognition, 36,* 17–34.

Westby, C. (2004). A language perspective on executive functioning, meta-cognition, and self-regulation in reading. In C. A. Stone, E. R. Silliman, B. J. Ehren, & K. Appel (Eds.), *Handbook of language and literacy: Development and disorders* (pp. 398–427). New York: Guilford Press.

White, T. G., Power, M. A., & White, S. (1989). Morphological analysis: Implications for teaching and understanding vocabulary growth. *Reading Research Quarterly, 24,* 283–303.

Windsor, J. (2000). The role of phonological opacity in reading achievement. *Journal of Speech, Language, and Hearing Research, 43,* 50–61.

Wolf, M., O'Brien, B., Adams, K. D., Joffee, T., Jeffrey, J., Lovett, M., et al. (2003). Working for time: Reflections on naming, speed, reading fluency, and intervention. In B. Foorman (Ed.), *Preventing and remediating reading difficulties: Bringing science to scale* (pp. 355–379). Baltimore: York Press.

Woodcock, R. W., & Johnson, M. B. (1989). *Woodcock–Johnson psychoeducational battery—Revised.* Allen, TX: DLM.

Wysocki, K., & Jenkins, J. R. (1987). Deriving word meaning through morphological generalization. *Reading Research Quarterly, 22,* 66–81.

CHAPTER 6

Morphological Structure Awareness, Vocabulary, and Reading

CATHERINE McBRIDE-CHANG

HUA SHU

JESSICA YUEN WAI NG

XIANGZHI MENG

TREVOR PENNEY

The purpose of this chapter is to highlight one concept of morphological awareness known as morphological structure awareness, and to explore its links to reading and vocabulary. The idea of *morphological structure awareness*, defined as awareness of and access to the structure of morphemes within words consisting of two or more morphemes, emerged out of an interest in cognitive correlates of word recognition in Chinese (McBride-Chang, Shu, Zhou, Wat, & Wagner, 2003). Preliminary results suggest that morphological structure awareness is a unique cognitive correlate of reading for some developmental periods, in at least some orthographies, and may be useful in understanding early vocabulary growth across languages. In this chapter, we first review the concepts of phonological awareness and morphological structure awareness, then demonstrate the usefulness of morphological structure awareness for predicting Chinese reading. Finally, we consider the potential importance of morphological awareness in relation to vocabulary skill in both Chinese and English. However, our conclusions are tentative, and we offer some cautions related to this perspective at the end of the chapter.

PHONOLOGICAL AWARENESS

In considering morphological structure awareness in relation to reading in Chinese, we begin by reviewing the cognitive construct that has been most compelling as a strong correlate of reading, particularly in English, over the past 40 years: phonological awareness. What can phonological awareness contribute to reading development in Chinese, and why might a concept such as morphological awareness be useful as a complement to it?

Although it is clear that phonological awareness is a strong correlate of reading in many alphabets, particularly among young children, the role of phonological awareness for reading Chinese has always been ambiguous. On the one hand, we have the *universal phonological principle* (Tan & Perfetti, 1999), which states that reading, across orthographies, involves phonological processing. On the other hand, the concept of phonological awareness for Chinese character recognition has at least three limitations when compared to phonological awareness in relation to alphabetic reading.

First, the phonetic component in any given Chinese character provides only a limited amount of information about how the character is pronounced (Shu, Chen, Anderson, Wu, & Xuan, 2003). Most (about 80%) Chinese characters are *compound characters*, which means that they are comprised of a *semantic radical*, which indicates something about the meaning of the character, and a *phonetic*, which may provide some information about the character's pronunciation. The information provided by the phonetic is limited in that, from character to character, the pronunciation of it might differ by onset, tone, or overall. Although letters can be unreliable within alphabetic words as well (e.g., the sounds represented by "p" in *psychology, philosophy,* and *pedigree* differ considerably), there is greater unreliability of phonological information in Chinese characters as compared to words represented in the English alphabet (Shu et al., 2003) and likely most or all other alphabets as well. Thus the extent to which awareness of and access to speech sounds, one definition of phonological awareness, matter for reading development in Chinese is unclear.

Second, measurement of phonological awareness is relatively easy and limited in Chinese as compared to English, German, or many other alphabetic languages. In particular, Chinese has virtually no consonant clusters, whereas English has many of them. The most difficult level of measurement of phonological awareness in English, phonemic awareness (e.g., *split* without the /l/ sound is *spit*), does not exist in Chinese.

Thus, from a purely practical perspective, children's performances on tasks of phonological awareness in Chinese may reach a ceiling at a young age. Limited variance on such tasks reduces the amount of variance that can be explained in reading itself.

Third, reading Chinese characters requires only syllable-level phonological awareness. Thus, even when phoneme-level awareness is tested in Chinese children, such awareness may not be independently associated with Chinese character recognition. For example, in one correlational study (McBride-Chang, Bialystok, Chong, & Li, 2004), when both phoneme- and syllable-level phonological awareness tasks were included in regression equations predicting Chinese character recognition in kindergarten and first-grade children from Hong Kong and Xian, China, only the syllable-level phonological awareness measure predicted unique variance in reading; the phoneme-level awareness measure did not. These results are relevant to a consideration of the importance of phonological awareness for reading in Chinese because syllable awareness seems to develop naturally and early (Treiman & Zukowski, 1991). Thus tasks of syllable awareness simply become too easy for children to be important cognitive correlates of reading past the age of about 6. The question then becomes, What else could be a useful cognitive skill in learning to read Chinese? In response to this question, we began to think about the concept of morphological awareness, first as a predictor of early Chinese character recognition and then, very modestly, of reading comprehension.

MORPHOLOGICAL STRUCTURE AWARENESS

We came up with a concept of morphological structure awareness based on the observation that the Chinese language is analytic and, at least intuitively, in relation to English, relatively semantically transparent. A brief introduction to the Chinese language and its orthography in comparison to English may highlight these features. Most Chinese words consist of two or more morphemes, and each morpheme simultaneously represents both a morpheme and a syllable. By way of contrast, morphemes, the smallest units of meaning in language, are typically represented in a variety of phonological units in English. The smallest English morpheme is a single phoneme, as in the *s*, indicating plural, in *cats*. Syllable-length morphemes are obvious in compound words, such as the morpheme *sun* in *suntan* or *Sunday*. In English, a morpheme might even comprise more than one syllable, as in the single-morpheme word *lettuce*. In comparison, Chinese is consistent in its one-to-one mapping of syllable to morpheme. Moreover, each of these morphosyllables is represented by a single Chinese character.

We refer to Chinese as an analytic and relatively semantically transparent language because Chinese words are built from single morphemes in language in a way that, to some extent, highlights their meaning. For example, whereas in English the words *backpack*, *teach*, and *read* do not appear, in linguistic structure, to have any association with one another, they are related in Chinese by the word *book* (書 shu1). *Backpack* is shu1bao1 (書包), *teach* is jiao4 shu1 (教書), and *read* is kan4 shu1 (看書). Another example involves the Chinese morpheme dian4 (electricity), which can be found in the words *movie* (電影 dian4 ying3) and *television* (電視 dian4 shi4). Naïve practical experience in examining the performance of children on tasks of receptive vocabulary translated from English to Chinese makes clear that Chinese children's vocabulary skills are difficult to measure because of the semantic transparency of some words. As some cross-cultural researchers have found, in a receptive vocabulary task in which vocabulary words are simply translated from English to Chinese, Chinese children are likely to perform much better than their English-speaking counterparts. This performance is, at least in part, a function of the semantic transparency of Chinese. Particularly in a forced-choice receptive vocabulary task, children can make use of the morphemes they know from previously learned words (e.g., *shu1*, *dian4*) to make an educated guess as to the meanings of newly encountered words. The morphological structures of words in English are less transparent, so educated guessing may be far less realistic in English. In addition, compounding is much more frequent in Chinese as compared to English; that is, generalizing morphemes to new words appears to be relatively common in Chinese. Generalizing morphological knowledge in English also occurs with some degree of regularity (e.g., Clark, 1995). However, in early childhood particularly, we wonder whether there may be more generalization of known lexical compounding morphemes in Chinese to novel Chinese words as compared to English.

We attempted to tap Chinese children's morphological awareness skills by having children combine familiar morphemes in new ways. An example of this in English relies on analogy, with scenarios such as the following: "Basketball is a game in which players throw a ball through a basket. What could you call a game in which you throw a ball into a bucket?" (The best example, according to our scoring thus far, would be *bucketball*.) An example from Hong Kong, in Cantonese, is the following: 有一種家庭電器可以用來*洗衣服*，我們叫它*洗衣機*。("There is a home appliance that is used to wash *clothes*; it is called a *washing machine* [literally, *washing clothes machine*]"). 有一種新的家庭電器可以用來洗鞋，我們會怎麼叫它呢？**[洗鞋機]**。("If that home appliance could be used to wash *shoes*, what would you call that?" [A good answer is *washing shoes machine*]). We thought this type of task might be a useful indicator of children's understanding of how to combine morphemes in their language. The idea behind this task is based on Chomsky's (1976) concept of generativity in language and on observations by Berko (1958), Clark (1995), and others that children look for logic in language from early on. Thus we sometimes find ourselves confronted with demands from young children to explain, for example, why *chestnut* has that name, given that it has nothing to do with one's chest. Another example of this assumption of logic in language comes from the assertion from an older child that a *genius* is someone who is both smart and magical because "*genius* comes from *genie*." Across languages, children are generative and creative with language (Chomsky, 1976). Given this well-known observation, we were curious about whether or not understanding of the morphology of words in one's native language would be useful for helping children to read, at least in Chinese.

Researchers similarly recognize children's analytic focus on the script in learning to read. In script, as in language, children try to capitalize on the logical aspects of the system. What is logical about learning to read English is that each of the letters of the alphabet represents only one or at most a few different phonemes in written words. This is the *alphabetic principle*. The importance of the alphabetic principle for reading English and many other alphabets is in the relative consistency offered by the letters. The importance of phonological awareness for learning to read English has been linked directly to this alphabetic principle (for a review, see Shankweiler, 1999). In contrast, as mentioned above, although generalizing phonological information in the phonetic of one Chinese character to another character containing the same phonetic may be somewhat helpful in learning to read Chinese, its utility is limited in comparison to the alphabet in English. On the other hand, what is perhaps most logical for those who are beginning readers of Chinese is the way in which morphemes can be combined to form new words.

As an adult beginning learner of Chinese, one of us authors (Catherine McBride-Chang) has had some personal experience with the logic of

Chinese morphemes. Although her spoken vocabulary level in Mandarin Chinese is perhaps at the high-beginner to low-intermediate college level, her Chinese character recognition skills are substantially below this. This mismatch has occurred because she did not subsequently practice the Chinese characters she learned in an introductory college Chinese course, whereas she employed the daily language skills she had learned at home with her Mandarin-speaking husband and in-laws. Fifteen years later, she sought to study Chinese in a formal course again. Given her vocabulary skills, she was permitted to take a second-year college-level Chinese course, provided that she very quickly memorize between 400 and 600 Chinese characters in preparation for the course. With intensive practice of these characters over a period of 6 weeks, she entered the second-year class. The course was well matched to her conversational skills, but she had particular difficulty when text reading was required. After all, 6 weeks did not seem sufficient for all of the characters to have crystallized in her mind. In class, she found that she often would make use of her vocabulary skills to make "educated guesses" about Chinese text. In particular, based on context, she could often recognize two-morpheme words while confidently visually recognizing only a single Chinese character in the word, based on context. Examples of this include recognizing xue2 xiao4 (學校, together meaning school) from the first character (meaning to study) only or ke3 ai4 (可愛, meaning lovely) from the second character (meaning to love). To what extent do children, who, like a second-language (L2) learner of Chinese, also may not recognize all Chinese characters learned equally well, make use of their knowledge of language structure to try to recognize words in text?

Although this case of an adult learning to read Chinese as an L2 could be criticized in many ways in relation to understanding how native-speaking Chinese children learn to read Chinese, it brings up some questions about Chinese literacy that remain relatively unanswered. First, do Chinese children, like adult L2 readers of Chinese, use their knowledge of the morphological structure of spoken Chinese to learn to read Chinese characters? Second, if children do make use of such knowledge, to what extent is morphological awareness dissociable from awareness of the syllable structure of Chinese, that is, phonological awareness at the syllable level? More broadly, is morphological structure awareness a uniquely important cognitive construct for reading Chinese, or is it merely associated with many other cognitive skills that have already been shown to correlate with Chinese character recognition, such as vocabulary skills, phonological awareness, or speeded naming? Third, is morphological awareness causally related to Chinese character recognition, or is it developed as a result of good Chinese character recognition skills?

MORPHOLOGICAL STRUCTURE AWARENESS AND READING IN CHINESE

We have begun to tackle some of these questions with data on children from both Hong Kong and Beijing. In several sets of data, we do observe a strong association of morphological structure awareness to Chinese character recognition. Most of these data sets are correlational only and do not address causality. In addition, we have not looked specifically at strategy use in early readers. Thus, the extent to which children, like adult L2 learners of Chinese, make use of their awareness of morphological structure to read Chinese (our first question) remains unclear. Nevertheless, the strong correlations of morphological structure awareness and Chinese character recognition across data sets suggests that these abilities may be bidirectionally associated with one another.

The second question, regarding the unique variance explained in Chinese character recognition by the morphological structure awareness task, is more easily answered. In one study of Hong Kong children in kindergarten and second grade (McBride-Chang et al., 2003), we demonstrated that our task of morphological structure awareness (which we then called "morphological construction") was a unique predictor of character recognition across grade levels. In fact, across all the reading-related tasks we administered, including measures of general speed, speeded naming (of both objects and numbers), phonological awareness, and vocabulary knowledge, the morphological structure awareness task was the only measure that was uniquely predictive of reading skill in both grade levels.

We then included the same tasks in a parallel study on Chinese children from Beijing. However, although Hong Kong and Beijing are both Chinese societies, they differ substantially in several aspects potentially relevant to literacy development. First, the medium of instruction in Beijing is Mandarin, whereas children are taught in Cantonese in Hong Kong. Mandarin and Cantonese are different languages. Second, whereas Beijing teachers use Pinyin, an alphabetic system, as an aid to teaching Chinese character recognition, Hong Kong teachers use no phonetic coding system as an aid to reading instruction. Rather, Hong Kong teachers use the "look-and-say" method of literacy instruction, in which children are encouraged to encode the character visually and holistically. The significance of this instructional contrast is particularly apparent in its relation to the importance of phonological awareness for learning to read Chinese. Beijing teachers make phonological access to symbols via Pinyin an explicit requirement in learning to read, whereas Hong Kong teachers do not. Third, formal reading instruction begins earlier in Hong Kong (at around age 3.5 years) than in Beijing (at around ages 5–6 years).

Given these differences, we were interested in examining the relative importance of morphological structure awareness for Chinese character recognition in Beijing kindergarten and second-grade children. Table 6.1 shows the results separately for Beijing and Hong Kong second graders. As demonstrated in Table 6.1, the association of morphological structure awareness to Chinese character recognition in Beijing was virtually identical to that found for Hong Kong second graders. Again, the morphological structure awareness construct was uniquely associated with Chinese character recognition, even controlling for the other reading-related tasks included in the battery.

As compared to our original Hong Kong sample, however, virtually none of the kindergarten children from Beijing could read when we tested them. Initially, this seemed like an exciting research opportunity because we hoped to follow them from the middle to the end of kindergarten when, presumably, their reading skills might have improved substantially. Unfortunately, the appearance of SARS (severe acute respiratory

TABLE 6.1. Regression Predicting Chinese Character Reading of Beijing and Hong Kong Grade 2 Students

Variables	Beijing		Hong Kong	
	Standardized beta	t	Standardized beta	t
Syllable deletion	−.09	−.91	−.12	−1.28
Phoneme-onset deletion	.05	.54	.16	1.72
Morphological structure awareness	.25	2.77**	.22	2.22*
Vocabulary	.19	2.08*	.18	1.99*
Number naming	−.47	−4.70***	−.15	−1.71
Object naming	.12	1.25	−.17	−1.91
Cross out	.26	2.37*	−.02	−.16
Visual matching	−.05	−.44	.25	2.40*

*$p < .05$; **$p < .01$; ***$p < .001$.

syndrome) in Beijing interfered with this plan. Happily, we managed to test the character recognition skills of 59 of the original 100 children initially included in the study approximately 9 months after initial testing. This was a difficult task because by that time the children had scattered from a single kindergarten to several different primary schools. The correlations of these children's cognitive skills at time 1 with Chinese character recognition at time 2 are displayed in Table 6.2. Approximately one-third of the sample still could not read by this time. Nevertheless, the correlations suggest that the morphological structure awareness task, in addition to speeded naming, found in other studies to correlate substantially with Chinese character recognition (e.g., Ho & Lai, 1999), were the strongest predictors of early reading skill over 9 months. In contrast, the phonological awareness measures do not appear to have been good longitudinal predictors of Chinese reading, at least in this small sample.

Might the morphological structure awareness task have practical value for understanding reading achievement? In a further analysis, we split the small Beijing sample of kindergartners from time 1 into those who scored 0 on the Chinese character recognition task and those who read one or more words correctly at our second testing time. There were 16 children in the first group and 43 in the second group. The latter group had a mean score of 4.49 (SD = 6.13) on our measure of Chinese character recognition at time 2. We then compared the two groups on the morphological structure awareness task at time 1. On this task, which consisted of 20 items, we found that the time 2 nonreaders had initially scored a mean of 10.63 (SD = 4.18), whereas the time 2 readers had scored approximately 10% higher on average (M = 12.84; SD = 3.05). The difference between these groups' morphological structure awareness scores at time 1 was significant ($t(58)$ = −2.23, $p < .03$). We therefore

TABLE 6.2. Correlations of Chinese Character Recognition at Time 2 with Other Variables among Beijing Kindergartners at Time 1

	Chinese character recognition, time 2
Syllable deletion	.00
Phoneme deletion	−.08
Vocabulary	.14
Morphological structure awareness	.32*
Number naming	−.33*

Note. n = 59.
*$p < .05$.

tentatively conclude that this task of morphological structure awareness might have some practical value in distinguishing those who may have difficulty learning to read from those who learn to read without difficulty. At the same time, however, we must caution that all of the children in this small sample were considered to be developmentally normal; no one at such a young age could be considered a "poor" reader.

In one more small study of Chinese reading and the morphological structure task, we focused on the reading comprehension of third graders. The reading comprehension task was a speeded one in which children were asked to read as many of the 90 sentences presented, in a paper-and-pencil test, as possible within 15 minutes. Each sentence was accompanied by five pictures, and students were asked to indicate the matching picture for each sentence by circling it. This task was group-administered in a classroom during school hours in Hong Kong. Fifty-nine third-grade students completed this task in addition to individually administered measures of phonological awareness (onset and rhyme detection), one orthographic task (lexical decision, involving distinguishing real from pseudoword printed characters), a measure of speeded number naming, and a Chinese character recognition test. All of these tasks were taken from the Hong Kong Test of Specific Learning Difficulties in Reading and Writing (HKT-SpLD) (Ho, Chan, Tsang, & Lee, 2000). Along with these tasks, these children were also administered a morphological structure awareness task. This task consisted of 11 of the original 20 items administered that were positively correlated with Chinese character recognition. Thus, in this study, we created new, more difficult items to measure morphological structure awareness. Of the original 20, only 11 were included in the analyses described below, because nine of the originals were found to be poor items either because they were confusing to the children or because they were not correlated with Chinese character recognition.

We focus here particularly on the utility of the morphological structure awareness measure in explaining variance in reading comprehension in correlational data. As shown in Table 6.3, when age and tasks of orthographic and phonological skills were entered first into the regression equation, they explained 19% of the variance in reading comprehension. The morphological structure awareness task, entered into the regression at step 2, contributed an additional 11% of the variance in this analysis. We repeated the analysis again, this time with Chinese character word reading included in step 1 as well. With this measure included, 29% of the variance in reading comprehension was explained.

TABLE 6.3. Hierarchical Regression Predicting Chinese Reading Comprehension in 58 Hong Kong Grade 3 Students

Step/variables	R^2	R^2 change
1. Age, digit naming, rhyme detection, onset detection, and lexical decision	.19	.19
2. Morphological structure awareness	.30	.11**
1. Age, digit naming, rhyme detection, onset detection, lexical decision, and Chinese character recognition	.29	.29**
2. Morphological structure awareness	.33	.04

Note. For the regression without Chinese character recognition, $F_{(56, 6)} = 3.54$; for the regression with Chinese character recognition, $F_{(56, 7)} = 3.74$.

The morphological structure task entered into the equation at step 2 contributed a unique 4% of the variance to the equation, so that 33% of the variance in reading comprehension was explained using all available measures. As shown in Table 6.4, with all reading-related measures included in the equation, the standardized beta of the morphological structure task was relatively large. It was significantly and uniquely associated with reading comprehension when Chinese character recognition was not included in the equation but did not attain conventional significance ($p < .10$) with character recognition included. Nevertheless, given the relatively small sample included and the large number of measures used to predict the comprehension measure, the morphological structure task may be worth pursuing as a possible unique correlate of Chinese reading comprehension in future studies.

TABLE 6.4. Final Beta Weights Predicting Chinese Reading Comprehension in 58 Hong Kong Grade 3 Students

Variables	Standardized beta	t
Age (months)	.11	.88
Chinese character reading (max. = 150)	.25	1.64
Digit rapid naming (in seconds)	−.18	−1.33
Rhyme detection (max. = 18)	.09	.60
Onset deletion (max. = 15)	−.13	−.93
Lexical decision (max. = 60)	.02	.13
Morphological structure awareness (max. = 11)	.28	1.72

Note. $R^2 = .33$.
*$p < .05$; **$p < .01$; ***$p < .001$.

With these analyses, we have tried to demonstrate why the concept of morphological structure awareness is of interest for understanding reading development in Chinese children. We have some evidence that morphological structure awareness is strongly correlated with early character recognition and is even associated with reading comprehension. This skill is to some extent dissociable from phonological awareness tasks in our data sets; indeed, the morphological structure awareness task emerges as a unique correlate of reading, at least in these data. However, as with the long-standing debate in studies of the relation of phonological awareness to English literacy development (e.g., Castles & Coltheart, 2004), we find it much more difficult to specify causal associations of morphological awareness to Chinese character recognition. Given the strong one (syllable) to one (morpheme) to one (character) associations of phonology, meaning, and print representation in Chinese, it is likely that morphological awareness and reading skill are bidirectionally associated from early on. The results of our correlational and group comparison of 59 Beijing kindergartners followed over time do suggest that there is some reason to suspect that morphological awareness may, in part, facilitate better character recognition in early readers; further studies will be needed to pursue this idea.

At the same time, however, children's morphological structure awareness must emerge from their processing of oral language. Early language develops primarily from whole to parts (for a review, see McBride-Chang, 2004). Parallel to the *lexical restructuring hypothesis*, which posits that phonological representation develops as a result of vocabulary acquisition (e.g., Fowler, 1991; Goswami, 2002; Metsala & Walley, 1998), morphological structure awareness also likely emerges with increased vocabulary knowledge. As a parallel to oral vocabulary development, in reading of Chinese, one study noted a pronounced developmental shift from a word-dominant pattern of reading Chinese characters in second graders to a character-dominant pattern in adulthood (Chen, Song, Lau, Wong, & Tang, 2003). At the same time, however, vocabulary knowledge and morphological structure awareness likely interact from a young age. For example, 2- and 3-year-olds can generate new terms for things they see in their environment by using their knowledge of morphemes (e.g., substituting the term *plantman* for *gardener;* see Clark, 1995). Causal mechanisms among morphological structure awareness, vocabulary knowledge, and reading development are thus likely to be complex.

MORPHOLOGICAL STRUCTURE AWARENESS
AND VOCABULARY KNOWLEDGE

The idea of morphological structure awareness emerged out of our explorations of Chinese reading. As described above, we were looking for a complement to phonological awareness that might account for reading skills in Chinese children. However, as we continued to think about the concept of morphological structure awareness as a cognitive construct, it became clear to us that this construct might be a useful link to understanding vocabulary development as well. The idea that morphology is associated with vocabulary knowledge seems almost so obvious as to be laughable. What is new in our conceptualization here is primarily a focus on a cognitive construct that might be practically, as well as theoretically, useful for understanding vocabulary growth. There is an important and somewhat varied literature on the extent to which different aspects of phonological processing are associated with vocabulary skills (Avons, Wragg, Cupples, & Lovegrove, 1998; Bowey, 2001; Gathercole, Service, Hitch, Adams, & Martin, 1999; Gathercole, Willis, Emslie, & Baddeley, 1992; Metsala, 1999). To what extent might the construct of morphological structure awareness explain unique variance in vocabulary knowledge in children?

To explore this question, we reanalyzed the data sets referred to previously from Hong Kong and Beijing. Each data set included approximately 100 children each from kindergarten and second grade. We also included a data set of approximately 100 children each from kindergarten and second grade from the United States; these data are presented elsewhere (McBride-Chang, Wagner, Muse, Shu, & Chow, 2005). Our measure of morphological structure awareness in the United States was similar to that in China. However, in this task, we also included some items measuring inflectional morphology in addition to the lexical compounding of items. An example of an inflectional morphology item is the following (following Berko, 1958): "Here is one hux. Now there are two of them. There are two _____ [huxes]." The purpose of this analysis in all three cultures was the same: we examined whether the morphological structure task could predict unique variance in concurrently collected data on vocabulary knowledge, controlling for other phonological-processing skills and word recognition ability. Given the strong associations of reading with vocabulary knowledge in some studies (see Nagy & Anderson, 1984), we thought it would be particularly important to control for reading ability in these analyses. As Table 6.5 in-

TABLE 6.5. Final Beta Weights Predicting Vocabulary Knowledge in Hong Kong, Beijing, and the United States, among Kindergarten and Second Grade Students

Variables	Hong Kong		Beijing		United States	
	Beta	t	Beta	t	Beta	t
Grade	−.23	−1.67	−.00	−.01	−.23	−1.73
Age	.26	2.04*	.11	.46	.30	2.39*
Morphological structure awareness	.30	3.59***	.22	3.16**	.38	6.28***
Phoneme-onset deletion	.06	1.05	.20	2.18*	.22	3.17**
Character recognition/word identification	.37	3.62***	.34	2.61*	.16	2.09*
Number naming	.07	1.21	.12	1.01	.02	.38
Object naming	−.09	−1.35	−.06	−.63	−.10	−1.66

$*p < .05; **p < .01; ***p < .001.$

dicates, in combined samples in all three cultures, the morphological structure awareness task was a significant predictor of vocabulary skill, even controlling for word recognition skill. What was the unique contribution of this task to vocabulary knowledge? In Beijing, the variance explained by all tasks combined excluding the morphological structure task was 51%; the morphological task contributed a unique 2% of variance to the equation. In Hong Kong, at step 1, the variables combined contributed 45% of the variance in vocabulary knowledge, and the morphological awareness task contributed 3% extra variance to the equation in step 2. In the U.S. data, 49% of the varance in vocabulary knowledge was contributed by all of the tasks in step 1; the morphological task contributed a unique 8% of the variance at step 2.

These data indicate that our task of morphological structure awareness is potentially useful for understanding vocabulary development, apart from phonological-processing and reading skills. Given the strong correspondences among syllables, morphemes, and Chinese characters in Chinese, it is particularly interesting that our measure of morphological awareness uniquely explained variance in vocabulary skills in both Chinese societies, controlling for all reading-related tasks measured. In the U.S. data, the unique percentage of variance contributed alone by this single task to explain variability in vocabulary knowledge was relatively great. Nevertheless, all of these data presented are correlational. Thus it is imperative that we follow up on these ideas about the interactions of phonological and morphological awareness in explaining vocabulary development longitudinally. We are currently testing this idea in approximately 280 children each from Beijing and Hong Kong followed from 9 months through (currently) ages 5 (in Beijing) and 4 (in Hong Kong). Preliminary analyses suggest that this task predicts unique variance in vocabulary knowledge in young children, even controlling for earlier vocabulary knowledge and phonological skills.

By way of contrast to these results relating morphological structure awareness to vocabulary knowledge in both Chinese and English, our measure of morphological structure awareness was not a unique predictor of word recognition in English. Given the centrality of phonological awareness for early decoding skills, this finding should not be particularly surprising. There is mounting evidence that specific types of morphological awareness that better distinguish derivational and inflectional morphology play a role in reading development of some alphabetic scripts, particularly among older children in primary and secondary school (e.g., Casalis & Louis-Alexandre, 2000; Rispens, 2004). Nevertheless, we are converging on one theme of universals and specifics of early vocabulary and reading development: whereas phonological awareness appears to be particularly important for beginning reading of English and some other alphabetic orthographies, morphological structure awareness may be particularly important for learning to read Chinese. We have presented some arguments and some data related to the potential importance of morphological structure awareness for learning to read Chinese throughout this chapter. Our second theme is that across cultures, both phonological awareness and morphological structure awareness are universally important for vocabulary development. This idea is outlined further below.

UNIVERSALS AND SPECIFICS OF MORPHOLOGICAL STRUCTURE AWARENESS

By definition, oral languages make use of both phonological and morphological information. These typically overlap substantially. An example of the overlap might be the fact that many words that are indicated as plural in English (e.g., *cats, tops*) end with a single letter *s*, pronounced /s/. At the same time, however, an indication of plural may be signaled by the different speech sound /z/ (as in *eggs, farms*). Likewise, these sounds, falling at the end of words, do not necessarily signal the same meaning consistently. For example, the /s/ sound in *dress* or *face* does not signal a plural version of these words; neither does the /z/ sound in *buzz* or *haze*. What we have shown in our correlational data is that both phonological and morphological awareness skills are associated with one another, but also that morphological structure awareness ability may uniquely explain variance in vocabulary knowledge, at least in Mandarin, Cantonese, and English. Given the undisputed importance of phonological and morphological information across all oral languages, it may be reasonable to conjecture that the associations among phonological awareness, morphological awareness, and vocabulary knowledge may be fairly consistent across languages. We have argued for this position in another paper that includes Korean data as well (McBride-Chang et al., 2005).

This idea is, however, subject to criticism on a number of fronts. First, the question of measurement is central to any conceptualization of the ways in which phonological awareness, morphological awareness, and vocabulary knowledge are associated across languages. Phonological differences across languages make phonological awareness particularly difficult to master in some languages, such as English, and easier, at least to measure, in others, such as Chinese. Measuring the cognitive construct of morphological awareness brings similar challenges. Particularly in young children, inflectional grammar in Chinese is relatively rarely required; compounding is relatively important. In English, far more inflectional morphology is required; compounding occurs less frequently. It is, therefore, overly simplistic to assert that our measures of morphological awareness, centering only on compounding in Chinese but on inflectional grammar and compounding in English, are cross-linguistically comparable for the age levels we have included in our studies. Across most studies of phonological awareness, there is also some confounding of semantics and phonology. Most phonological awareness tasks make use of real words because they are easier for young children to think about and manipulate. In some tasks, morphology and phonology overlap. For example, syllable deletion tasks require the deletion of a syllable that most often represents a morpheme, particularly in Chinese. This is also a problem for a conceptualization of the ways in which morphological awareness and phonological awareness are associated with one another and with vocabulary skills.

From an evolutionary perspective, however, the idea that morphological structure awareness and phonological-processing skills are both important for vocabulary growth is reasonable. Geary (1995) conceptualizes biologically primary abilities as those that arose in all human societies as a consequence of evolutionary pressures. Within language, morphological awareness, phonological processing, and vocabulary knowledge are all biologically primary abilities. All are universally involved in spoken language with development. Although it is true that in very young children conscious awareness of morpheme structure or phonological structure is not necessary for language to develop, with age and growth in vocabulary knowledge such awareness develops, perhaps bidirectionally with vocabulary. This conscious awareness can be measured, and variability among children in it can be demonstrated, across human societies. Reading, on the other hand, is a biologically secondary ability (Geary, 1995) because it did not evolve across all human societies. Rather, reading has arisen from certain symbol systems created in different societies over very short periods of time. Although all normally developing human beings around the world have language, many human beings cannot read. Moreover, the scripts that are read in different societies differ markedly and make greater and lesser use of certain biologically primary abilities. Thus it is logical that whereas phonological awareness and morphological structure awareness may be universally associated with vocabulary development, their relations to reading may differ markedly depending upon the script to be read. We hope to continue to pursue this theme in future research.

Despite the many theoretical and methodological issues involved in making cross-cultural comparisons of the associations of cognitive constructs to vocabulary or reading, we think this research is well worth pursuing. We have found that, in thinking about different scripts and what makes them easy or difficult to read, we have perhaps discovered a construct, morphological structure awareness, that may have different functions in different societies. Admittedly, we have a lot to do in terms of refining measurement of this idea. Measuring it using analogy only, for example, may limit its usefulness because we have thus far scored children's answers as right or wrong only. As Berko (1958) demonstrated, children show a great deal of variability in their etymological understanding of vocabulary. Answers are not strictly right or wrong much of the time. Therefore, in future work, we would like to expand our measurement of this concept to solicit open-ended answers as well as structured ones and to explore additional measures of morphological awareness. Such exploration may be both theoretically useful in understanding the universals and specifics of vocabulary and literacy development and also practically meaningful as we come up with new tools to assess those who may be at risk for early language or reading problems across societies.

ACKNOWLEDGMENTS

This study was supported by RGC Grant Nos. 4325/01H and 4257/03H.

REFERENCES

Avons, S. E., Wragg, C. A., Cupples, L., & Lovegrove, W. J. (1998). Measures of phonological short-term memory and their relationship to vocabulary development. *Applied Psycholinguistics, 19*(4), 583–601.

Berko, J. (1958). The child's learning of English morphology. *Word, 14,* 150–177.

Bowey, J. A. (2001). Nonword repetition and young children's receptive vocabulary: A longitudinal study. *Applied Psycholinguistics, 22*(3), 441–469.

Casalis, S., & Louis-Alexandre, M.-F. (2000). Morphological analysis, phonological analysis and learning to read French: A longitudinal study. *Reading and Writing: An Interdisciplinary Journal, 12,* 303–335.

Castles, A., & Coltheart, M. (2004). Is there a causal link from phonological awareness to success in learning to read? *Cognition, 91*(1), 77–111.

Chen, H.-C., Song, H., Lau, W. Y., Wong, K. F. E., & Tang, S. L. (2003). Developmental characteristics of eye movements in reading Chinese. In C. McBride-Chang & H.-C. Chen (Eds.), *Reading development in Chinese children* (pp. 157–169). London: Praeger.

Chomsky, C. (1976). Creativity and innovation in child language. *Journal of Education, 158*(2), 12–24.

Clark, E. V. (1995). The lexicon and syntax. In J. L. Miller & P. D. Eismas (Eds.), *Speech, language, and communication* (pp. 303–337). San Diego, CA: Academic Press.

Fowler, A. E. (1991). How early phonological development might set the stage for phoneme awareness. In S. A. Brady & D. P. Shankweiler (Eds.), *Phonological processes in literacy: A tribute to Isabelle Y. Liberman* (pp. 97–117). Hillsdale, NJ: Erlbaum.

Gathercole, S. E., Service, E., Hitch, G. J., Adams, A. M., & Martin, A. J. (1999). Phonological short-term memory and vocabulary development: Further evidence on the nature of the relationship. *Applied Cognitive Psychology, 13*(1), 65–77.

Gathercole, S. E., Willis, C. S., Emslie, H., & Baddeley, A. D. (1992). Phonological memory and vocabulary development during the early school years: A longitudinal study. *Developmental Psychology, 28*(5), 887–898.

Geary, D. C. (1995). Reflections of evolution and culture in children's cognition: Implications for mathematical development and instruction. *American Psychologist, 50*(1), 24–37.

Goswami, U. (2002). In the beginning was the rhyme?: A reflection on Hulme, Hatcher, Nation, Brown, Adams, and Stuart. *Journal of Experimental Child Psychology, 82,* 47–57.

Ho, C. S.-H., Chan, D. W.-O., Tsang, S.-M., & Lee, S.-H. (2002). The cognitive profile and multiple deficit hypothesis in Chinese developmental dyslexia. *Developmental Psychology, 38,* 543–553.

Ho, C. S.-H., & Lai, D. N.-C. (1999). Naming-speed deficits and phonological memory deficits in Chinese developmental dyslexia. *Learning and Individual Differences, 11,* 173–186.

McBride-Chang, C. (2004). *Children's literacy development.* London: Arnold.

McBride-Chang, C., Bialystok, E., Chong, K., & Li, Y. P. (2004). Levels of phonological awareness in three cultures. *Journal of Experimental Child Psychology, 89,* 93–111.

McBride-Chang, C., Cho, J.-R., Liu, H., Wagner, R. K., Shu, H., Zhou, A., et al. (2005). Changing models across cultures: Associations of phonological awareness and morphological structure awareness with vocabulary and word recognition in second graders from Beijing, Hong Kong, Korea, and the United States. *Journal of Experimental Child Psychology, 92,* 140–160.

McBride-Chang, C., Shu, H., Zhou, A., Wat, C. P., & Wagner, R. K. (2003). Morphological awareness uniquely predicts young children's Chinese character recognition. *Journal of Educational Psychology, 95,* 743–751.

McBride-Chang, C., Wagner, R. K., Muse, A., Chow, B. W.-Y., & Shu, H. (2005). The role of morphological awareness in children's vocabulary acquisition in English. *Applied Psycholinguistics, 26,* 415–435.

Metsala, J. L. (1999). Young children's phonological awareness and nonword repetition as a function of vocabulary development. *Journal of Educational Psychology, 91,* 3–19.

Metsala, J. L., & Walley, A. C. (1998). Spoken vocabulary growth and the segmental restructuring of lexical representations: Precursors to phonemic awareness and early reading ability. In J. L. Metsala & L. C. Ehri (Eds.), *Word recognition in beginning literacy* (pp. 89–120). London: Erlbaum.

Nagy, W., & Anderson, R. C. (1984). How many words are there in printed school English? *Reading Research Quarterly, 19,* 304–330.

Rispens, J. E. (2004). *Syntactic and phonological processing in developmental dyslexia.* Groningen, The Netherlands: Grodil.

Shankweiler, D. (1999). Words to meanings. *Scientific Studies of Reading, 3,* 113–127.

Shu, H., Chen, X., Anderson, R. C., Wu, N., & Xuan, Y. (2003). Properties of school Chinese: Implications for learning to read. *Child Development, 74*(1), 27–48.

Tan, L.-H., & Perfetti, C. A. (1999). Phonological activation in visual identification of Chinese two-character words. *Journal of Experimental Psychology: Learning, Memory, and Cognition, 25,* 382–393.

Treiman, R., & Zukowski, A. (1991). Levels of phonological awareness. In S. A. Brady & D. P. Shankweiler (Eds.), *Phonological processes in literacy: A tribute to Isabelle Y. Liberman* (pp. 97–117). Hillsdale, NJ: Erlbaum.

CHAPTER 7

Large Problem Spaces
The Challenge of Vocabulary for English Language Learners

CATHERINE E. SNOW
YOUNG-SUK KIM

Practitioners as well as researchers have recurrently noted that acquiring enough English vocabulary to perform well in the reading and writing tasks expected of middle- and secondary-school students is a huge challenge for many language-minority students. It is worth considering why vocabulary acquisition is such an intractable challenge for so many second-language (L2) learners. Understanding the degree of difficulty of the task of English vocabulary learning, and the complexities involved in adding a new item to one's vocabulary, will help us establish reasonable goals for L2 learners' vocabulary acquisition, and should guide us in the allocation of time and instructional resources to vocabulary in elementary and secondary classrooms.

Furthermore, in order to help students meet the challenge of vocabulary learning, it is important to try to ascertain the optimal conditions for L2 vocabulary acquisition. Perhaps if we better understand the conditions under which L2 vocabulary is most easily and efficiently acquired, we can recreate those conditions in more classrooms. And if those conditions include more time and more instructional attention to vocabulary than is typical today, the implications for teacher professional development and for curricular emphasis should be broadcast widely.

In addition, it is useful to determine which language-minority students are most likely to do well at L2 vocabulary learning, either on their own or as a result of normal instruction, and which ones are likely to need extra help, enhanced prevention, or perhaps intervention focused on vocabulary learning. For example, do learners with large first-language (L1) vocabularies easily acquire vocabulary in the L2? If so, that would suggest positive transfer in the lexical domain, and would support the pedagogical value of attention to first-language vocabulary in order to support second-language outcomes. Alternately, if L1 and L2 vocabulary sizes are, in fact, unrelated or possibly even negatively correlated, that would suggest that instructional time is better spent focusing on L2.

The goal of this chapter is to summarize what the research literature has to say about these three questions: How big is the challenge of L2 vocabulary learning, for English language learners (ELLs) in particular? What activities support L2 vocabulary acquisition? And how does L1 vocabulary knowledge relate to L2 vocabulary-learning processes and levels of achievement?

THE SIZE OF THE CHALLENGE

On the one hand, it is not surprising that vocabulary acquisition is a huge challenge. It is estimated that high-school graduates need to know 75,000 words in English—that means having learned 10–12 words every single day between the ages of 2 and 17. ELLs who start even just a few years late need to increase their daily learning rate if they are to match the outcomes of English-only (EO) learners.

On the other hand, vocabulary is the aspect of L2 learning that is often assumed to be maximally tractable. Whereas later language learners often display persistent traces of nonnative accents or grammar, they can match or even transcend native speaker levels of vocabulary knowledge—consider Joseph Conrad, Vladimir Nabokov, Eva Hoffman, and other late learners of English whose lexical resources send native speakers off to consult their dictionaries. In a study of postadolescent L2 learners of English who achieved near-native performance levels, Marinova-Todd (2003) found that a higher proportion scored within the range of equally well-educated native English speakers on measures of receptive vocabulary than on other dimensions of English skill (pronunciation, morphology, syntax, narrative), and that a small subgroup matched the best native speakers on productive vocabulary knowledge as well. Snow and Hoefnagel-Höhle (1978) found that school-age L2 learners of Dutch approached native speaker levels of vocabulary knowledge within 1 year of residence in The Netherlands—suggesting that rapid L2 vocabulary learning is entirely possible, under the right circumstances.

It is clear, then, that L2 vocabulary acquisition to native levels is possible, though it is probably not a common outcome of second-language learning. We know little from large sample studies of natural, untutored second-language learning about how fast vocabulary is acquired. It is clear from findings like those of Snow and Hoefnagel-Höhle (1978) and Marinova-Todd (2003) that L2 vocabulary learning can proceed more rapidly than L1 vocabulary learning typically does; otherwise L2 learners would never achieve the fully or close-to-fully native speaker levels that many do manage. Given its relative rapidity, achieving high levels of vocabulary in an L2 is very likely mediated by L2 literacy skills, that is, by exposure to the L2 vocabulary during reading. For those who develop particularly large L2 vocabularies, acquisition may depend on study skills and explicit, intentional learning as well, rather than resulting only from casual exposure and normal inferential processes concerning the meanings of newly encountered words.

But given that even adolescent and adult L2 learners are capable of impressive L2 vocabulary feats, why are we so worried about younger language-minority students? They have more time to catch up to their native speaker peers, and they are spending their days in school settings where literacy activities and vocabulary teaching are regular occurrences. Should they not acquire large L2 vocabularies naturally? Unfortunately, considerable evidence suggests that ELLs of preschool-through elementary-school age, particularly those whose first language is Spanish (perhaps because this is the most widely studied group), suffer from very limited vocabulary knowledge in English. For example, Tabors, Páez, and López (2003), in a study of Latino children in Head Start, found a mean score below 70 on a standardized test of English vocabulary productive knowledge, and Miccio, Tabors, Páez, Hammer, and Wagstaff (2005) found a mean score of about 80 on a receptive task in a sample from the same population. Rolla San Francisco, Mo, Carlo, August, and Snow (2004), studying Latino kindergartners and first graders, found mean standardized productive vocabulary scores of 80 for those receiving English instruction and 60 for those receiving Spanish instruction. Proctor, Carlo, August, and Snow (2005), studying Latino fourth graders who were all at time of testing in English-only classrooms, found that the children scored at mid-first-grade range in vocabulary knowledge, whereas their listening and reading comprehension scores were equivalent to early second- and third-grade expectations, respectively.

Finally, a study of EO and ELL fourth graders all studying in the same classrooms showed that ELL students scored on average more than one standard deviation below the expected mean, whereas EO children were scoring at or slightly above the expected mean, on a measure of receptive vocabulary (see Figure 7.1) (August, Carlo, Lively, McLaughlin, & Snow, 2006; August, Carlo, Dressler, & Snow, 2005). These same group differences showed up on researcher-designed tests of knowledge about polysemy (see Figures 7.2 and 7.3). The polysemy tasks involved recognizing the multiple meanings that very common words like *run*, *bug*, and *cup* can express; despite the ubiquity of polysemy in English, the ELLs were often unable to recognize or produce more than a single meaning for such words.

In summary, then, ELLs from Spanish-speaking families typically arrive at school needing to learn a very large amount of English vocabulary; and they show up as farther behind EO age-mates on productive than on receptive vocabulary, but even their comprehension vocabulary is quite limited. Though these children certainly acquire English vocabulary at school, their speed of acquisition seems in many cases not to be adequate to bring them up to native speaker levels by first or even fourth grade. In other words, they learn English vocabulary at a steady pace that approximately matches that of their EO classmates, with the result that they remain on average about one standard deviation below

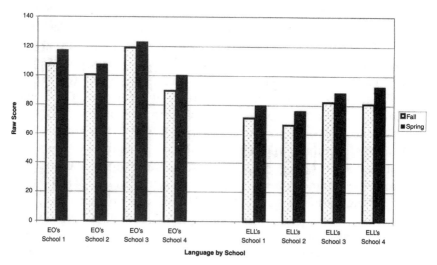

FIGURE 7.1. Average fourth-grade fall and spring performance on the PPVT as a function of language and school.

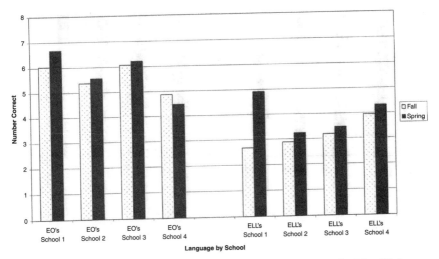

FIGURE 7.2. Average fourth-grade fall and spring performance on the Word Polysemy task as a function of language and school.

EO children on vocabulary assessments. Given that vocabulary is one key predictor of reading comprehension outcomes, it seems clear that the consequences of this vocabulary deficit for success in the middle grades and the capacity to learn the content presented in textbooks are quite severe. There is some consolation in the suggestion (Proctor et al., 2005) that listening and reading comprehension outcomes are less severely retarded than are vocabulary outcomes—at least in the primary grades, but they too fall well below the desired levels.

OPTIMAL CONDITIONS FOR L2 VOCABULARY ACQUISITION

There are two major sources of data about optimal conditions for L1 vocabulary development: studies of the home environments in which children typically acquire large vocabularies and studies of instructional practices that support vocabulary. Both these types of data are quite extended in supporting conclusions about vocabulary acquisition in a first language. Comparative data for L2 acquisition are considerably more constrained.

The best predictors of young children's vocabulary acquisition in L1 are the quantity of speech heard (Hart & Risley, 1995; Huttenlocher, Haight, Bryk, Selzer, & Lyons, 1991); exposure to a wide variety of words,

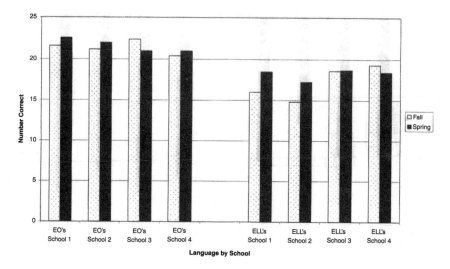

FIGURE 7.3. Average fourth-grade fall and spring performance on the Sentence Polysemy task as a function of language and school.

including some low-frequency lexical items (Snow, Tabors, & Dickinson, 2001; Tabors, Roach, & Snow, 2001; Tabors, Snow, & Dickinson, 2001); and the occurrence of new lexical items in semantically rich (Weizman & Snow, 2001) and recurrent contexts, such as book reading (de Temple & Snow, 1998, 2003) and extended conversations (Tabors, Beals, & Weizman, 2001). Evidence from Pearson and Fernandez (1994) suggests that these same features predict efficient lexical acquisition for bilingual as well as monolingual children.

The instructional conditions that support vocabulary acquisition for EO students have been widely studied and constitute a strong foundation for thinking about how best to support vocabulary acquisition among L2 learners (see, e.g., Beck, McKeown, & Omanson, 1987; Beck, Perfetti, & McKeown, 1982; Beck, McKeown, & Kucan, 2002; Stahl & Clark, 1987; Stahl, 1999). At the same time, the literature on vocabulary instruction for EO students does not offer great hope that extreme disparities in vocabulary achievement can be overcome instructionally. For example, Stahl and Fairbanks (1986), in a review of vocabulary instruction effectiveness, concluded that good instructional programs ensure that students learn about 300 lexical items per year—hardly enough to compensate for the ELLs' deficits in vocabulary knowledge.

In addition, L1 vocabulary development is supported by reading, since many of the rare and more sophisticated lexical items are encountered only in print. On the other hand, the likelihood of learning an unfamiliar word encountered in print is rather small (Swanborn & de Glopper, 1999), so several exposures to any particular word are needed to ensure it is learned. Furthermore, only readers who know most of the words in a text are capable of acquiring new lexical items from reading the text (Carver, 1994), so simply engaging in wide reading is not a useful strategy for ELL students with limited English-reading skills.

Evidence about L2 vocabulary acquisition suggests that precisely these same factors operate, and in much the same way. For example, an observational study of interaction in the homes of 51 Latino immigrant families (Quiroz, 2005) showed that the amount of maternal speech during book reading and the use of appropriate pedagogical techniques in a simulated homework task correlated significantly with children's L2 (English) vocabulary scores. These were, of course, precisely the same kinds of activities that have been demonstrated to promote L1 acquisition.

Carlo et al. (2003) reported the effectiveness of a vocabulary intervention designed to incorporate research-based knowledge about excellent vocabulary instruction from studies of EO learners into a curriculum that offered particular supports for Spanish speakers. The principles underlying the Vocabulary Improvement Project (VIP) were the following:

- Words to be studied should be encountered first in meaningful text; nonproficient speakers of English were thus provided with Spanish versions of the source texts.
- Each target word should be encountered in several different contexts to display its semantic breadth.
- Studying the spelling of the target words is important because it helps develop clear phonological representations and build orthographic knowledge.
- Because there is insufficient time to teach all the words children need to know, instruction should focus on powerful mechanisms for learning about words, rather than on long lists of target words.
- Morphological analysis and knowledge about key derivational morphemes should be taught explicitly.
- Information about multiple meanings and practice in recognizing and using multiple meanings of words should be an explicit part of instruction.
- Possibilities for inferring meaning from context, and limitations on those possibilities, should be taught explicitly.

- Students who speak and read Spanish should be taught explicitly to recognize and use cognates, both to hypothesize meanings for English words and to recognize cross-linguistically predictable morphological structures.

A 15-week curriculum built around these principles was written (see Lively, August, Carlo, & Snow, 2003) and evaluated with Spanish-speaking fifth-grade ELLs and their EO classmates, in four schools serving large numbers of Latino students. Baseline data were collected, and students were assigned to intervention or control groups at the classroom level. Assessments targeted mastery of the taught words, polysemy, morphological analysis, recognition of cognates, and reading comprehension. The results showed strong and significant improvement for the intervention group but not the control group on all measures except morphological analysis. Most impressively, the intervention group performed better on the reading comprehension measure, suggesting that students were indeed using the strategies they had been taught to infer word meaning in novel texts.

While these results were encouraging, the advances produced by the intervention were no greater for the ELL participants than for the EO participants. In other words, the intervention did not contribute to closing the gap between the groups. Nonetheless, one might in an optimistic mood focus on the advances in reading comprehension produced by the curriculum; better comprehension would be expected to generate enhanced vocabulary knowledge in the future—at least if students have regular opportunities to read material at an appropriate level.

A very successful aspect of the intervention involved teaching Spanish speakers to use cognate vocabulary items and predictable similarities between Spanish and English in their morphologies. As Hancin-Bhatt and Nagy (1994) have reported, Spanish-speaking elementary-school students are not likely to recognize or use cognate relations spontaneously. Thus explicitly drawing their attention to these relations is important, and our study provided further evidence that it could be effective. Furthermore, including attention to cognates as part of the classroom activities promoted effective collaborative learning in which the Spanish speakers were accorded higher status than they usually enjoyed because of their privileged knowledge of Spanish.

We must be realistic, though, about the value of cognate-focused instruction. First, students who could not read Spanish had a much more difficult time recognizing cognates, since the cross-language similarities are more obvious in the orthography than in the pronunciation—for example, *tranquil* and *tranquilo* look very similar, but sound quite different, as do *jocose* and *jocoso* and many other such pairs. Second, using the predictable relationships in the morphological system—for example, *prosperity/prosperidad, servitude/servidumbre*—requires both metalinguistic sophistication and knowledge of rather complex vocabulary to be optimally helpful. Third, teaching about cognates can be both difficult and intimidating for teachers who have little knowledge of Spanish or of the likely etymological sources of English vocabulary. While bilingual students can be a resource, their knowledge of Spanish is sometimes too unexamined to support the teacher's instructional goals.

Furthermore, fully and directly translatable cognates (cases like *prosperity/prosperidad* or *amorous/amoroso*) are not sufficiently frequent to solve most reading comprehension problems. The true value of thinking about cross-language lexical relationships requires incorporating attention to issues of polysemy, so as to explore words that are clearly cognate and whose semantic relationships can be discerned, but that have slightly (or even extremely) different meanings in English and Spanish (e.g., *advertisement/advertencia; compromise/compromiso; embarrassed/embarazada*). Ideally, such pairs would be studied and the similarities as well as the differences in their meanings probed, rather than, as often happens, simply being dismissed as false cognates. Furthermore, the great potential of cognate relationships comes from seeing relationships of morphological relatives (*difficult* is harder to relate to its translation *difícil* than to the noun form *dificultad*) and of Spanish word roots to entire word families in English; for example, *escribir* is not cognate to its English translation *to write*, but is of course a source of information (in the hands of a lexically gifted teacher) about the meanings of words like *scribe, scrip, script, scripture, inscribe, describe, conscribe, circumscribe, prescribe, proscribe, subscribe,* and *transcribe*. Fully exploiting these cross-linguistic relations is unlikely to happen in classrooms where neither teacher nor students are highly bilingual, yet is it arguably the availability of this sort of linguistically sophisticated analysis that would support high levels of English proficiency characteristic of sophisticated Spanish users such as Pablo Neruda and Carlos Fuentes.

RELATIONS OF L1 TO L2 VOCABULARY KNOWLEDGE

Teachers who have experience with ELLs frequently comment that those children with well-developed first-language skills have the easiest time acquiring English. Indeed, there are many reasons that one might expect a positive relationship between first- and second-language skills of all types, including vocabulary. Whatever aptitudes enabled a child to develop rich L1 skills are presumably available to support the acquisition of L2 skills, so one might well expect a positive correlation. Furthermore, if vocabulary acquisition is thought of as having two components—learning new concepts and learning new phonological forms—then clearly the L2 learner who already has many L1 lexical items indexing concepts is advantaged in that only the new forms need to be learned in the L2, whereas the child who is lexically limited in the L1 will have to acquire both the conceptual and the phonological component for many items in L2. Thus, if there is an L1–L2 relationship, it might be hypothesized to reflect a mechanism of transfer of concepts from the L1 to the L2. One might also expect that the L2 learner seeks to express in the L2 everything he or she was able to express in the L1, leading to an effort at least to match the L1 vocabulary in the L2. Finally, it seems plausible that having a large L1 vocabulary generates some metalinguistic sophistication that leads to greater ease in L2 vocabulary acquisition; for example, larger vocabularies lead to greater understanding about polysemy and about morphological analysis, and offer a richer knowledge base that could be exploited if cross-linguistic cognate relationships exist. This hypothesis suggests another path for L1–L2 transfer.

These speculative explanations for positive L1–L2 vocabulary relationships all relate to a situation in which the L2 learner has a well-established L1 in which lexical knowledge has already accumulated. The vast majority of ELLs in U.S. schools are, however, still firmly in the period of L1 lexical acquisition while acquiring English as an L2. And many ELLs come from families in which their parents have little education and low literacy levels—factors that lead to smaller vocabularies in the L1. Can we expect positive correlations between L1 and L2 vocabulary knowledge in cases where the L1 and the L2 are being acquired simultaneously, and may even be in competition with one another? Or does that situation lead to negative cross-language correlations?

A data set strongly suggesting that language competition occurs for many ELL students was collected by Mariela Páez (2001), studying Chinese, Dominican, and Haitian immigrants to the United States. All the participants in Páez's study were adolescents who had been in U.S. schools at least 3 years and had immigrated within the previous 3–5 years. Páez found that all three groups scored, on average, very poorly on an English proficiency assessment, but that better levels of English were achieved by the Haitian group, who also were least likely to maintain their native language. In other words, language outcomes among these adolescents were evidently to some extent determined by their distribution of time over their two languages: those who spent the most time talking English and the least time speaking their native language ended up with the best knowledge of English vocabulary.

But within language groups, is there any relationship between knowledge of the L1 and the L2? Studies of bilingual children's vocabulary appear to converge on the conclusion that cross-language correlations of vocabulary breadth are minimal in *magnitude* (Lindsey, Manis, & Bailey, 2003; Verhoeven, 1994). For instance, in a study that followed 74 Turkish children age 6 to age 8 living in The Netherlands, the children's vocabulary knowledge in Turkish (L1) predicted their vocabulary in Dutch only at a very low level (structural equation model coefficients were .14 and .10 at age 6 and age 8, respectively). While some studies have generated slightly larger correlations than this, no published study we have found has reported substantial relationships between L1 and L2 vocabulary size.

Furthermore, the studies show conflicting results concerning the *direction* of the L1–L2 vocabulary relationship. For example, Páez, Tabors, and Lopez (in press) found negative correlations between Spanish and English vocabulary for 139 Spanish–English bilingual pre-K children ($r = -.27$ and $r = -.12$, for fall and spring, respectively). This study assessed vocabulary using the picture vocabulary subtest of the Woodcock Language Proficiency Battery (WLPB-R), which includes mostly items measuring productive vocabulary knowledge. A similar result ($r = -.23$) was reported for older children, fourth- and fifth-grade Spanish–English bilinguals, using receptive vocabulary measures, the PPVT, and the TVIP (the Spanish version of PPVT) by Ordóñez, Carlo, Snow, and McLaughlin (2002).

In contrast, as noted above, 6- and 8-year-old Turkish-speaking children's L1 vocabulary was positively related to their L2 (Dutch) vocabulary, though the correlation was very small (Verhoeven, 1994). Another longitudinal study with younger Turkish–Dutch bilinguals revealed similar results (Leseman, 2000). For 3-year-old Turkish-speaking Dutch learners, the average correlations between Turkish vocabulary and Dutch vocabulary at three different waves of data collection were positive ($r = .26$ and $r = .04$ for receptive and productive vocabulary, respectively). The study also suggested that the frequency of high-level language interaction at home (use of decontextualized language) may have been a mediator for the positive relationship. When high-level language interaction at home was partialed out, the cross-language correlations became zero or negative. The results of this study may suggest the importance of home-environment factors in developing L1 knowledge that can be the basis for transfer to the L2, a suggestion reinforced by Pearson and Fernandez's (1994) findings concerning the importance of the home language environment in bilingual infants' vocabulary development.

Evidence suggests that when children are growing up bilingual from birth, the breadth and depth of their vocabulary in either L1 or L2 is more limited than that of monolinguals (Umbel, Pearson, Fernandez, & Oller, 1992). However, bilinguals' total conceptual vocabulary—the number of different referents for which words are known—is as large as that of monolinguals. So, for example, bilinguals may label some concepts only in English and other, different concepts only in Spanish, as well as knowing some translation equivalents (or *doublets*). In a longitudinal study of 20 Spanish–English bilingual infants from age 3 months to age 36 months, Pearson and Fernandez (1994) reported that bilingual children's vocabulary development followed the same trajectory as monolingual children's vocabulary development, but only if both languages were taken into account. Because bilingual infants' vocabulary is distributed across two languages, their average vocabulary size tends not to match monolingual norms in either language. Doublets accounted for an increasing percentage of total vocabulary knowledge as children grew older. Thirty percent of bilingual infants' words were doublets, but 60% of 6-year-olds' words, 70% of 10-year-olds' words, and 90% of college-age students' words were doublets (Pearson, 2002). Cross-language competition is reflected in the phonological forms known, but not evidently in acquiring the capacity to refer to concepts linguistically.

All these studies looked at cross-linguistic relationships at the same age. A longitudinal study of 249 Spanish–English bilingual kindergartners showed a positive time-lagged relationship between children's vocabulary size in Spanish at kindergarten and in English at first grade (Lindsey et al., 2003). Children's Spanish vocabulary, assessed with the Picture Vocabulary subtest of the WLPB-R, in the fall and spring semester of kindergarten year, was positively associated with their vocabulary in English in the spring of first grade ($r = .15$). Of course this positive relation is very small, and it is entirely possible that the simultaneous cross-language correlation was negative even though the lagged correlation was positive.

Clearly much more data is needed, on bilinguals of different ages and learning their L2 under a variety of conditions, to resolve the question how L1 and L2 vocabulary knowledge relate. The available studies do not provide much information about the language environments in which either L1 or L2 skills were acquired. Furthermore, due to the small number of studies identified here, it is not possible to compare systematically different subgroups of bilinguals (e.g., those growing up bilingual, those learning the L2 on entry to school, or those learning the L2 only after considerable L1 language and literacy proficiency has been achieved). Furthermore, studies need to differentiate students' receptive and productive vocabulary knowledge when examining relationships between L1 and L2 vocabulary. For instance, in Leseman's (2000) study with Turkish–Dutch bilingual preschoolers the magnitude of productive and receptive vocabulary correlations differed. It is also striking that there is no distinction in strength of cross-language associations as a function of the typological relationships between the L1 and the L2; correlations for Spanish and English, languages characterized by many related lexical items, are not higher than those for Turkish and Dutch, two languages that share almost no lexical stock. Obviously, more systematic study of pairs of languages would be of considerable value. It seems clear that if there is strong positive transfer from the L1 to the L2 in the domain of vocabulary, that it does not emerge strongly for young children and that it may well be dependent on relatively sophisticated and well-consolidated L1 vocabulary knowledge; in other words, transfer might support development of L2 vocabulary breadth only for adolescent or adult L2 learners, and be available to younger L2 learners only if strong literacy skills in both the L1 and the L2 are present.

THE NATURE OF THE PROBLEM

We have seen that ELLs face a large but not insoluble problem of lexical acquisition, that the same factors that promote L1 vocabulary learning—exposure to sophisticated vocabulary multiple times in rich semantic contexts, combined for older children with explicit teaching about strategies for word analysis and learning—also promote L2 vocabulary, and that, despite the opportunities for positive L1 to L2 transfer in the domain of vocabulary, there is little convincing evidence that such transfer occurs, at least for breadth of vocabulary knowledge.

Vocabulary can be characterized as an extremely large problem space. In comparison to learning to recognize 26 letters, to distinguish 44 phonemes, to mastering a couple hundred spelling rules, or even to learning the complexities of English syntax and morphology, acquiring 75,000 separate words, each with its own meaning(s), syntactic and morphological affordances, pronunciation, and orthographic representation, is a gargantuan task (see Figure 7.4). It is not surprising that so many ELLs, and for that matter many EOs, who perform perfectly well on other aspects of knowledge of English, fall short in the domain of lexical knowledge. This failure is even more likely for ELLs who read rather little, or for those who read with limited comprehension of the texts, since literacy is the only context in which many of these words are likely to be encountered.

Nonetheless, we must take seriously the lesson from those L2 learners of English who do achieve a very high level of English lexical knowledge. Lexical acquisition could be a more central and vibrant focus in early childhood settings, should be included as a robust part of basic literacy instruction in the primary grades, and can be demonstrably supported across the school years, if intensive instruction, lexically rich environments, high student motivation, and lots of opportunities to encounter and use novel vocabulary are provided. When the L1 and the L2 are related, there is also an important role for building metalinguistic awareness and literacy skills in the L1, as a scaffold for the intentional use of L1 knowledge in learning L2 vocabulary. Small problem spaces are easier to teach and easier to test, but it is in mastering the large problem spaces that students become truly literate.

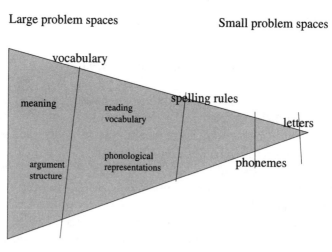

FIGURE 7.4. A representation of the various problem spaces associated with literacy.

REFERENCES

August, D., Carlo, M., Dressler, C., & Snow, C. (2005). Avoiding the misidentification of English language learners as learning disabled: The development of vocabulary. *Learning Disabilities Research and Practice*, *20*, 50–57.

August, D., Carlo, M., Lively, T., McLaughlin, B., & Snow, C. (2006). The Vocabulary Improvement Project: A research-based program for building vocabulary in English-language learners. In T. Young & N. Hadaway (Eds.), *Helping English language learners in regular classrooms* (pp. 96–112). Newark, DE: International Reading Association.

Beck, I., McKeown, M., & Kucan, L. (2002). *Bringing words to life: Robust vocabulary instruction*. New York: Guilford Press.

Beck, I., McKeown, M., & Omanson, R. (1987). The effects and use of diverse vocabulary instructional techniques. In M. McKeown & M. Curtis (Eds.), *The nature of vocabulary acquisition* (pp. 147–163). Hillsdale, NJ: Erlbaum.

Beck, I., Perfetti, C., & McKeown, M. (1982). Effects of long-term vocabulary instruction on lexical access and reading comprehension. *Journal of Educational Psychology*, *74*, 506–521.

Carlo, M., August, D., McLaughlin, B., Snow, C., Dressler, C., Lippman, D., et al. (2004). Closing the gap: Addressing the vocabulary needs of English language learners in bilingual and mainstream classrooms. *Reading Research Quarterly*, *39*, 188–215.

Carver, R. P. (1994). Percentage of unknown vocabulary words in text as a function of the relative difficulty of the text: Implications for instruction. *Journal of Reading Behavior*, *26*, 413–437.

De Temple, J., & Snow, C. E. (1998). Mother–child interactions related to the emergence of literacy. In M. Zaslow & C. Eldred (Eds.), *Parenting behavior in a sample of young mothers in poverty: Results of the New Chance Observational Study* (pp. 114–169). New York: Manpower Development Research Corporation.

De Temple, J., & Snow, C. E. (2003). Learning words from books. In A. van Kleeck, S. A. Stahl, & E. B. Bauer (Eds.), *On reading books to children: Teachers and parents* (pp. 16–36). Mahwah, NJ: Erlbaum.

Hancin-Bhatt, B., & Nagy, W. E. (1994). Lexical transfer and second language morphological development. *Applied Psycholinguistics*, *15*, 289–310.

Hart, B., & Risley, T. (1995). *Meaningful differences in the everyday experiences of young American children*. Baltimore: Brookes.

Huttenlocher, J., Haight, W., Bryk, A., Seltzer, M., & Lyons, T. (1991). Early vocabulary growth: Relation to language input and gender. *Developmental Psychology*, *27*, 236–244.

Leseman, P. M. (2000). Bilingual vocabulary development of Turkish preschoolers in The Netherlands. *Journal of Multilingual and Multicultural Development*, *21*, 93–112.

Lindsey, K. A., Manis, F. R., & Bailey, C. E. (2003). Prediction of first-grade reading in Spanish-speaking English-language learners. *Journal of Educational Psychology, 95,* 482–494.

Lively, T., August, D., Carlo, M., & Snow, C. (2003). *Vocabulary improvement program for English language learners and their classmates.* Baltimore: Brookes.

Marinova-Todd, S. (2003). *Comprehensive analysis of ultimate attainment in adult second language acquisition.* Unpublished doctoral dissertation, Harvard Graduate School of Education, Cambridge, MA.

Miccio, A., Tabors, P., Páez, M., Hammer, C., & Wagstaff, D. (2005). Vocabulary development in Spanish-speaking Head Start children of Puerto Rican descent. In J. Cohen, K. McAlister, K. Rolstad, & J. MacSwan (Eds.), *ISB4: Proceedings of the 4th International Symposium on Bilingualism.* Somerville, MA: Cascadilla Press.

Ordoñez, C. L., Carlo, M. S., Snow, C. E., & McLaughlin, B. (2002). Depth and breadth of vocabulary in two languages: Which vocabulary skills transfer? *Journal of Educational Psychology, 94*(4), 719–728.

Páez, M. (2001). *Language and the immigrant child: Predicting English language proficiency for Chinese, Dominican, and Haitian students.* Unpublished doctoral dissertation, Harvard Graduate School of Education, Cambridge, MA.

Páez, M. M., Tabors, P. O., & López, L. M. (in press). Bilingual language and literacy development of Spanish-speaking children. *Applied Developmental Psychology.*

Pearson, B. Z. (2002). Bilingual infants: Mapping the research agenda. In M. M. Suarez-Orozco & M. Páez (Eds.), *Latinos: Remaking America* (pp. 301–320). Berkeley and Los Angeles: University of California Press.

Pearson, B. Z., & Fernandez, S. C. (1994). Patterns of interaction in the lexical growth in two languages of bilingual infants and toddlers. *Language Learning, 44*(4), 617–653.

Proctor, P., Carlo, M., August, D., & Snow, C. (2005). The English reading of Spanish-speaking English language learners: Towards a model of comprehension. *Journal of Educational Psychology, 97,* 246–256.

Quiroz, B. (2005). *Home-language skills and family characteristics predicting the vocabulary skills of Spanish–English bilinguals.* Unpublished doctoral dissertation, Harvard Graduate School of Education, Cambridge, MA.

Rolla San Francisco, A., Mo, E., Carlo, M., August, D., & Snow, C. (2004). *The cross-linguistic influences of English and Spanish vocabulary and literacy instruction in English spelling.* Paper submitted for publication.

Snow, C. E., & Hoefnagel-Höhle, M. (1978). Critical period for language acquisition: Evidence from second language learning. *Child Development, 49,* 1263–1279.

Snow, C. E., Tabors, P. O., & Dickinson, D. K. (2001). Language development in the preschool years. In D. K. Dickinson & P. O. Tabors (Eds.), *Beginning literacy with language* (pp. 1–25). Baltimore: Brookes.

Stahl, S. (1999). *Vocabulary development.* Cambridge, MA: Brookline Books.

Stahl, S., & Clark, C. (1987). The effects of participatory expectations in classroom discussion on the learning of science vocabulary. *American Educational Research Journal, 24,* 541–556.

Stahl, S., & Fairbanks, M. (1986). The effects of vocabulary instruction: A model-based meta-analysis. *Review of Educational Research, 56,* 72–110.

Swanborn, M. S. L., & de Glopper, K. (1999). Incidental word learning while reading: A meta-analysis. *Review of Educational Research, 69,* 261–286.

Tabors, P., Beals, D., & Weizman, Z. (2001). "You know what oxygen is?": Learning new words at home. In D. K. Dickinson & P. O. Tabors (Eds.), *Beginning literacy with language* (pp. 93–110). Baltimore: Brookes.

Tabors, P. O., Páez, M., & López, L. (2003). Dual language abilities of bilingual four-year-olds: Initial findings from the Early Childhood Study of Language and Literacy Development of Spanish-Speaking Children. *NABE Journal of Research and Practice, 1,* 70–91. Also available online at www.uc.edu/njrp.

Tabors, P. O., Roach, K. A., & Snow, C. E. (2001). Home language and literacy environment final results. In D. K. Dickinson & P. O. Tabors (Eds.), *Beginning literacy with language* (pp. 111–138). Baltimore: Brookes.

Tabors, P. O., Snow, C. E., & Dickinson, D. K. (2001). Homes and schools together: Supporting language and literacy development. In D. K. Dickinson & P. O. Tabors (Eds.), *Beginning literacy with language* (pp. 313–334). Baltimore: Brookes.

Umbel, V. M., Pearson, B. Z., Fernandez, M. C., & Oller, D. K. (1992). Measuring bilingual children's receptive vocabularies. *Child Development, 63,* 1012–1020.

Verhoeven, L. T. (1994). Transfer in bilingual development: The linguistic interdependence hypothesis revisited. *Language Learning, 44,* 381–415.

Weizman, Z., & Snow, C. E. (2001). Lexical input as related to children's vocabulary acquisition: Effects of sophisticated exposure and support for meaning. *Developmental Psychology, 37,* 265–279.

CHAPTER 8

Tapping the Linguistic Resources of Spanish–English Bilinguals
The Role of Cognates in Science

MARCO A. BRAVO
ELFRIEDA H. HIEBERT
P. DAVID PEARSON

Vocabulary is unarguably a critical factor in building proficiency in reading. This role of vocabulary in reading is one that reading researchers have long recognized. Whipple (1925), for example, stated that growth in reading means "continuous enriching and enlarging of the reading vocabulary and increasing clarity of discrimination in appreciation of word values" (p. 76), and Davis (1942) described comprehension as comprised of two skills: word knowledge, or vocabulary, and reasoning.

Words vary on many dimensions, with frequency of use (How likely are language users to encounter it in oral and written discourse?), complexity of meaning (How concrete or abstract is the underlying concept represented by the word?), and ambiguity of meaning (How many possible meanings must be considered in order to settle on a precise meaning for the local context?) being three of the most salient in determining the difficulty students will encounter in learning new words. Words must be understood in particular contexts, some oral and some written. Other things being equal, everyday oral texts tend to be limited to a few thousand common words that we use to get through the business of life and communicating with others on everyday affairs. Written texts complicate language comprehension by introducing students to words that they will not necessarily have encountered in everyday oral discourse. But there is a silver lining to the cloud of difficulty introduced by written texts: written texts also provide a rich resource for expanding vocabulary, particularly in elaborating the set of words that can be used to name a given concept (e.g., by adding "gorgeous," "stunning," and "dazzling" to the description of a painting).

Not only are students expected to understand words in texts, but texts also introduce students to many new words. The vocabulary of written language is much more extensive and diverse than the vocabulary of oral language (Hayes, Wolfer, & Wolfe, 1996).

The degree to which vocabulary of texts serves as an obstacle in the reading of U.S. schoolchildren is difficult to establish because the effects of vocabulary are often difficult to separate from reasoning in assessments. However, according to the National Assessment of Educational Progress (NAEP; Donahue, Finnegan, Lutkus, Allen, & Campbell, 2003), a fairly consistent number of U.S. fourth graders—around 40%—fail to comprehend a grade-level text at a basic level and approximately one in four comprehends at a proficient level. The profile of the NAEP on science is quite similar (O'Sullivan, Lauko, Grigg, Quan, & Zhang, 2003).

Closer examination of these data indicates that traditionally marginalized students (i.e., low-income and racial or linguistic minority students) are more likely to perform at the below-basic level and less likely to perform at the proficient level or higher in either reading comprehension or science achievement. A breakdown of the data by ethnic group indicates that Hispanic and black students account for a disproportionate percentage of the below-basic group, while white students account for a disproportionate percentage of the proficient and above group. The racial gap is even wider in NAEP science achievement (compared to reading), with approximately 10% more nonwhite students in the below-basic group and 10% more white students in the proficient category (O'Sullivan et al., 2003).

Numerous policies have been initiated to narrow this gap between Hispanic and black students and their white counterparts. In this chapter, we examine a set of linguistic resources that bilingual Latino students bring to the task of learning English—the shared cognates of Spanish and English—and we propose that if these resources were made a centerpiece of educational initiatives in the states where significant numbers of children speak Spanish as their native language, it might dramatically increase access to academic language and learning for this sizable population. Particularly in a content area such as science where the performance of Latino students is substantially discrepant from their

English peers, this potential resource deserves consideration. As a content area, science is unforgiving in terms of the constant need to build knowledge and the terminology needed to express that knowledge. Native-Spanish-speaking students need to use every resource available to them to make meaning and build control over science vocabulary and conceptual knowledge; cognates seem a ripe area to exploit as a fundamental building block.

In the first section of this chapter, we review the relevant literature on cognate learning to develop the empirical and theoretical arguments for examining cognates as a resource for enhancing science learning. In the second section, we present the findings of an analysis of the core words of an elementary science program to assess the viability of the cognate strategy. In the final section, we unpack some of the ideas we have developed for moving the cognate agenda along, proposing needed research and plausible practices for teachers to include when teaching science to first-language Spanish speakers.

THEORETICAL AND EMPIRICAL FOUNDATIONS

Our work is based on three areas of scholarship: (1) the nature of science vocabulary, (2) the nature of English, and (3) the nature of instruction and learning for students at risk for failure (i.e., those students whose achievement lags behind expected standards).

The Nature of Science Vocabulary

Vocabulary in science texts differs from vocabulary in narratives. It is our claim that these differences demand a different allocation of attentional resources while reading. To illustrate these differences, consider these two text excerpts taken from the middle portion of the appropriate content-area, sixth-grade textbook of the same publisher.

Excerpt A (Science)

In a transverse wave, energy moves in one direction, while the crests and troughs move at right angles to that direction. Sound energy travels in compressional waves. In a compressional wave matter vibrates in the same direction as the energy waves that travel through it. (Cooney, DiSpezio, Foots, Matamoros, Nyquist, & Ostlund, 2003, p. B141)

Excerpt B (Reading/Language Arts)

Ten thousand eyes were on him as he rubbed his hands with dirt;
Five thousand tongues applauded when he wiped them on his shirt.
Then while the writhing pitcher ground the ball into his hip, Defiance gleamed in Casey's eye, a sneer curled Casey's lip. (Thayer, 2003,
p. 17)

Science texts deal with aspects of the world with which students
may have daily contact but that they have never consciously analyzed
or addressed. An overwhelming majority of the students who read the
science text in Excerpt A have heard sounds throughout their lives. Surely
they have experienced sound waves thousands of times. But they are
not likely to have examined sound waves as "an object of intentional
study." Few are likely to have either the concept or the vocabulary to
envision a "compressional" wave of sound energy. Their introduction to
the concept will likely co-occur with their introduction to the vocabulary. Understanding of a compressional wave involves much more than
pronouncing the word; it requires understanding a complex, conceptual construct. In this manner, science texts contain many words of the
most difficult of the three word-learning tasks described by Graves (2000):
words that represent new concepts for students rather than words that
are synonyms for concepts that students already have or words that students know at some level but that have multiple meanings. Science texts
also involve many words of the latter type where known words need to
be given nuanced or new meanings. An excellent example of this type
of word is the word *energy* in the science excerpt. While sixth graders
will be familiar with the use of the word *energy* to imply "level of activity" ("I have lots of energy today"), most will not have the technical
understanding that is implied by the word's use in the phrase "energy
moves in one direction." In science, words such as *energy* have precise
meanings that differ from the manner in which the words are used in
narrative text or everyday life. While synonyms can be given for *energy*
in a narrative text—*lively* or *full of life*—students need to understand a
particular and precise meaning of *energy* in science texts.

The easiest type of word to learn is the first of Graves's (2000) categories where students already have a concept but are confronted with
an unfamiliar synonym. These synonyms are likely to imply a nuance or
connotation that is different from the original word, but students will
have some background knowledge for the concept. Many of the new
words in the narrative text are of this type. While some students may

not have background knowledge of baseball (the setting for the narrative text in Excerpt B), most sixth graders are likely to understand the stance of an arrogant athlete. Thus, while they may never have encountered the words *defiance* and *sneer*, they will get the gist of the text. And should the word *sneer* be unfamiliar, a quick explanation by the teacher that *sneer* is the same as "laughing at" could provide access to the word.

Another aspect of science vocabulary that makes it difficult is that a new topic typically involves a number of unknown concepts and vocabulary. In science texts, new words come in groups since complex concepts are situated in a semantic network that includes related words. Gaining active control of these words is achieved when students know where the word fits in relation to other words. Since science is a discipline with a host of complex concepts (e.g., *erosion, decomposition, dissolving* in our units), and because students need these concepts to talk about the science they experience, we feel students should learn concepts as organized networks of related information. Further, because ideas are developed in a science text, the new vocabulary is repeated more often than in narrative text (Hiebert, 2003). Thus, if a student does not know what *compressional* means, the gist of the text will be difficult to establish. Words such as *defiance* can be glossed over in a narrative. Words such as *energy, compressional, angles, and vibrates* in a science text cannot be ignored if meaning is to be gained.

The learning of science vocabulary is particularly challenging since there are few contexts other than the school lesson in which the technical vocabulary of science is used or heard. A word such as *applauded* in a narrative text may be heard on a television program or at a school assembly. For science vocabulary such as *erosion* and *decomposition*, students simply do not have the background knowledge nor can they build experiences with the concept without the support of classroom lessons. Science has never received much of the curricular pie in elementary schools, and it is receiving even less time as a result of recent reading mandates (Spillane, Diamond, Walker, Halverson, & Jita, 2001). As a consequence, students have few opportunities to engage in the inquiry-based science that will provide the background to understand the vocabulary when they see it in a text. Without real experiences, the words may mean little to students when they do encounter them (Carlisle, Fleming, & Gudbrandsen, 2000).

If students are lucky, they will gain this conceptual knowledge in a rich, hands-on, inquiry-based science curriculum. If they are even luckier, they will also have a teacher who will connect the visual form of the word with the rich experiential examination of the phenomenon. And if they are still luckier, they will also be reading texts in which this new vocabulary is encountered with sufficient frequency and clarity to stabilize both the pronunciation and the meaning of these new terms. Unfortunately, as we have suggested, we see too few curricular opportunities for this highly integrated approach that mixes experience and text to achieve conceptual understanding.

The Nature of English

While English has its linguistic roots in the Germanic languages of the Angles and the Saxons, it also borrowed heavily from its Romance language neighbors and thus has many Latin-based words. The nature of the Latin-based English words deserves attention in thinking about the task of the vocabulary of texts for all children, but it has unique applications for children whose native language is Spanish.

Latin-based words in English have two main sources: the use of Latin words in science and French. The former source is common to many languages. Because of the use of Latin among scholars and the clergy during the Middle Ages, the early language of science was Latin. The tradition of attaching Latin names (that often drew on Greek) to new discoveries in science continued for many centuries.

These Latin-origin words for science and technical vocabulary are similar in English and Spanish. The following examples from the life sciences illustrate these similarities: *hydroponics/hidroponía; deciduous/deciduo; ecology/ecología; penicillium/penicilium*. Thousands of additional examples could be given. For most schoolchildren, whether speakers of English or of Spanish, these terms will be unfamiliar until they encounter this vocabulary in school contexts. Latin-origin words that are used in science and technical fields account for a large number of the cognates that are listed in compilations of English–Spanish cognates (see, e.g., Nash, 1997). Spanish-speaking students do not necessarily have an advantage over their native-English-speaking peers when they are introduced to these words. Yet the translation process for these cognates is transparent for speakers of Spanish: once they know the word in either language, producing or recognizing it in the other language is easy. As an aside, notice that the speaker of English trying to learn Spanish has the same advantage.

Spanish-speaking students may have an advantage, however, with another group of Latin-derived words that have come into English through another route. Historically these words came into English from the use of French as the language of the aristocracy and of government when French-speaking Normans became the ruling class of England after 1066. Commoners continued to use English, but within the court, the church, the judiciary, and other facets of life related to the upper classes, French was dominant. This pattern continued for more than 200 years until, in 1399, a native English speaker again sat on the English throne (Barber, 2000).

Even after English regained its dominant position among the upper classes, the influence of French remained in the form of vocabulary. Historians of the English language note that the French loan words that remained were many (Barber, 2000). In particular cases, the French vocabulary became the dominant vocabulary of the cultural and political domains of the ruling classes: ecclesiastical matters (e.g., *religion, saint, sermon, service, parish, clergy*), the law (e.g., *court, attorney, accuse, justice, judge, crime, prison, punish, verdict, sentence*), hunting, heraldry, the arts and fashion (e.g., *apparel, costume, dress, fashion, romance, column, music*), and administration (e.g., *council, country, crown, government, nation, parliament, people, state*).

French loan words can also be found in the domain of hearth and home. Because commoners continued to use English after the Norman Conquest, these French loan words exist alongside the Germanic-origin words of English. Take, for example, the English–French pairs of *doom/judgment, folk/nation, hearty/cordial*, and *stench/odor*. As these examples show, the German-origin words are typically used in colloquial or everyday settings, while the French words are typically used for purposes that might be regarded as more formal or refined.

Because written language typically employs more formal vocabulary, these French-origin words are often found in literary and academic texts. For example, a writer of literary or academic text may use the word *frigid* rather than the word *cold* to describe the temperature of a building; a crawling creature may be described as an *insect* rather than as a *bug*. For native Spanish speakers, these literary words are close to the common words in their native language: *frío, insecto*. These cognates can be useful in the learning of English, particularly academic English.

The Nature of Learning and Instruction

Students with home languages and dialects that differ from the language of school are frequently evaluated on their inadequacies rather than on their strengths (Allington & McGill-Franzen, 1991). This perception has too often led to lowered academic expectations for these students. Lower academic perceptions, in turn, lead to lower academic performances (Moll & Ruiz, 2002).

The funds-of-knowledge perspective of Moll and his colleagues (Moll, Amanti, Neff, & Gonzalez, 1992) directs attention to the intellectual resources that students, particularly culturally or linguistically different students, bring to school. The funds of knowledge that Moll and his associates have emphasized pertain to the bodies of knowledge that are essential to a household's functioning and well-being. For example, some members of a Latino/a community have knowledge about auto or bicycle mechanics that they share with other community members, while others are knowledgeable about home improvement (e.g., electrical wiring, plumbing). As these funds of knowledge are shared within the community, children observe and participate as community members perform tasks, such as measuring the opening for replacing a faucet. Such funds of knowledge create "zones of possibilities," in which classroom learning might be enhanced by the bridging of community ways of knowing with the expected classroom curriculum.

Spanish–English cognates can also be regarded as a "fund of knowledge" that can be used to bridge community with classroom ways of knowing. As the preceding review of the history of English showed, academic English contains vocabulary that has close connections to a Romance language such as Spanish. To date, researchers have examined the "transfer" value of these cognates, but they have not studied whether interventions that capitalize on this resource deliver benefits for learning English.

For example, research by Nagy and his colleagues has shown that, when students are aware of Spanish–English cognates, they do better on vocabulary tasks (Nagy, García, Durgunolgu, & Hancin-Bhatt, 1993). However, students' ability, even among upper-elementary students, is not fully developed or an automatic condition of bilinguals (García & Nagy, 1993). There does appear to be a developmental trend (Hancin-Bhatt & Nagy, 1994), with older students more aware and capable of using cognates than younger ones. Some of this developmental effect appears to be a function of English proficiency, but it also appears to be a function of the degree to which the word is understood in Spanish (Nagy et al., 1993).

Research has yet to be conducted on how this linguistic knowledge can be consistently recognized and drawn upon. While instructional studies exist in cognate use in learning French as a foreign language (Tréville, 1996) or even in learning Spanish as a foreign language (Cunningham & Graham, 2000), there have been few studies aimed at developing cognate understanding among native Spanish speakers learning English. Even among the teachers' manuals of programs that were adopted for use in the state of California (and that provide the foundation for the Reading First initiative in the state), we can find no evidence that cognates are listed or even emphasized as a strategy. We can, however, assume that the literary and academic texts that students encounter in school contain at least some cognates. Evidence for this conclusion comes from a vocabulary intervention conducted by Carlo et al. (2004). Even though Carlo et al. did not choose texts based on the presence of cognates, approximately 68% of the challenging and targeted vocabulary in the trade books and newspaper articles used in the intervention consisted of cognates.

Our particular interest in the cognate question came about because of our work on a science curriculum project aimed at increasing literacy and science connections. A portion of this work involved identifying a set of conceptually challenging words that would be introduced to students through both firsthand (active science investigations) and secondhand (reading science texts) inquiry. When the language and literacy members of the team viewed the words chosen by science educators for explicit teaching within each unit, they quietly generated a hypothesis: namely, that many of these critical science words were English–Spanish cognates. In particular, we thought that many of the Spanish cognates might fall into that category for which Spanish speakers have a distinct advantage: where the rarer academic word in English (e.g., *frigid* or *insect*) is a cognate for an everyday word in Spanish (e.g., *frío* or *insecto*). These words, we thought, could be a resource for bilingual students who are being asked to learn science content in English.

We also knew from our reviews of both reading and science textbooks that, even in states with large number of Spanish speakers (specifically, California, Texas, and Florida), state-adopted curricula do not highlight cognates as a strategy for native-Spanish-speaking students. It seemed such a transparently inviting practice, we wondered why. One possibility is that we have no research documenting the efficacy of the practice of emphasizing cognates in introducing academic vocabulary. This may be especially true when it comes to science texts. To gauge the potential benefits of embedding an English–Spanish cognate strategy into large-scale science curriculum and instruction efforts, data on the size and kind of the vocabulary in particular areas of science are needed. After all, if the cognate strategy could be applied to only a handful of words for a given topic, it might not be worth the energy and effort to create a special strand. Further, an understanding of the diversity of cognate types is also essential in designing curriculum and instruction for bilingual students. The cognate strategy works only if the language of science in English classrooms relies on a substantial set of words that appear infrequently in English but frequently in Spanish. Thus the present study was designed to test the potential efficacy of the cognate strategy by examining the types and number of English–Spanish cognates among a critical set of science words that might well be taught explicitly in a science curriculum.

AN EXAMINATION OF ENGLISH–SPANISH COGNATES IN SCIENCE CURRICULUM

The purpose of this study was to identify and classify the English–Spanish cognates within a set of words that science educators had identified as critical to the learning of three science topics. This analysis was set within a larger curriculum development process aimed at increasing literacy and science connections. A portion of this work involved identifying a set of conceptually challenging words that would be introduced to students through both firsthand (active science investigations) and secondhand (reading science texts) inquiry. The current study provides a linguistic existence proof on the kind and number of English–Spanish cognates in science content.

Methods of the Study

The development of the classification scheme and the identification of words for this linguistic analysis involved three steps: (1) establishing the critical science word list, (2) developing the cognate classification scheme, and (3) identifying the frequency of words in English and Spanish.

Identification of Critical Science Words

The analysis of critical science words occurred as part of a federally funded grant to increase the quality and quantity of literacy activities within a nationally recognized science curriculum, the Great Exploration in Math and Science (GEMS), carried out at the University of California's Lawrence Hall of Science. For prototypes of literacy–science connections, a set of three topics was chosen from among the 70 science curriculum units that have been published by GEMS. These three topics were chosen for their relevance to the curricula of the primary grades and representations of each of the three areas identified within national science standards: life, earth, and physical sciences. The three content areas and topics were: life science: Terrarium Investigations; earth science: Shoreline Science; and physical Science: Designing Mixtures.

For each topic, a team of four science educators with graduate degrees in the area and considerable material and professional development experience met to identify a group of critical words. These words were to be emphasized in the subsequent creation of student materials, books, and activities, and teacher guides. Over at least three meetings that occurred over a 6-week period, each of these three teams identified 20–26 words. In addition, all teams contributed to a group of words that described science processes across all three of the units. Across the three topics and the science process words, 86 words were represented: (1) science process: 14; (2) Shoreline Science: 26; (3) Terrarium Investigations: 25; and (4) Designing Mixtures: 21.

Some words appeared in more than one topic and some appeared with several derivatives within a topic (e.g., *decompose, decomposer, decomposition*). However, because the teams of science educators represented different disciplines and had conducted independent analysis of the critical words in their content area, all forms and occurrences of words were regarded as distinct words.

Cognate Classification Scheme

Cognates were defined as words with a similar spelling and meaning across languages. The classification of cognate types began with a study of the available databases including Nash's (1997) grouping of 20,000 Spanish/English words. The analysis yielded the following cognate types:

1. No shared cognate
2. False cognate (*globe/globo*)
3. Low-frequency English word: low-frequency Spanish word (*organism/organismo*)
4. High-frequency English word: low-frequency Spanish word (*question/cuestión*)

5. High-frequency English word: high-frequency Spanish word (*animal/animal*)
6. Low-frequency English word: high-frequency Spanish word (*frigid/frío*)

If the cognate strategy is to work, there must exist a substantial pool of words in categories 3 through 6 but especially in categories 5 and 6; in the final analysis there must be a sizable pool of words that Spanish speakers are likely to know from everyday Spanish use.

Establishing the Frequency of Spanish and English Words

The 86 English words were translated into Spanish by one of the principal investigators, who is a native Spanish speaker with three degrees in language-related study. The translations were checked with two on-line resources: (1) the on-line database of the Real Academia Española (2003), the official agency of the Spanish government that regulates the Spanish language, and (2) the English–Spanish On-Line Dictionary (2000).

Frequency of words in written English was established by consulting Zeno, Ivens, Millard, and Duvvuri (1995). Zeno et al. based their frequencies on approximately 17.25 million words drawn from a representative sampling of grade levels (kindergarten–college) and content areas. Criteria for establishing the word frequencies were as follows: (1) high frequency: words that occur at least 10 or more times per 1-million-word corpus and (2) low frequency: words that occur less than 10 times per 1-million-word corpus. There are approximately 5,500 words that occur 10 times or more per 1-million-word corpus. These words have been reported to account for approximately 90% of the words that students read from grades three through nine (Carroll, Davies, & Richman, 1971).

The Spanish word frequencies were tabulated using the online *Corpus del Español* (Davies, 2001). The corpus is based on 100 million words containing both spoken and written Spanish. Two-thirds of the corpus comes from the written register, while one-third comes from spoken Spanish. Approximately half of the spoken corpus comes from transcriptions of natural conversations from 11 different countries. The written corpus includes newspaper articles, essays, encyclopedias, letters, and humanistic texts from both Latin America and Spain. All texts were written between 1975 and 2000. Criteria for establishing the word frequencies was as follows: (1) high frequency: words that occurred 10 or more times per-million-word corpus in written form, and (2) low frequency: words that occurred fewer than 10 times per 1-million-word corpus in written form.

Results

The distribution of different cognate types among the words for each topic as well as for the entire corpus of words is provided in Table 8.1. Of the 86 critical science words, a large number were Spanish–English cognates (76%). Within the entire corpus, 38% (or half of the words with cognates) were high-frequency words in Spanish. By contrast, the percentage of cognate pairs with a high-frequency English word was considerably less: 13% of the entire corpus.

EXTENSIONS AND IMPLICATIONS

This analysis addressed a corpus of science vocabulary from the three disciplines that are central within national science standards (National Research Council, 1996) and those of large states: life, earth, and physical sciences. It included as well process words that extend across topics. Within this sample of words, three of every four words shared a Spanish–English cognate and, in one of every three words, the cognate was a common word in Spanish but not in English. This prima facie test

TABLE 8.1. Distribution of Words from Four Science Topics across Six Cognate Categories

Science topic	Number of words	No shared cognate	False cognate	LF English/ LF Spanish	HF English/ LF Spanish	HF English/ HF Spanish	LF English/ HF Spanish
						Cognate type	
Shoreline	26	5	0	11	1	3	6
Terrarium	25	7	0	10	0	1	7
Designing mixtures	21	5	1	6	0	1	8
Process	14	1	1	4	1	4	3
Entire corpus	86	18	2	31	2	9	24

Note. LF, low frequency; HF, high frequency.

suggests that the corpus of cognates is sufficiently large to merit adopting an explicit cognate instruction strategy. The paucity of existing research means that information on the amount of instructional time that needs to be devoted to this strategy is uncertain. However, we can point to two projects to illustrate the nature of research that has begun.

While the Vocabulary Improvement Program of Carlo et al. (2004) was not specifically focused on cognates, the set of target words included cognates. The intervention included lessons on vocabulary tools that were aimed at promoting general word analysis strategies, not specific knowledge of the target words. For three of the 15 lessons of the intervention, the cognate strategy was the tool of focus. Thus, in the Carlo et al. intervention, students were provided information on cognates in the texts that they read and were also introduced to a strategy that they were encouraged to use independently. While application of the cognate strategy was not assessed as a separate measure, the English language learners who received the intervention consistently outperformed their peers in the control group.

A second example comes from the implementation of the science/literacy curriculum that we have been involved in designing. At the present time, data collection continues on the effects of simultaneous participation in the science and literacy curriculum. However, we can outline what we believe to be imminently straightforward and also justified, based on our findings: the identification of cognates within science vocabulary and a reminder in the teachers' manual of a metacognitive strategy related to cognates. This metacognitive strategy is presented in a series of simple steps, including identifying a word (e.g., *plant*), asking students to look carefully at the spelling of the word and to identify a word in Spanish that sounds or looks like the target word, and giving a hypothesis about the meaning of the Spanish word and the new word.

Application of this strategy requires either teachers or program developers to identify cognates in advance of instruction. Inclusion of such lists as part of textbook programs would not place undue demands on program developers and could increase both teachers' and students' awareness of the linguistic derivations of words. However, more extensive and elaborate policies and practices for teaching cognates must await additional research. The replication of the analysis to a more extended corpus is needed and, as we have already described, we also need studies of the level of instructional time and consistency that students require to use the strategy. Research also needs to consider the effects of such a strategy on the learning of native English speakers and English language learners whose native language is not a Romance language.

Even when students' native languages do not have many high-frequency words that are cognates to words in academic English, understanding the manner in which Latin-based words work in science vocabulary is essential for all students.

As the current analysis showed, a significant portion of science vocabulary does relate to high-frequency Spanish words. To fail to capitalize on native language knowledge to support academic English language use would be to miss an opportunity to enhance the performance of a group of students who lag behind their non-Hispanic peers in science (Lee & Fradd, 1998). Transforming these linguistic differences into funds of knowledge (Moll et al., 1992) and infusing them into state standards and into both science and reading programs should be a high priority, especially since students whose first language is Spanish comprise the fastest growing sector of the U.S. school-age population (U.S. Census Bureau, 2001).

REFERENCES

Allington, R. L., & McGill-Franzen, A. (1991). *Educational reform and at-risk children: Exclusion, retention, transition, and special education in an era of increased accountability* (Final report to the U.S. Department of Education, Office of Educational Research and Improvement). Gainsville: University of Florida.

Barber, C. (2000). *The English language: A historical introduction.* Cambridge, UK: Cambridge University Press.

Carlisle, J. F., Fleming, J. E., & Gudbrandsen, B. (2000). Incidental word learning in science classes. *Contemporary Educational Psychology, 25,* 184–211.

Carlo, M. S., August, D., McLaughlin, B., Snow, C. E., Dressler, C., Lippman, D. N., et al. (2004). Closing the gap: Addressing the vocabulary needs of English-language learners in bilingual and mainstream classrooms. *Reading Research Quarterly, 39*(3), 188–215.

Carroll, J. B., Davies, P., & Richman, B. (1971). *The American Heritage word frequency book.* Boston: Houghton Mifflin.

Cooney, T., DiSpezio, M. A., Foots, B. K., Matamoros, A. L., Nyquist, K. B., & Ostlund, K. L. (2003). *Scott Foresman science* (Grade 6). Glenview, IL: Pearson Education.

Cunningham, T. H., & Graham, C. R. (2000). Increasing native English vocabulary recognition through Spanish immersion: Cognate transfer from foreign to first language. *Journal of Educational Psychology, 92,* 37–49.

Davies, M. (2001). *Corpus del Español.* Retrieved 20 September 2004 from www.corpusdelespañol.org.

Davis, F. B. (1942). Two new measures of reading ability. *Journal of Educational Psychology, 33,* 365–372.

Donahue, P. L., Finnegan, R. J., Lutkus, A. D., Allen, N. L., & Campbell, J. R. (2001). *The nation's report card for reading: Fourth grade.* Washington, DC: National Center for Education Statistics.

English–Spanish On-Line Dictionary. (2000). Retrieved 15 October 2004 from dictionaries.travlang.com/SpanishEnglish/.

García, G. E., & Nagy, W. E. (1993). Latino students' concept of cognates. In D. Leu & C. K. Kinzer (Eds.), *Examining central issues in literacy research, theory, and practice: Forty-second yearbook of the National Reading Conference* (pp. 367–374). Chicago: National Reading Conference.

Graves, M. F. (2000). A vocabulary program to complement and bolster a middle-grade comprehension program. In B. M. Taylor, M. F. Graves, & P. van den Broek (Eds.), *Reading for meaning: Fostering comprehension in the middle grades* (pp. 116–135). New York: Teachers College Press/Newark, DE: International Reading Association.

Hancin-Bhatt, B., & Nagy, W. (1994). Lexical transfer and second language morphological development. *Applied Psycholinguistics, 15,* 289–310.

Hayes, D. P., Wolfer, L. T., & Wolfe, M. F. (1996). Schoolbook simplification and its relation to the decline in SAT-Verbal scores. *American Educational Research Journal, 33,* 489–508.

Hiebert, E. H. (2003, April). *An examination of the effects of two types of text on second graders' fluency.* Paper presented at the annual meeting of the American Educational Research Association, Chicago.

Lee, O., & Fradd, S. H. (1998). Science for all, including students from non-English language backgrounds. *Educational Researcher, 27*(4), 12–21.

Moll, L. C., Amanti, C., Neff, D., & Gonzalez, N. (1992). Funds of knowledge for teaching: Using a qualitative approach to connect homes and classrooms. *Theory into Practice, 31*(2), 132–141.

Nagy, W. E., García, G. E., Durgunoglu, A. Y., & Hancin-Bhatt, B. (1993). Spanish–English bilingual students' use of cognates in English reading. *Journal of Reading Behavior, 25,* 241–259.

Nash, R. (1997). *NTC's dictionary of Spanish cognates: Thematically organized.* Lincolnwood, IL: NTC Publishing Group.

National Research Council. (1996). *National science education standards.* Washington, DC: National Academy Press.

O'Sullivan, C. Y., Lauko, M. A., Grigg, W. S., Quan, J., & Zhang, J. (2003). *The nation's report card: Science 2000.* Washington, DC: National Center for Education Statistics.

Real Academia Española. (2003). Retrieved October 12, 2004 from www.rae.es/diccionario/drae.htm.

Spillane, J. P., Diamond, J. B., Walker, L. J., Halverson, R., & Jita, L. (2001). Urban school leadership for elementary science instruction: Identifying and activating resources in an undervalued school subject. *Journal of Research in Science Teaching, 38*(8), 918–940.

Thayer, E. L. (2003). *Casey at the bat: A ballad of the republic sung in the year 1888*. New York: Simon & Schuster Books for Young Readers.

Tréville, M. C. (1996). Lexical learning and reading in L2 at the beginner level: The advantage of cognates. *Canadian Modern Language Review, 53*, 1–23.

U.S. Census Bureau. (2001). *The Hispanic population*. Retrieved October 10, 2004 from www.census.gov/population/www/socdemo/hispanic/ppl-172.html.

Whipple, G. (Ed.). (1925). *The twenty-fourth yearbook of the National Society for the Study of Education: Report of the National Committee on Reading*. Bloomington, IL: Public School.

Zeno, S. M., Ivens, S. H., Millard, R. T., & Duvvuri, R. (1995). *The educator's word frequency guide*. New York: Touchstone Applied Science Associates, Inc.

CHAPTER 9

Implications of New Vocabulary Assessments for Minority Children

JILL DE VILLIERS
VALERIE JOHNSON

The goal of this chapter is to discuss the ramifications of the status of the child's home language for the study of vocabulary and reading. The researchers at this conference have extensive data on how vocabulary and grammar prepare the way for the child's first experiences with literacy and reading. But what are the implications for this process if the vocabulary and grammar of the child are not the ones encountered in the school setting? In the case of the child whose parents speak a language other than English, the assumption is that the child is a competent speaker of that particular language, and must therefore be transitioned as quickly as possible to English if teaching him or her reading and writing English is the desired goal. The case of the African American child has created more perplexity, because English is the language being spoken, but educators do not think it is being spoken *correctly*. Mainstream American English (MAE) is the language of instruction, but the African American child's English often departs in significant ways from that dialect. Furthermore, it often displays features that educators associate with much younger children, such as dropped tenses, and so those parts that are like MAE superficially resemble the kind of speech that children have when they have language delays or disabilities (Craig & Washington, 1994; Wyatt, 1995). And to make matters worse, when the children are given standard tests for language, the scores they receive can fall into the dubious range, both on inflectional morphology (tenses, plurals, copulas, etc.) and in known vocabulary (Stockman, 1999, 2000). Thus the African American child, unlike the child raised by parents who come from another country, is suspected of being a less than competent speaker of his native language. Many educators have a ready-made explanation for this failure in what they perceive as the material conditions of too many African American families: undereducated parents, a high frequency of single parents with insufficient support for childrearing, a lack of stimulating materials in the home, and inadequate childcare (National Center of Education Statistics, 2001; Washington, 2001). Thus, the child's home life is regarded as the cause of the *deficit* seen in primary language skills (Bereiter & Englemann, 1966; Hart & Risley, 1995).

It would be dangerous to assert that there is no such problem. However, we offer in this chapter a different perspective on the issue. In the course of doing so, we hope to reveal the strengths of the African American child's language competence that are too often squandered in the early school years. The *differences* are there, but considering them *deficits* can blind us to the possibilities for a more successful transition to schooling.

As Snow (2004) remarked, African American children do not enter kindergarten with a bias against reading. They arrive as eager as any child to begin to learn and are excited to become competent in this grown-up skill. What discourages them? By fourth grade, an estimated 60% have failed to reach appropriate competence, and the gap between African American and white children continues through eighth and eleventh grade (National Center for Education Statistics, 2001; Washington, 2001). Everyone agrees that this is a situation not to be tolerated, but then the different accounts of the process begin to part company. In this chapter we consider the "language factor" and speculate that its ramifications have the potential to extend into other domains, such as student motivation and student and teacher attitudes.

THE LANGUAGE FACTOR

Minority children in the United States, especially those with African American heritage, often speak languages or dialects other than MAE. African American English (AAE) is a dialect defined by a commonality of speech spoken primarily by African Americans, but not by all. AAE is less geographically defined than other dialects of English. Historical evidence suggests it originated in the language used by slaves and then spread with the major black migrations to the large urban centers. Because of continued segregation in work, community, and schooling, it gained a certain separation from the speech of white Americans (Baugh, 1983; Dillard, 1972; Green, 2002; Labov, 1972; Rickford, 1999). AAE may be defined in terms of the features that distinguish a pattern of morphology, semantics, syntax, and phonology in the speech used by *culturally identified* African Americans. Several decades of careful linguistic work have revealed that it is a language dialect of English as rich and complex as any other variety, though it is frequently considered to be a degenerate form of English by nonlinguists (Vaughn-Cooke, 1999; Wolfram, 1999). Though regional dialects are often considered quaint, or even heralded as resources reflecting our linguistic heritage, this has not been the common attitude toward AAE.

Since at least the 1970s, the American Speech–Language–Hearing Association (ASHA) has recognized these negative attitudes toward AAE as creating a risk for children when they face language assessment. Most tests of English language are normed for MAE. The problem takes two forms: (1) content bias, in which MAE target forms are the standard, with departures from them often considered as mistakes; and (2) sampling bias, in that too few AAE speakers are sampled in the norms for existing tests. Even when African American children are represented in the sampling norms, their data are often not considered separately, so if they happen to constitute a disproportionate share of the lowest quartile it is not considered to be test bias.

Although speaking AAE is not a disorder, it can be misinterpreted as one on such tests. The overidentification of African American children in caseloads of speech–language pathologists is only one symptom. Because of the centrality of language testing (especially of vocabulary) to the diagnosis of special education categories, it is probable that some overrepresentation there is also caused by the unsuitability of existing language tests (Seymour, 2003).

In 1998, a research group at the University of Massachusetts headed by Harry Seymour received a contract from the National Institutes of Health (National Institute on Deafness and Other Communication Disorders) to develop norms, and ultimately a new kind of language test, for children speaking non-Standard English, that is, AAE (website: www.umass.edu/aae). Our goals were ambitious:

1. To develop a comprehensive language assessment of syntax, semantics, pragmatics, and phonology between ages 4 and 9 years.

2. To be able to determine whether language variation in children is due to development, dialect, or disorder.
3. To create a test that is not biased against dialect speakers, especially AAE speakers.

In order to do this successfully, it became obvious that such a test needed to avoid some surface aspects of language, because focusing on morphosyntactic elements such as plural, past tenses, and copula verbs only highlights the grammatical differences between MAE and AAE. Selection of such items places AAE speakers who are normally developing language learners in the same category as MAE speakers with specific language impairment (SLI) (de Villiers, 2003; Seymour, Bland-Stewart, & Green, 1998). Instead the focus should be on those aspects of language that do not differ between AAE and MAE, that is, on the deeper principles on which all languages are based and which connect to the concepts of Universal Grammar. This is tantamount to making a test that is harder and more challenging than existing tests.

The ideal items for such a test must have the following properties:

1. Show a clear developmental progression from age 4 to age 9 years.
2. Show no bias against AAE speakers.
3. Show a clear differentiation of a priori identified "impaired" children in each dialect.

The astute reader may realize that (3) is not easily achieved if we doubt the ability of existing tests to reliably identify "impaired" children who speak AAE! However, there are two ways to ameliorate the difficulty. First, we can see how successful we are at identifying MAE speakers using our test versus traditional tests. If we trust the traditional tests with MAE speakers (and we may still be doubtful), at least our test should identify most of the same children despite its theoretically different content. Second, we can use a variety of indices to identify impaired AAE speakers: not just the traditional tests, but parental report, teacher report, advice from seasoned clinicians familiar with the population, and so on. That is, converging indicators allow more secure determination even if the "gold standard" here is more like "tin" (de Villiers, P., 2003)!

The test that Seymour and colleagues developed, the Diagnostic Evaluation of Language Variation (DELV; Seymour, Roeper, & de Villiers, 2003, 2005) is discussed in detail in Seymour and Pearson (2004). The

DELV does seem to meet the requirements outlined above, in that when socioeconomic class is carefully matched, the child who speaks AAE is not differentially successful compared to the child who speaks MAE. That meets the requirements by ASHA (1983) that speech–language pathologists should not treat dialect variations as a speech and/or language disorder. Of course, such a result would be trivial if the test failed to also identify children in need of services, regardless of the dialect they spoke. The test fulfills that requirement too—though, as expected, the convergence between its identification and that of existing tests is not perfect, especially for AAE speakers. It will take some years of clinical practice to determine if the test has merit in identifying the right children who can benefit from services. Before describing the way that the DELV tests semantic development, it is first necessary to introduce the general problem of vocabulary assessment in African American youngsters.

WHY IS VOCABULARY ASSESSMENT A CHALLENGE?

Current standardized tests of receptive vocabulary such as the Peabody Picture Vocabulary Test–III (PPVT-III; Dunn & Dunn, 1998) and the Receptive One-Word Picture Vocabulary Test (ROWPVT; Gardner, 1985) measure a child's performance in matching the meaning of a word to a corresponding list of possible referents, with one being the best match. However, children for whom certain experiences may not be common or may be different because of diverse cultural and linguistic backgrounds can be at a decided disadvantage when taking such tests.

This disadvantage appears to be reflected in the poorer performance of AAE-speaking children when compared to their MAE-speaking peers (Stockman, 2000; Washington & Craig, 1992, 1999) on some tests. One likely factor in lower performance on word learning is differences in input. As J. de Villiers (2004) points out, word learning is dependent on frequency of input; however, children grow up in various conditions and may develop vocabularies that differ from each other.

Although the source of poor performance scores by AAE-speaking children on various standardized tests remains controversial (Seymour & Bland, 1991; Washington & Craig, 1999), Stockman (1999, 2000) argues that the popular and commonly used index of receptive vocabulary is likely to be the most vulnerable to bias when assessing culturally and linguistically diverse populations. Most picture-based vocabulary tests rely heavily on nouns due to the difficulty of capturing verb meaning in a picture format (de Villiers, 2004). Blake (1984) contended that verbs may be a more salient part of the vocabulary for AAE-speaking children, as they are in other cultures (Choi & Gopnik, 1995). Children who come from families with different vocabularies, or who may not emphasize object labeling (Heath, 1983, 1989; Peña, 1996) may be at a disadvantage on noun-laden vocabulary tests. Thus there is the need for developing more culturally and linguistically fair ways of assessing children's semantic competency.

One potential method for assessing lexical learning that does not depend so much on prior knowledge or experience, regardless of linguistic background, is fast mapping (Carey & Bartlett, 1978). *Fast mapping* consists of quickly inferring a preliminary idea of a novel word's meaning. Carey and Bartlett (1978) argue that this process involves a restructuring of the lexicon and of the underlying conceptual domain that can be achieved by a single exposure to the novel word. For example, fast mapping of nouns requires establishing an association between the word and the entity, a process that plays a major role in early lexical acquisition. However, in the fast mapping of verbs, such a direct association is inadequate (Tomasello, 1995). Additional information for fast mapping of verbs is needed because actions indirectly involve either an object undergoing change or two or more objects with dynamic relationships (Slobin, 1978). As a result, often the action is over before the verb is heard, or is still impending (Tomasello, 1995; Gleitman, 1990), making ostensive reference much more difficult than for nouns. Instead, syntactic frames play a more significant role in verb learning (Gleitman, 1990; Gleitman & Gleitman, 1992). During fast mapping of verbs, children can learn meaning by noticing the range of syntactic frames in which the word appears. In other words, children use relations among nouns and verbs to support mapping by using each syntactic frame or argument to narrow the choice of possible interpretations for the verb.

EXPERIMENTS ON FAST MAPPING

In an early study of the role of syntax in fast mapping, Brown (1958) found that preschool children, 3–5 years of age, were sensitive to the sentence context in choosing different word meanings for the novel word *sib*. The pictures contained a character doing a strange action to a mass substance with an unknown implement. For example:

Look, a sib! (Child picks out implement.)
Look, sibbing! (Child picks out action.)
Look, some sib! (Child picks out mass substance.)

More recently, Klibanoff and Waxman (2000) showed children could differentiate adjectives from nouns by using linguistic context, as in the following examples:

Look, a sib! (Child notices object.)
Look, a sib one! (Child notices attribute.)

Researchers have shown that for verbs, sentence context, namely, the argument frame, is crucial (e.g., Naigles, 1990; Gleitman, 1990; Fisher, 1996). They have demonstrated that young children can guess the kind of event that is being referred to in an utterance based on the sentence context. For example, in work conducted by Fisher (1996), children between the ages of 3 and 5 were shown a video of person B sitting on a swivel stool, who was being spun by person A, who was pulling off a scarf wrapped around the waist of person B. This action was labeled with either a transitive (1) or an intransitive (2) argument frame:

1. She's mooping *her* over there.
2. She's mooping over there.

For (1), "mooping" was associated with person A. For (2), "mooping" was more often considered to be the action person B, though not exclusively, just as with adult judgments.

Johnson (2001) extended Fisher's work to include more complex forms, with the goal of investigating whether such a procedure could be used for the fairer assessment of semantic knowledge in children speaking AAE or MAE. It was reasoned that such a procedure, involving the readiness to learn new verbs, might level the playing field for children who come from different backgrounds and so have different preparation for standard vocabulary tests.

Thirty AAE-speaking children and 30 MAE-speaking children were included in this study, 10 children from each group at ages 4, 5, and 6 years. The AAE-speaking group was recruited from working-class communities in central Connecticut where the neighborhoods included primarily African American families. The MAE-speaking group was recruited from working-class communities in western Massachusetts where the neighborhoods consisted primarily of Caucasian families. The teachers provided background demographic and educational information for each student. All children were reported to be performing at expected levels for their age and grade level.

Fast mapping of verbs was the measure of semantic knowledge examined in this study; however, the PPVT-III (Dunn & Dunn, 1998) was also administered to all children to compare against the novel test. In order to study fast mapping in detail, four argument structures judged to be the same across the two dialects were included: intransitive, transitive, transfer, and infinitival complement structures (see Table 9.1). Naigles (1990), Fisher (1996), Gleitman (1990), and Gleitman and Gleitman (1992) have conducted studies that demonstrated children can bootstrap verb meaning from *intransitive* and *transitive* argument structures, and have argued that *complement* structures are important sources of verb meaning. However, complement structures had not been investigated experimentally with children.

In Johnson's (2001) study, a design similar to that of Naigles (1990) and Fisher (1996) was used by pairing the argument structures with the same pictured stimuli: intransitive with transitive; *to-* complement with transfer. The study utilized sequential picture sets to simulate a "movie" of the main event to be presented to the participants (see Figures 9.1 and 9.2). For example, a participant would see a strange event (Figure 9.1) in which a boy was performing some novel action on his own, and a woman was performing some other novel action to the boy, over a set of three pictures in sequence. The participant then heard: (1) "The woman is *temming* the boy" or (2) "The boy is *temming*." The participant hearing (1) would likely associate the novel verb *temming* with the woman's action on the boy and hearing (2) would associate it with the boy's own action.

To see which meaning the child mapped to each verb, questions that included the novel verb were presented to each participant (Table 9.2). To test this, participants were shown a set of four pictures (e.g.,

---

TABLE 9.1. Argument Structures and Examples

- Intransitive: *The boy* is sneezing.
- Transitive: *The girl* is pushing *the wagon*.
- Transfer: *The woman* is handing *the letter* to *the man*.
- Infinitival complement: *The man* is asking *the girl* to throw *the ball*.

Note. Data from Johnson (2001).

FIGURE 9.1. A sample transitive/intransitive picture sequence for the sentence "The woman is temming the boy." Copyright 2001 by Harcourt. Reprinted with permission.

the boy, the woman, an instrument from the picture, and another incidental object) to choose from when asked: (1) "Which one was the temmer?" and (2) "Which one got temmed?"

Participants were randomly assigned to be administered Form A or its counterbalanced version, Form B, in which the alternate argument structure was used, as in Fisher (1996). By this design, the child's choice of an agent could not be attributed to the picture alone, but instead had to be based on the argument structure heard. A total of eight novel verbs were presented to each participant (two novel verbs per argument structure). Each participant had the opportunity to fast-map two novel verbs per argument structure. (For more details of the design of materials, see Johnson, 2001.)

The six question types and examples using novel verbs are classified in Table 9.3. Notice that not all questions are equally appropriate for all verb types. Question types 5 and 6 did not contain any bound or derivational morphology because they were designed to assess whether the child could determine the object of the complement and subject of the complement in the complement argument structure (see Figure 9.2).

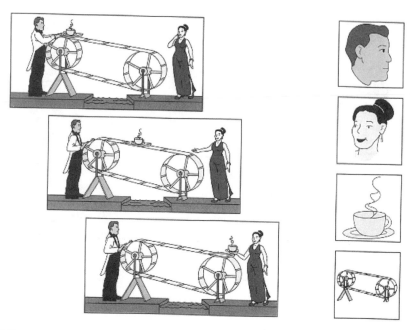

FIGURE 9.2. A sample transfer/complement picture sequence for the sentence "The woman is ganning the waiter to send the coffee." Copyright 2001 by Harcourt. Reprinted by permission.

The child has to use the full argument structure to answer questions regarding the subject and object of the complement. Of course, a child could fail on the questions because of the morphology or syntax of those questions, not because of a failure to map the novel verb meaning. To control for that possibility, the test was introduced and modeled first with real verbs that the children were likely to know, and they were asked parallel questions about those verbs. This ensured that they had practice with the task with familiar verbs first, and also determined whether the questions caused difficulty with familiar verbs.

Johnson's results suggested a promising future for the tasks. Children between the ages of 4 and 6 could glean meaning about the verbs from the argument structures, as shown by their differential answers to the probe questions. Some of the questions proved hard for this age group even with the novel verbs—for example, the *-able* morpheme was often misinterpreted as an agent marker: the actor was considered "handable" if he handed something to someone! (See also Roeper, 1987.) Furthermore, complement structures were difficult for this age group compared to transitive argument structures. Most importantly, only minor differences were

TABLE 9.2. Question Types and Examples

Question type 1: Included derivational morpheme -er
     Which one was the temmer?

Question type 2: Included bound morpheme present progressive -ing
     Which one was temming?

Question type 3: Included bound morpheme -ed in a passive construction (-ed$_{passive}$)
     Which one got temmed?

Question type 4: Included bound derivational morpheme -able
     Which one was temmable?

Question type 5: Designed to address the object of the complement (OC)
     Which one did the woman gan the waiter to send?

Question type 6: Designed to address the subject of the complement (SC)
     Which one did the woman gan to send the coffee?

Note. Data from Johnson (2001).

found in performance between AAE-speaking children and MAE-speaking children, who did equally well in mapping novel verb meanings. This is significant in the light of their performance on the PPVT-III; despite attempts to match socioeconomic status (SES), the MAE speakers averaged 13 points higher than the AAE speakers (Johnson, 2001).

But the important question then becomes, Is this equality of performance a sign that the playing field has been leveled, or might it mean that important differences in ability have been ignored by the test? The acid test is whether the test distinguishes typically developing children from children with language impairment.

In the preparation for the new test, the DELV (Seymour et al., 2003), Johnson's thesis idea was adapted to study how children ages 4–9 years

TABLE 9.3. Matrix of Argument Structures and Question Types Presented to the Participants to Test the Comprehension of Real and Novel Verbs

Question Types	Real and novel verbs			
	Intransitive	Transitive	Transfer	Complement
1 (-er)	X	X	X	X
2 (-ing)	X	X	X	X
3 (-ed$_{passive}$)		X	X	
4 (-able)		X	X	
5 (OC)				X
6 (SC)				X

from various dialects of English including AAE could fast-map verbs from argument structures. The task held the promise of being nonbiased, though it was untried with clinical populations. We reasoned that the case of verbs might prove especially vulnerable in language impairment given the work of Rice and Bode (1993) on the insufficiency of early verb lexicons in language-impaired children.

The general characteristics of the tryout, or field testing, of the DELV are contained in Table 9.4. The sample was a large one, and contained a larger than usual proportion of children diagnosed as having language impairments (33%). In addition, the sample contained 60% AAE speakers, which is a much greater sampling of those children than the usual standardization procedure that matches U.S. census proportions. Both dialect grouping and language impairment status were categorized by testing clinicians based on their experience with the children as well as a variety of standardized testing that they had carried out. Confirmation of these categorizations was then sought from the DELV screener (Seymour, Roeper, & de Villiers, 2003).

Because this was field testing of a test, not an experiment, it was not possible to balance the stimuli as in Johnson's (2001) study, so one-half of the children received one kind of prompt for a given picture sequence and one-half the alternative prompt. However, Johnson's work had provided the background we needed to show that the pictures were balanced, and that the sentences were what led the child to one answer or another. The stimuli were adapted from Johnson's work and contained the same kinds of exemplars, representing four kinds of argument structures (Table 9.1) and six kinds of questions (Table 9.2) to allow the examiner to determine which action the child had associated the novel

TABLE 9.4. Composition of the DELV Tryout Sample

- $N = 1,014$
- Ages: 4 years, 0 months–9 years, 11 months
- Working-class background, matched parent education levels at high school or below
- From all regions of the United States.
- 60% AAE speakers
- 40% MAE speakers
- AAE and MAE speakers matched for parental education level
- Approximately 33% diagnosed as language-impaired at each age-level in each dialect group

Note. Data from Seymour, de Villiers, and Roeper (2003).

verb with. From the large amount of data this generated, a selection was made for inclusion on the final DELV. For example, everyone found the intransitive forms too easy, so they were dropped. The point was to find items that showed steady changes with age. The amount of information gleaned from the "real verb" use was less useful than the information gleaned from the novel verbs in discriminating impaired children from typically developing children, so that section was also truncated so that it served merely as an introduction to the procedure for the child.

The graph in Figure 9.3 shows the results from the field testing. Recall that ideal items would have the properties of (1) steady developmental growth and (2) no bias against AAE speakers. The graphs show that promise was met. But as before, such item sets would only be useful if they also discriminated language-impaired children from typically de-veloping children. Figure 9.4 shows that the fast-mapping test also has that characteristic. Hence, the verb fast-mapping test has some desirable properties for assessing how much children can begin to establish a meaning from a new verb, regardless of the dialect they speak. This is to be distinguished from standard acquired vocabulary tests that assess what the child has learned but not what they *can* learn, possibly con-founding experience and potential.

The results of these investigations suggest that children can fast-map a novel verb at least partially from a single exposure to it in intransitive,

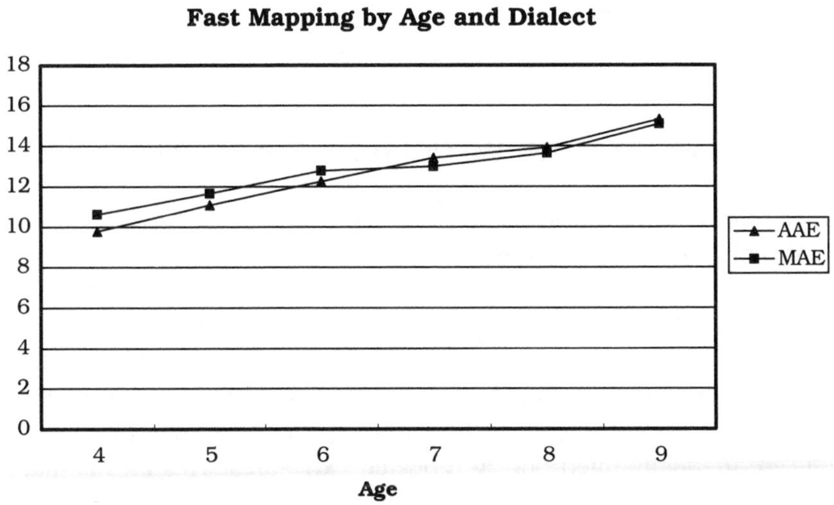

FIGURE 9.3. Results from the DELV-CR: dialect groups compared by age.

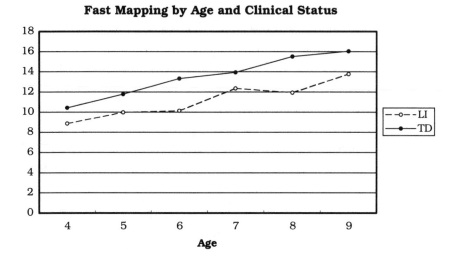

FIGURE 9.4. Results from the DELV-CR: clinical status groups compared by age.

transitive, transfer, and complement syntactic structures, as long as there are supporting pictures. However, multiple exposures, across multiple frames, are likely needed to fix it more firmly (Gleitman, 1990). Pinker (1994) has argued that the structures themselves allow a kind of zooming in on the right domain of meaning, but contextual support is necessary for more specific mapping of the meaning. Gleitman (1990) has argued that converging evidence across a variety of sentence structures might be necessary to delimit the meaning further.

WHAT ARE THE IMPLICATIONS FOR READING?

How Might "Fast Mapping" Relate to Reading, as Opposed to Vocabulary Knowledge?

The source of new vocabulary lies in the conversation with adults in school or home environments, where ostensive definition of new words is not the norm for any child. Instead, meanings are picked up from their sentence contexts, categorized by part of speech, and then their meanings are gradually filled out by repeated exposures. This means that a child needs the skills that are tapped by the fast-mapping assessments in order to acquire vocabulary past the baby stage. These skills increase as the child masters more syntactic varieties, and also as a function of the other words that he or she knows that allow anchors to bridge to the new words, and also serve as clues to the potential semantic domain. So a child hearing a conversation about firemen, hoses, and burning might hear the new word *extinguish*, and pragmatic inferences as well as syntax might allow the meaning of "put an end to" to emerge. Ideally, early texts or readers are made up of highly frequent words that are in every child's experience. Once the basic word attack skills are mastered, then reading actually promotes vocabulary development (Nagy, Anderson, & Herman, 1987). A major source of new vocabulary words once a child learns to read is from written material, and the skills of fast mapping are needed in a parallel way to glean meaning from text, make provisional guesses about word meaning, and then pick up clues to narrow meanings (de Villiers & Pomeranz, 1992). As education proceeds, we become adept at reading materials where virtually nothing is familiar, but we know how to play the game and answer the questions. An example of this process is often provided in cognitive psychology texts (Table 9.5).

It is rather frightening to consider how much of student learning takes this form. However, in abstract domains (e.g., microscopic science, abstract philosophy) this is how words are first learned, and the networks of such uses constitute their "meaning." So fast mapping via syntactic bootstrapping is not just one of the major ways that vocabulary is acquired, but also an essential component of skilled reading (Sternberg & Powell, 1983; de Villiers & Pomeranz, 1992). Nevertheless, it is also clear that prior domain knowledge plays a large role in helping this process of making words meaningful (Drum & Konopak, 1987). A child with more experience in the relevant domain, biology, for example, will have more chance to connect the new words to established networks.

TABLE 9.5. The Information in Text When Reading New Words

A phlogian can enterporate for many minicols if it is not depertoned. In order to depertone a phlogian, one should first ciphirate it into smaller flegpols. After this depertoning, phlogians should not enterporate.

So, how do you depertone a phlogian?
What if it isn't depertoned?
What can a phlogian be ciphirated into?
How can you protect a phlogian from enterporation?
Are flegpols parts of phlogians?

However, we also have evidence that the grammar may be a significant variable here. In a follow-up study, Johnson, de Villiers, Deschamps, D'Amato, and Huneke (2002) explored the role of concrete nouns in helping the child to fast-map novel verbs. That is, could the argument structure stand alone as a reliable clue to verb meaning if the concrete nouns were absent? In this study, 55 MAE-speaking children heard sentences with "empty" nouns such as those in Table 9.6, that is, with the same pictured support and argument structures as before, and also the same probe questions. Real verbs were used as an introduction to the task and to test whether children could answer the probe questions, as in Johnson (2001).

The results suggest the children's success depended on the particular argument structure used. A single exposure to a novel verb in a *transitive* or *transfer* structure permitted successful mapping—even with empty nouns. However, a single exposure to a novel verb in an *intransitive* structure was not successful with empty nouns: the meaning was ambiguous (as in Fisher, 1996). A single exposure to a novel verb in a *complement* structure was not successful with empty nouns, and even adults had difficulty. These results are important for delineating which aspect of the stimulus context is providing the crucial information for the child to map a preliminary meaning. At least with spoken exposure, sometimes surrounding words are necessary for fast mapping, and sometimes they are not.

Are These Dynamic Assessments of Vocabulary Better Indicators Than Acquired Vocabulary Tests of the Child's School Readiness?

If we successfully assess whether a child *can* learn new words from context, how can that help? First, it may help describe the source of difficulty:

1. The child cannot use context to learn new words. This child needs help in basic structures of sentences and inferences, that is, is a *language-impaired* child.

TABLE 9.6. Empty Nouns in Argument Positions

- Intransitive: Someone is meeping.
- Transitive: Someone is meeping someone.
- Transfer: Someone is meeping something to someone.
- Infinitival complement: Someone is meeping someone to send something.

Note. Data from Johnson, de Villiers, Deschamps, D'Amato, and Huneke (2002).

2. The child can learn easily from context but has not had much opportunity to do so, so the child's vocabulary is low, that is, is a *vocabulary-deprived* child.
3. The child can learn easily from context and has had the opportunity to do so but the words he or she knows are not in the texts he or she encounters, that is, he or she is a *culturally mismatched* child.

Depending on the outcome, different educational strategies would be called for.

We argued that because of cultural variation, the vocabulary a child knows may be underestimated on standard tests. However, their capacity to acquire words through discourse may be developing normally. The question is, Which is more important for reading success? Clearly the answer to this depends on how well matched the reading texts are to the language of the child. If the reading texts contain much vocabulary that the child does not know, then the child who has a different acquired lexicon will be disadvantaged, and will need to use fast mapping and inferencing strategies much more than the child who encounters familiar vocabulary. The child with a different lexicon would have to work harder to achieve the same understanding. In this sense, acquired vocabulary tests do assess the child's upcoming workload if school texts are biased to represent one cultural norm.

We have shown that AAE-speaking and MAE-speaking children alike have fast-mapping skills needed to infer new word meaning from sentence context in spoken discourse. Might differences show up if the task involved reading? If a child's vocabulary does not match that of the text, then more inferencing work will be needed than for a child for whom most of the words are familiar. Second, there is the risk that a child might "guess" a word from its first sound, a strategy that Labov, Baker, Bullock, Ross, and Brown (1998) found to be common in AAE speakers in which the phonics curriculum taught first-letter matches too thoroughly at the expense of other code-cracking skills. A child who guesses at an unknown word without reading it thoroughly may then go astray in recognizing its morphological variant. Imagine, to return to the exaggerated example in Table 9.5, that the word encountered was *flegpolation*. If a reader skims-reads it as "flagellation," then he or she will be bewildered by questions about "flegpols." For reasons of both different vocabulary and inadequate phonics training, the transition to fast mapping in reading may impact AAE speakers and MAE speakers differentially. But knowing exactly how would lead to potential solutions.

THE LARGER FRAMEWORK

The bigger questions emerge at this juncture. If AAE-speaking children enter school eager and able to learn vocabulary, eager and able to learn to read, then why do AAE-speaking children in reading assessments continue to differ from their MAE-speaking counterparts with grade level? The claim is that as reading requires higher level skills, the problems expand (Craig, Conner, & Washington, 2003). As a result, it appears unlikely that this is directly dialectal in origin, that is, that phonology and morphology are mismatched to orthography (Hart, Guthrie, & Winfield, 1983; Labov, Baker, Bullock, Ross, & Brown, 1998). However, Labov (1995; Labov et al., 1998) argued for a restructuring of phonics-based reading programs to take into account the differences between written forms and the surface realization of words in AAE speech.

We have suggested the increasing strains that might develop in the child who encounters vocabulary mismatch between home and school environments. There are several solutions: use vocabulary that is culturally familiar and neutral so that the children all have the same aid from known words, or use texts with vocabulary tailored to the child's cultural background (LeMoine, 1999; Rickford & Rickford, 1995). The latter solution seems very sensible except that the broader bias issues emerge, in which African American lives and circumstances are considered unsuitable reading material (Gilyard, 1991; Rickford, 1999) or African American parents worry that they promote stereotypes, as with the case of the book *Nappy Hair* (Herron, 1998). The impact is likely to be most effective if it is two-way: preschool programs that boost vocabulary skills in children from different backgrounds toward a more traditional school-ready vocabulary (Craig et al., 2003), and concerted efforts by educators to make schools a better match to the skills that AAE-speaking children bring (Adger, Christian, & Taylor, 1999; LeMoine, 2001; Boykin & Allen, 2003; Vernon-Feagans, Scheffner-Hammer, Miccio, & Manlove, 2001).

What are some other sources of the problems for AAE speakers learning to read? As material becomes more difficult and more and more inferencing is required, it is probable that motivation becomes much more significant than ability. The danger is that the child who is AAE-speaking is accumulating experiences that tell him or her that his or her native language and speech are degenerate, and that he or she is not speaking "right" by the school's standards. Those children who take that lesson to heart and/or begin to see the value in bidialectalism, begin code-switching in school environments. A recent report suggests that code-switchers, that is, children who manifest fewer dialect features in their speech, achieve higher standardized test scores and reading scores than children who retain more features (Craig & Washington, 2004). Given Labov's (Labov et al., 1998) findings, this is probably not just because the languages are in increasing synchrony at the superficial level. Possibly, it is because some children have adopted school norms and are assimilating into the more powerful mainstream school culture. Gilyard (1991) movingly describes this tension in his own schooling, where he also cites Hudson (1980) about a child's choices: ". . . he will probably model his speech largely on that of the others in the group he has chosen. In other words, at each act of utterance his speech can be seen as an ACT OF IDENTITY in a multi-dimensional space" (p. 14).

Washington (2001) clearly describes some of the pressures that AAE-speaking children are subject to in the classroom.

1. Teachers judge reading by read-alouds, and constantly "correct" dialectal pronunciations, sometimes at the cost of attention to the child's understanding of the text. Yet, in order to switch from the written MAE into spoken AAE, the child is demonstrating bidialectal competence with the language of the text (Washington, 2001).

2. It is well documented that many teachers are biased against dialect speakers. Studies have taken the same text and read it with the voice quality associated with black or white speakers and judges give higher ratings to the white speech qualities (Washington, 2001). In numerous small ways, teachers can indicate their distaste for and misunderstanding of features of dialect (Cazden, 1999; Washington, 2001). These are the reasons that educators such as LeMoine (1999, 2001), Baugh (1999), and Wolfram (1999) argue that teachers need linguistic knowledge about AAE before they can teach AAE speakers effectively.

3. Because texts are written in MAE, children who speak AAE do not feel represented. Many school texts do not portray African American characters or things of interest/familiarity to them (Barrera, 1992; Harris, 1995). A major stimulus in the educational history of Professor Keith Gilyard (Gilyard, 1991) occurs when his teacher suggests a poetry book written by an African American, Langston Hughes. Rickford and Rickford (1995) call for a reconsideration of the idea of dialect readers as a bridge to reading for AAE speakers.

4. Stories are structured in a way counter to the cultural practices of African American storytelling. This latter fact is a controversial one, as some earlier work suggested that African American storytelling has a unique "topic-associating" style associated with oral cultures (Michaels, 1981; Gee, 1991). However, more recently Champion (2002) finds that grade-school AAE-speaking children are capable of a wide range of styles in storytelling, including the linear story grammar type (see also Hyon & Sulzby, 1994). Nevertheless, the ethnographic work of Heath (1983, 1989) and others (Vernon-Feagans et al., 2001) reminds us that there are different ways that different cultural groups have to "make meaning," and that, at least at first, children might be better off with a match than a mismatch (Boykin & Allen, 1999; Le Moine, 1999). In particular, several studies have found differences in the style and quantity of questioning that African American mothers use to engage their children compared to white mothers reading to their children (Washington, 2001; Vernon-Feagans et al., 2001).

REMAINING RESEARCH QUESTIONS

Given the larger issues of culture fairness in school-reading instruction and assessment, the following research questions remain.

1. Do fast-mapping measures of semantic knowledge correlate at all with standard reading comprehension measures? How do they compare with acquired vocabulary tests? Do the two types predict differently for AAE than for MAE?
2. Suppose these fast-mapping measures do not correlate with *standard* measures of reading comprehension. Is it that the tests of reading comprehension rely more on nets of familiar (to some) words than on syntactic decoding? A test of fast mapping in reading could be devised along the same lines as the materials for spoken language to see when and if children benefit from the skills they have in oral vocabulary learning.
3. If not, can we improve the "fit" of the text in the fast mapping to the child's dialect, and see if reading improves? That is, would children benefit from using their fast-mapping skills on a passage of culturally familiar or interesting material?

These are some of the important directions future work might take.

REFERENCES

Adger, C., Christian, D., & Taylor, O. (1999). *Making the connection: Language and academic achievement in African American students.* McHenry, IL: Center for Applied Linguistics and Delta Systems Co.

American Speech–Language–Hearing Association. (1983). Position paper: Social dialects and implications of the position on social dialects. *ASHA, 25*(9), 23–27.

Baugh, J. (1983). *Black street speech: Its history, structure and survival.* Austin: University of Texas Press.

Baugh, J. (1999). *Out of the mouths of slaves: African American language and educational malpractice.* Austin, TX: University of Texas Press.

Bereiter, C., & Englemann, S. (1966). *Teaching disadvantaged children in the preschool.* Englewood Cliffs, NJ: Prentice-Hall.

Berrera, R. (1992). The cultural gap in literature-based instruction. *Education and Urban Society, 24,* 227–243.

Blake, I. (1984). *Language development in working-class black children: An examination of form, content, and use.* Unpublished doctoral dissertation, Columbia University, New York, NY.

Boykin, A. W., & Allen, B. (2003). Beyond deficit and difference: Psychological integrity in developmental research. In C. C. Yeakey (Ed.), *Edmund Gordon: Producing knowledge, pursuing understanding.* Stamford, CT: JAI Press.

Brown, R. (1958). *Words and things.* Glencoe, IL: Free Press.

Carey, S., & Bartlett, E. (1978). Acquiring a single new word. *Papers and Reports on Child Language Development, 15,* 17–29.

Cazden, C. (1999). The language of African American students in classroom discourse. In C. Adger, D. Christian, & O. Taylor (Eds.), *Making the connection: Language and academic achievement in African American students.* McHenry, IL: Center for Applied Linguistics and Delta Systems Co.

Champion, T. (2002). *Understanding storytelling among African American children: A journey from Africa to America.* Mahwah, NJ: Erlbaum.

Choi, S., & Gopnik, A. (1995). Early acquisition of verbs in Korean: A cross-linguistic study. *Journal of Child Language, 22,* 497–529.

Craig, H., Connor, C. M., & Washington, J. (2003). Early positive predictors of later reading comprehension for African American students: A preliminary investigation. *Language, Speech, and Hearing Services in Schools, 34,* 31–43.

Craig, H., & Washington, J. A. (2004). Grade-related changes in the production of African American English. *Journal of Speech, Language and Hearing Research, 47,* 450–463.

de Villiers, J. G. (2004). Cultural and linguistic fairness in the assessment of semantics. *Seminars in Speech and Language, 25,* 73–90.

de Villiers, P. A. (2003, June). *Validating assessment: Establishing a gold standard.* Paper presented at the Symposium in Research in Child Language Disorders, University of Wisconsin, Madison.

de Villiers, P. A., & Pomeranz, S. (1992). Hearing-impaired students learning new words from written context. *Applied Psycholinguistics, 13*, 409–431.

Dillard, J. (1972). *Black English: Its history and usage in the United States.* New York: Vintage Books.

Drum, P. A., & Konopak, B. C. (1987). Learning words meanings from written context. In M. McKeown & M. Curtis (Eds.), *The nature of vocabulary acquisition.* Hillsdale, NJ: Erlbaum.

Dunn, L., & Dunn, L. (1998). *Peabody Picture Vocabulary Test—Third Edition.* Circle Pines, MN: American Guidance Service.

Fisher, C. (1996). Structural limits on verb mapping: The role of analogy in children's interpretations of sentences. *Cognitive Psychology, 31*, 41–81.

Gardner, M. F. (1985). *Receptive one-word picture vocabulary.* Novato, CA: Academic Therapy Publications.

Gee, J. P. (1991). Memory and myth: A perspective on narrative. In A. McCabe & C. Peterson (Eds.), *Developing narrative structure.* Hillsdale, NJ: Erlbaum.

Gilyard, K. (1991). *Voices of the self: A study of language competence.* Detroit, MI: Wayne State University Press.

Gleitman, L. (1990). The structural sources of verb meanings. *Language Acquisition, 1*, 3–50.

Gleitman, L., & Gleitman, H. (1992). A picture is worth a thousand words, but that's the problem: The role of syntax in vocabulary acquisition. *Current Directions in Psychological Science, 1*, 31–35.

Green, L. J. (2002). *African American English: A linguistic introduction.* Cambridge, UK: Cambridge University Press.

Harris, V. (1995). Using African American literature in the classroom. In V. Gadsden & D. Wagner (Eds.), *Literacy among African-American youth.* Cresskill, NJ: Hampton Press.

Hart, B., & Risley, T. R. (1995). *Meaningful differences in the everyday experience of young American children.* Baltimore: Brookes.

Hart, J., Guthrie, J., & Winfield, L. (1983). Black English phonology and learning to read. *Journal of Educational Psychology, 72*, 636–646.

Heath, S. B. (1983). *Ways with words.* New York: Cambridge University Press.

Heath, S. B. (1989). What no bedtime story means: Narrative skills at home and school. In B. Schieffelin & E. Ochs (Eds.), *Language socialization across cultures.* Cambridge, UK: Cambridge University Press.

Herron, C. (1998). *Nappy hair.* New York: Dragonfly Books. For notes on criticism and censorship, see www.scils.rutgers.edu/~kvander/nappy12.html.

Hudson, R. A. (1980). *Sociolinguistics.* Cambridge, UK: Cambridge University Press.

Hyon, S., & Sulzby, E. (1994). African American kindergartners' spoken narratives: Topic associating and topic centered styles. *Linguistics and Education, 6*(2), 121–152.

Johnson, V. E. (2001). *Fast mapping verb meaning from argument structure.* Unpublished doctoral dissertation, University of Massachusetts, Amherst.

Johnson, V. E., de Villiers, J., Deschamps, C., D'Amato, K., & Huneke, S. (2002,

July). *Can syntax give you complements?* Poster presented at the Symposium on Research in Child Language Disorders, Madison, WI.

Klibanoff, R. S., & Waxman, S. R. (2000). Basic level object categories support the acquisition of novel adjectives: Evidence from preschool-aged children. *Child Development, 71*, 649–659.

Labov, W. (1972). *Language in the inner city: Studies in the black English vernacular.* Philadelphia: University of Pennsylvania Press.

Labov, W. (1995). Can reading failure be reversed: A linguistic approach to the question. In V. Gadsden & D. Wagner (Eds.), *Literacy among African-American youth.* Cresskill, NJ: Hampton Press.

Labov, W., Baker, B., Bullock, S., Ross, L., & Brown, M. (1998). *A graphemic-phonemic analysis of the reading errors of inner-city children.* Unpublished manuscript, Department of Linguistics, University of Pennsylvania.

LaMoine, N. (1999). *English for your success: A language development program for African American students.* Maywood, NJ: Peoples Publishing Group.

LaMoine, N. (2001). Language variation and literacy acquisition in African American students. In J. L. Harris, A. G. Kamhi, & K. E. Pollock (Eds.), *Literacy in African American communities.* Mahwah, NJ: Erlbaum.

Michaels, S. (1981). Sharing time: Children's narrative styles and differential access to literacy. *Language and Society, 10*, 423–442.

Naigles, L. (1990). Children use syntax to learn verb meanings. *Journal of Child Language, 17*, 357–374.

Nagy, W. E., Anderson, R. C., & Herman, P. A. (1987). Learning words from context in normal reading. *American Educational Research Journal, 24*, 237–270.

National Center for Education Statistics. (2001). *Educational achievement and black–white inequality.* Available at nces.ed.gov/pubsearch/pubsinfo.asp?pubid=2001061.

Peña, E. D. (1996). Dynamic assessment: The model and its language applications. In K. N. Cole, P. S. Dale, & D. J. Thal (Eds.), *Assessment of communication and language.* Baltimore, MD: Brookes.

Pinker, S. (1994). *The language instinct.* New York: William Morrow.

Rice, M. L., & Bode, J. (1993). GAPS in the verb lexicons of children with specific language impairment. *First Language, 13*, 113–131.

Rickford, J. (1999). *African American vernacular English: Features, evolution and educational implications.* Oxford, UK: Blackwell.

Rickford, J., & Rickford, A. (1995). Dialect readers revisited. *Linguistics and Education, 7*, 107–128.

Roeper, T. (1987). The acquisition of implicit arguments and the distinction between theory, process and mechanism. In B. Macwhinney (Ed.), *Mechanisms of language acquisition.* Mahwah, NJ: Erlbaum.

Seymour, H. (2003, November). *Preventing overrepresentation of culturally/linguistically diverse students.* Seminar presentation at American Speech and Hearing Association Convention, Atlanta, GA.

Seymour, H., & Bland, L. (1991). A minority perspective in diagnosis of child language disorders. *Clinics in Communication Disorders, 1*, 39–50.

Seymour, H., Bland-Stewart, L., & Green, L. (1998). Difference versus deficit in child African American English. *Language, Speech, and Hearing Services in the Schools, 29*, 96–108.

Seymour, H., & Pearson, B. Z. (Eds). (2004). Evaluating language variation: Distinguishing development and dialect from disorder. *Seminars in Speech and Language, 25.*

Seymour, H., Roeper, T., & de Villiers, J. (2003). *The diagnostic evaluation of language variation: Screener (DELV-SC) and criterion referenced (DELV-CR).* San Antonio, TX: Psychological Corporation.

Seymour, H., Roeper, T., & de Villiers, J. (2005). *The diagnostic evaluation of language variation: Norm referenced (DELV-NR).* San Antonio, TX: Psychological Corporation.

Slobin, D. (1978). Cognitive prerequisites for the development of grammar. In L. Bloom & M. Lahey (Eds.), *Readings in language development.* New York: Wiley.

Snow, C. (2004). *Getting African American kids to love reading* [Interview on NPR with Travis Smiley]. Available at www.npr.org/features/feature.php?wfId=1501664.

Sternberg, R., & Powell, J. S. (1983). Comprehending verbal comprehension. *American Psychologist, 38*, 878–893.

Stockman, I. J. (1999). Semantic development of African American children. In O. L. Taylor & L. B. Leonard (Eds.), *Language acquisition across North America: Cross-cultural and cross-linguistic perspectives* (pp. 61–108). San Diego, CA: Singular.

Stockman, I. J. (2000). The new Peabody Picture Vocabulary Test–III: An illusion of unbiased assessment? *Language, Speech, and Hearing Services in the Schools, 31*, 340–353.

Tomasello, M. (1995). Pragmatic contexts for early verb learning. In M. Tomasello & W. E. Merriman (Eds.), *Beyond names for things.* Mahwah, NJ: Erlbaum.

Vaughn-Cooke, A. (1999). Lessons learned from the Ebonics controversy: Implications for language assessment. In C. Adger, D. Christian, & O. Taylor (Eds.), *Making the connection: Language and academic achievement in African American students.* McHenry, IL: Center for Applied Linguistics and Delta Systems Co.

Vernon-Feagans, L., Scheffner-Hammer, C., Miccio, A., & Manlove, E. (2001). Early language and literacy skills in low-income African American and Hispanic children. In S. B. Neuman & D. K. Dickinson (Eds.), *Handbook of early literacy research* (pp. 192–210). New York: Guilford Press.

Washington, J. (2001). Early literacy skills in African-American children: Research considerations. *Learning Disabilities Research and Practice, 16*, 213–221.

Washington, J., & Craig, H. (1992). Performances of low-income African American preschool and kindergarten children on the Peabody Picture Vocabulary Test—Revised. *Language, Speech, and Hearing Services in the Schools, 23*, 329–333.

Washington, J., & Craig, H. (1999). Performances of at-risk African American preschoolers on the Peabody Picture Vocabulary Test–III. *Language, Speech, and Hearing Services in the Schools, 30*, 75–82.

Washington, J., & Craig, H. (2001). Reading performance and dialectal variation. In J. L. Harris, A. G. Kahmi, & K. E. Pollock (Eds.), *Literacy in African American communities*. Mahwah, NJ: Erlbaum.

Wolfram, W. (1999). Repercussions from the Oakland Ebonics controversy: The critical role of dialect awareness programs. In C. Adger, D. Christian, & O. Taylor (Eds.), *Making the connection: Language and academic achievement in African American students*. McHenry, IL: Center for Applied Linguistics and Delta Systems Co.

Wyatt, T. (1995). Language development in African American English child speech. *Linguistics and Education, 7*, 7–22.

CHAPTER 10

Different Ways for Different Goals, but Keep Your Eye on the Higher Verbal Goals

ISABEL L. BECK
MARGARET G. McKEOWN

In the early 1980s our understanding of several aspects of word knowledge commingled to stimulate our academic interest in vocabulary. These aspects of knowledge eventually became integral to our principles of vocabulary learning. One aspect emerged from Mary Beth Curtis's presentation of findings from investigations of college students' vocabulary knowledge (as described in Curtis, 1987). Her research indicated that high vocabulary students not only knew more words than those with not so high vocabularies, but the former knew more about the words that they knew. Curtis pointed out that lower vocabulary students tended to define words in terms of a specific context—for example, in the case of *surveillance*, low vocabulary people said something like "That's what the police do," whereas high vocabulary individuals were more likely to talk about *surveillance* in terms of "watching." What high vocabulary people seemed to know more about was how to generalize and decontextualize word meaning. These notions played a role in the vocabulary instruction we eventually developed for use in several studies, in that we provided multiple contexts for target words and prompted students to generalize across contexts to decontextualize target words.

In co-occurrence with the Curtis seminar, our inert knowledge that there were different kinds of word knowledge came to the fore. In particular, we were reminded that as long ago as 1942 Cronbach presented descriptions of the knowledge and abilities involved in knowing a word as *generalization*, the ability to define a word; *application*, the ability to select or recognize situations appropriate to a word; *breadth*, knowledge of words' multiple meanings; *precision*, the ability to apply a term correctly to all situations and to recognize inappropriate use; and *availability*, the actual use of a word in thinking and discourse. Later, Dale (1965) suggested four stages of word knowledge that an individual may possess: Stage 1—never saw/heard it before; Stage 2—heard it, but don't know what it means; Stage 3—recognize it in context as having something to do with . . . ; Stage 4—know it well. Consideration of Curtis's findings and the implications of levels of word knowledge would later lead us to develop instruction to enable the kind of knowledge Cronbach described as *application*, *precision*, and *availability*.

During the same time period our understanding of the important role of decoding automaticity, or efficiency, in comprehension prompted us to reason that word-meaning efficiency was similarly important for comprehension. The need for fast lexical access to a rich representation arises because comprehension is a very complex process in which several components of the process may vie for attention at the same time (Beck & Carpenter, 1986; Perfetti, 1985). Reducing the need for attention on some components, in the case at hand, a lexical search, may free attention to deal with other components, in particular constructing meaning of the ideas represented by words. With lexical access in mind, we included in our instructional design frequent encounters and thoughtful activities with target words so that students had opportunities to develop fast access to strong representations of word meanings.

In close proximity to the events described above, we began an analysis of vocabulary instruction for intermediate-grade students as represented in two widely used basal series (Beck, McKeown, McCaslin, & Burkes, 1979). It was what we saw in the basals, in association with the theoretical notions discussed above, that sparked our subsequent vocabulary research. In this chapter we begin by discussing issues that arose from that original work and led us to develop our vocabulary research agenda. We then describe the features of instruction used in our research and the results of the research. We then turn to current issues in vocabulary, with a focus on identifying which words to target for instruction.

VOCABULARY INSTRUCTION IN OLDER AND UPDATED
BASALS FOR INTERMEDIATE GRADES

Our original analyses were conducted on the fourth- and fifth-grade materials from two 1979 widely used basals (Beck et al., 1979). We subsequently reviewed vocabulary instructional materials in 1990 basals and found that the issues we raised about the old basals were still present in the updated basals. The issues that arose concerned the words that were selected for teaching and the kind of instruction that was provided for the words. Consider the words in a 1979 basal that were selected for instruction before students read the Arachne myth, in which the haughty Arachne brags about her superior spinning ability, thereby offending the goddess Athena, who initiates a contest to determine whose ability is greater. With Athena's victory, she turns Arachne into a spider who is destined to spin forever. The words selected for instruction were *agreement, Athena, bargain, fleece, Greece, skeins, spindle, warf,* and *woof.*

Two of the words, *agreement* and *bargain,* are related to the theme or plot of the story, as the plot revolves around an *agreement* made between Athena and Arachne and the *bargain* that was established. Two of the words—*Athena* and *Greece*—are context-setting words. The remaining five words are specific to spinning: *fleece, skeins, spindle, warp,* and *woof* (Beck, McKeown, & Omanson, 1987). It would seem that the plot-related words—*agreement* and *bargain*—are most important to comprehension of the story, and *Greece* and *Athena* are likely useful for providing some context. But the five specific spinning words provide details of spinning that are not needed for understanding how the events play themselves out to the conclusion.

Given the differential use and value of knowing the meanings of the words within the set, one needs to question whether the spinning words should have been identified for meaning instruction. These words could have simply been pointed out as words having to do with spinning and the amount of instruction for the four other more conceptually important words given some elaborate treatment. But all the words received the same amount and kind of instruction.

Having taken issue with the choice of words targeted for instruction and that sameness of instruction for all words, we also identified a third concern. That is, we found typical instruction to be limited. Specifically, typical instruction often included just a brief definition or synonym (e.g., *quarrel,* a disagreement) and a sentence or example of the word (e.g., "The teacher told the boys to stop quarreling."). Occasionally there was some short associative task such as matching the target word with synonyms or short phrases.

DEVELOPING RICH VOCABULARY
INSTRUCTION FOR RESEARCH

On the basis of the issues we raised about vocabulary instruction, we undertook a series of three classroom studies in which we attempted to provide better instruction toward improving comprehension and assessed the instruction by comparing experimental and control students as well as experimental and control words (Beck, Perfetti, & McKeown, 1982; McKeown, Beck, Omanson, & Perfetti, 1983; McKeown, Beck, Omanson, & Pople, 1985). The goal of our research was to improve how students learn words to the extent that they would be able to access the words quickly and flexibly in the course of engaging in higher level verbal tasks. By "higher level verbal tasks," we meant comprehending and interpreting novel contexts containing the taught words.

So What Is Better Instruction?

Briefly, our "better" instruction was aimed at developing flexible and multifaceted representations of target words. Over the years we have come to call this kind of instruction "rich" instruction. Most of the features of rich instruction have roots in the theory noted at the beginning of this chapter. Below we present the full range of components of rich instruction.[1]

    1. *Introduce words through explanations in everyday connected language, rather than dictionary definitions.* As we developed the instruction for our first study, we became quite dissatisfied with dictionary definitions for introducing word meanings to intermediate-grade students. We began to develop our own informal ways to explain the meanings that we thought would be clearer and more helpful to stu-

---

[1]In other places we have combined some of the features of rich instruction into three or four components. Here we spell the features out in smaller pieces. Additionally, the term *rich* describes features of the instruction itself. In addition, aspects of the way the instruction is delivered influence its impact on comprehension. When these aspects are combined with rich instruction, we use the term *robust*.

dents for developing understanding of the new words. This was the seed of our notion of student-friendly explanations. Since then, we have become familiar with research showing that definitions are not effective for students (Miller & Gildea, 1985; Scott & Nagy, 1989), and have done research developing our notions of explanatory definitions more systematically (McKeown, 1993).

2. *Provide several contexts in which the word can be used.* Several sources of evidence demonstrated to us the need to design into the instruction multiple and varied contexts for each word. One source was Curtis's finding that lower knowledge vocabulary college students tended to talk about words that they knew in association with a single context in contrast to higher vocabulary adults, who talked about the meaning of words in more general ways. Another source was Werner and Kaplan's (1952) classic study showing that learners often imported features of the context into their developing understanding of an unfamiliar word. We found that, as former teachers, these sets of findings struck a chord of memory about students tending to stick to the context in which a word had been initially introduced. For example, when learning the word *forlorn* from a story about a sad, abandoned puppy, a student might think that being a lost animal was part of the meaning of *forlorn.* Thus in the instruction we developed, multiple contexts were an important keystone.

3. *Get students to interact with word meanings right away.* A good explanation of word meaning and several contexts can provide a strong idea of a word's meaning, but it is still static information. To develop deep understanding, a student needs to interact with word information in some way. This perspective makes contact with current theories of learning, which stress the active nature of successful learning, as well as with conceptions about levels of word knowledge. We implemented the notion of interaction with word meaning by providing quick activities with the words as soon as their meanings were introduced. For example, after encountering an explanation for *commotion*, students might be asked, "Would there more likely be a commotion on the playground or in the library?", and then asked to explain "why."

4. *Develop activities that require students to process the meanings of words in deep and thoughtful ways.* Here we reasoned that engaging students in simple associative tasks, such as matching a word with a synonym or a definition, required surface-level mental activity and as such may only bring about minimal learning results. Our thinking was related to the notion that lower levels of mental effort would produce lower levels of knowledge. Because our goal was to ensure that words be known

deeply and flexibly enough to enhance higher level verbal tasks, we needed to develop instruction that required deep processing. All this led us to arrange instruction that required students to *think* about words and their meanings, identify and explain appropriate uses, create appropriate contexts, and engage in various other reflective and analytical activities.

5. *Provide examples, situations, and questions that are interesting.* In the course of looking at commercial vocabulary instructional materials we noted that most examples were obvious and ordinary. A prime example was the context sentence provided in the basal for *quarrel*, which we presented earlier: *The teacher told the boys to stop quarreling.* Note that the sentence has an obvious protagonist (the teacher) and obvious antagonists (boys). It is of some irony that in trying to provide students with the building blocks of language, there wasn't much of an attempt to use engaging examples or to present novel contexts. Consider an alternative such as *Dale's sister got tired of quarreling with him about not using her CDs, so she set up an alarm system around her CD collection.*

6. *Provide many encounters with target words.* The importance of repetition in learning has a long history of research, and we adhered to that literature by providing many encounters for target words. We included this feature in our instruction beginning in 1980. Subsequently, reviews by Stahl and Fairbanks (1986) and Mezynski (1983) identified frequency of encounters as one component that differentiated successful vocabulary instruction.

7. *Word Wizard gimmick.* We considered that if students' learning of their new vocabulary was simply a classroom activity, their understanding and use of the words could be limited, and the words would be less likely to become a permanent part of their vocabulary repertoires. So another goal of instruction was to move students' learning beyond the classroom to increase their encounters with words and to enhance the decontextualization of the words. To encourage outside learning, we developed a gimmick called *Word Wizard* in which students could earn points by reporting having seen, heard, or used target words outside of class.

RESULTS OF THE CLASSROOM STUDIES

As noted, the features described above were incorporated into three studies. Extensive research articles are available about the results. Here we briefly note that in an initial study and a replication (Beck et al., 1982; McKeown et al., 1983) we focused on the assessment of three aspects of verbal skill: (1) accurate knowledge of word meanings, (2) accessibility of word meanings during semantic processing, and (3) reading comprehension. In the initial and replication studies, experimental children significantly outperformed control children on word knowledge as measured on multiple-choice tests and accessibility of word meanings. Accessibility of word meanings was measured by children's reaction time on word categorization tasks. That is, children were shown a word on a screen and asked to press a Yes or No button to indicate if the word was, for example, "a person." Experimental children's performance on the accessibility task was also faster for instructed words compared to uninstructed words. The results of the task suggest that the words were learned well enough to be readily available for complex processing.

The results of comprehension in the second study, the replication study, were that recall of a story containing taught words was superior to that of the story with uninstructed words and of children who had not received the instruction. From these two studies we concluded that instruction that improved accurate word knowledge, and that speed of semantic access could also influence reading comprehension.

A third study was designed to investigate the role of specific features of the instruction used in the first two studies: frequency, type of instruction, and extension of instruction. Frequency was implemented as either four or 12 encounters with each target word. Type of instruction was either rich or traditional, with traditional providing only definitions and synonyms for the words. Extension meant that the Word Wizard activity was included or not included (McKeown et al., 1985). The results of the two types of instruction and two frequency conditions indicated that even a few—in this case, four—encounters with a word within traditional instructional activities will produce some limited results: specifically, knowledge of a word's meaning as measured on a multiple-choice test. Second, a greater number of encounters with words is generally more helpful toward a variety of vocabulary-learning goals. One exception to this was that even a higher number of encounters with traditional instruction did not enhance reading comprehension.

Two measures were used to assess comprehension. One was a context interpretation task, which assessed students' understanding of the implications of a word's meaning within a context. Students were presented with a sentence containing a target word and then asked a question about the context. For example, "After the contest winners were announced, Tricia ran over to console Meg. How do you think Meg did in the contest?"

The second was a story comprehension task, which presented stories with target words. Only rich instruction, and only in the high-encounter condition, was powerful enough to affect comprehension. Instructional conditions that encouraged extension beyond the classroom by including use of the Word Wizard device held advantage in making knowledge about the words more readily available for processing. Specifically, both rich and rich/extended instruction showed a similar strong advantage over traditional instruction in the context interpretation task. Advantage for rich instruction was smaller in the story comprehension task in comparison to rich/extended instruction.

VOCABULARY ISSUES IN THE PRIMARY GRADES

Vocabulary instruction has long been incorporated in reading instruction, ostensibly with dual goals: to assist with comprehension of the text at hand and to build students' vocabulary repertoires. By the intermediate grades the texts students read in school are a natural source for building their vocabulary, as texts at that level often contain some vocabulary that is beyond the familiar oral conversational vocabulary that students have, for the most part, already mastered.

To select the words to teach for the studies discussed earlier we began with fourth-grade texts in a widely used basal program. From these texts, words were selected for our studies if they were judged as likely to be unknown, yet useful and interesting for students to learn, and other words were added that exhibited similar criteria. On a vocabulary multiple-choice pretest the mean percentage of words known by both experimental and control groups was about 30%. We took this as an indication that the words were appropriate for instruction.

In contrast, the texts that primary-grades children read, especially in the kindergarten, first, and even second grades, are *not* good sources for increasing children's meaning vocabularies. This is because the task of beginning reading instruction is to teach children a new representation, the written representation, for the language they already know aurally. As such it would be inappropriate to complicate that task by requiring children to deal with words whose meanings they cannot match with already known forms.

Perhaps in order not to complicate the learning to read task, increasing young children's meaning vocabulary repertoires has not been a focal objective of primary-grades curricula. Evidence of this lack of focus can be seen in a review of the earliest materials in basal teacher's editions that show that in practice "vocabulary" is used to mean instruction of high-frequency sight words, such as *have, was,* and *give,* and pronunciation of words with new or difficult spelling patterns, such as *pour, head,* and *how.* Thus it should not be surprising to learn that there is evidence that primary-grades curricula do not influence the acquisition of the meaning of new words (Biemiller, 2005).

But adding vocabulary to children's repertoires need not be held back until their word recognition skill becomes adequate to read texts that include unfamiliar words. The good news here is that young children's listening and speaking competence develops in advance of their reading and writing competence. That is, they can understand much more from oral language than they can from reading independently. As children are developing their reading and writing competence, advantage can be taken of their listening and speaking competence to enhance their vocabulary development.

Tradebooks that are read to children are a major source for interesting words that are well in advance of young children's typical oral vocabularies. So the read-aloud has been viewed by a number of researchers as a useful vehicle for adding new words to children's meaning repertoires (Biemiller & Boote, 2004; Coyne, Simmons, Kame'enui, & Stoolmiller, 2004; Elley, 1989; Nicholson & Whyte, 1992; Penno, Wilkinson, & Moore, 2002; Robbins & Ehri, 1994; Sénéchal, Thomas, & Monker, 1995). Moreover, there is an emerging consensus that attention needs to be given to enhancing children's vocabulary repertoires and that it should begin at the very beginning of schooling (Biemiller & Slonim, 2001; Coyne et al., 2004). A current issue, then, is how to use tradebooks to develop young children's word knowledge.

Our attempt to increase children's vocabulary repertoires was undertaken through *Text Talk,* a research and development project based on read-alouds (Beck & McKeown, 2001; McKeown & Beck, 2003). One of the purposes of Text Talk was to develop vocabulary by taking advantage of sophisticated words that can be found in young children's tradebooks by explicitly teaching and encouraging use of several words from a story. Rich instruction was developed for several words from each story. The instruction occurred after a story had been read, discussed, and wrapped up.

To provide a sense of the kinds of words targeted, kindergarten words included *appropriate, charming, concentrate, forlorn,* and *exhausted.* As an illustration of the kind of instruction provided, consider the vocabulary instruction from the story *Rusty Trusty Tractor* (Cowley, 1999), about an old man who will not buy a new tractor because of his confidence in his old tractor, which ends up getting the tractor salesman's car out of some mud. The words *regret*, *sprout*, and *partial* were selected from the story. Here is the way *regret* was handled.

- First, the word was contextualized for its role in the story. ("In the story, Mr. Hill promised Granpappy that he would not regret it if he looked over his new tractors. That means he would not be sorry.")
- Next, the meaning of the word was explained. ("If you regret something, you feel badly about it and wish it hadn't happened.")
- The children were asked to repeat the word so that they could create a phonological representation of the word. ("Say the word with me: *regret*.")
- Examples in contexts other than the one used in the story were provided. ("You might regret having a fight with your best friend. You might regret eating a whole pizza.")
- Children made judgments about examples. ("Would you regret buying a surprise for your best friend? Why?"; "Would you regret getting into trouble in your school? Why?")
- Children constructed their own examples. ("Have you ever done something that you regret? Start your sentence with 'I regret _____.'")
- The word's phonological and meaning representation were reinforced. ("What's the word that means feeling bad about something and wishing it hadn't happened?")

In addition to formally introducing words in the manner shown above, teachers were asked to reinforce target words on subsequent days. For example, all teachers kept charts of the words from several stories posted on the wall. If children heard or used one of the words, a tally mark was placed next to the word. Teachers attempted to use the words in the regular classroom activities. For instance, target words appeared in the morning message, such as "Today is Wednesday. The sun is *radiant*."

Two studies were undertaken to assess the extent to which the kind of instruction above applied to sophisticated words was effective for kindergarten and first-grade children (Beck & McKeown, 2004). In the first study, a between-subjects design, across both grade levels and within grade level, children in the experimental groups showed significantly higher gains than children in comparison classes. This finding suggested that it is feasible to teach words that are associated with mature language users to young children.

A second study, a within-subjects design, was undertaken to determine the extent to which an increased amount of instruction would enhance learning. The approach was to provide the same initial rich instruction (as described above) for all words and then to provide additional rich instruction for a subset of words. The results demonstrated that more instruction did pay off, with gains about twice as large for those words given more instruction.

WHICH WORDS TO TEACH

The issue of which words to teach has received surprisingly little attention. In fact Coyne et al. (2004) point out that while knowledge about how to effectively teach vocabulary is accumulating, what to teach remains elusive. Studies aimed at teaching vocabulary through read-alouds uniformly describe selecting words from the stories to be read that are likely to be unfamiliar to children and that are important to the story. Few researchers offer criteria beyond this.

However, when discussing how to select words to teach with others in the field, inevitably, the notion of using printed word frequency comes to the fore. In this regard, Thorndike's 1921 *Teacher's Word Book*, which ranked words by frequency of occurrence in general reading materials, has been cited as an early landmark in vocabulary research (Clifford, 1978). Although we do not discount a possible contribution of word frequency as one feature for selecting words, we caution that reliance on frequencies has a history in reading instruction that is not altogether positive. Specifically, the *Word Book* was utilized to develop a corpus of words for use in creating readable texts. Such utilization of the *Word Book* had a huge impact on instruction, chiefly through the implementation of readability formulas. Specifically, word frequencies in terms of difficulty (low frequencies) and ease (high frequencies) is one of the two pillars of readability formulas; the other pillar is sentence length.

Unfortunately, the formulae institutionalized the virtually exclusive use of vocabulary frequency and sentence length to control readability. Although these two features are predictive of easier reading materials, their use does not bring about greater ease in grasping the concepts represented or in establishing relations among concepts (Anderson & Davison, 1988; Beck & McKeown, 1986; Davison & Kantor, 1982; Duffy & Kabance, 1981; Rubin, 1985).

Analogously, use of the *Word Book's* modern-day counterpart, the *Word Frequency Book* (Carroll, Davies, & Richman, 1971), for selection of words for meaning instruction would suffer from the lack of any conceptual basis for words to be taught at a certain level. For example, if a young learner has the concept of *sad* under control, there is little reason that *forlorn* cannot be taught since the two words are close in meaning, albeit far apart in frequency. Other drawbacks with relying on printed frequency are, first, that frequency does not give information on whether words are known at a given grade, simply whether they appear in materials at that grade. Second, word forms are listed only once, and thus not differentiated for different meanings. Third, each derivational form of a word has a separate frequency, so that *run* is listed separately from *running*, and so forth. So in using printed frequency to select appropriate words for instruction, we get, for example, the words *breaking* and *complicated* looking identically relevant, that is, they share the same frequency level. But clearly they are not equally good candidates for instruction in meaning. *Breaking* is simply *break* with a common suffix, which most young children likely know the meaning of by age 3 or 4. *Complicated*, on the other hand, is an interesting word that young learners are not likely to be familiar with, but could learn and use.

Biemiller (2005) has also questioned the use of frequencies for selecting instructional words. Instead, he recommends using a developmental sequence to identify words based on his research that suggests that primary-grade children follow an identifiable sequence in acquiring word meanings. The sequence is related to children's vocabulary size and not to grade. Biemiller's strategy for identifying words to be taught in the primary grades is to focus on words that he describes as "partially known," in particular, words known by between about 20% and 70% of children, because Biemiller asserts that these tend to be rapidly learned at each vocabulary-size group.

Given that such words are likely to be rapidly learned, one could argue that they do not need special attention as they can be readily learned from grade-level materials and simple teacher input. Although we have made the argument that many children come to school with inadequate vocabulary and remain at risk, it is the case that all children's vocabulary does grow during the school years, and we venture that the growth more likely takes place among the 20–70% words noted by Biemiller.

In contrast, it has been our position for a long time that the kind of words that should be given significant instructional attention are sophisticated words, those we have labeled Tier 2 words. We thus favor expending instructional capital in a place least likely to be affected in any other way, that is, to target words that are less likely to be learned through grade-level materials and everyday contextual input.

Although our rationale differs from Biemiller's, some of our word choices would overlap with his; for example, we would judge the following words used in Biemiller's (Biemiller & Boote, 2004) studies as Tier 2 words: *rage, command, obstacle, loyal, admire, grateful, dwindle, quirk, precious, reveal,* and *cautious.* Others on Biemiller's list we would not have selected, some because of their specific or limited roles in the language, such as *bullseye, landlubber, gunpowder, cannon, pirate, boil, wicker, alas,* and *pantry*; others because they seem either likely known or readily explained when encountered in use, such as *tip, through, mop, whenever,* and *paddle.*

Even if Biemiller is correct in arguing that children tend to *learn* words in an order, it does not necessarily follow that children should be *taught* words in that same order. Consider the loquacious 2-year-old who was able to describe her clothing as "saturated," or another who indicated that her drawing was "creative," or the 3-year-old who told her mother that her plans for the day were not "realistic." There is no reason that children with smaller vocabulary repertoires need to focus their learning on lower level vocabulary before they are taught more sophisticated words.

This is not to say that we do not see value in directly teaching the kinds of words Biemiller suggests. Indeed, we think a strong vocabulary program can attend to words at a variety of difficulty levels, but the instruction needs to be differentiated. This is a key point that Graves (1987) has suggested as a foundation for classroom vocabulary work. Consider that teaching young learners the meaning of *paddle,* from Biemiller's list, will not need the same kind of effort as teaching *precious,* also from Biemiller's list. Yet too often teachers tend to "bring out the band" to get across simple concepts—simply because they have resources to do so readily at hand. It would be relatively easy to find pictures of a paddle or come up with ways to demonstrate its use. Teaching *precious,* however, takes a bit more reflection. This is one reason why we stress applying instructional resources toward teaching hard concepts, and believe it is so important to develop support for teachers to do so.

Tier 2 Words

Since the publication of our recent book (Beck, McKeown, & Kucan, 2002), our notion about thinking of the words of the language as comprising three tiers seems to have made an impact on the field. Here we elaborate our rationale for why we think that Tier 2 words are significant for literacy growth. The tiers were first developed in the mid-1980s (Beck et al., 1987) as a means of countering a widely held position against a significant role for direct vocabulary because there are just too many words to teach (Nagy & Herman, 1987).

The "too many words to teach directly" argument was based on considering the whole corpus of English words. Hence we thought we could reduce the "too many words" to a potentially manageable set of words by thinking about which words could most benefit from instructional attention. For this reason, we have developed three tiers. We designated the first tier as consisting of the most basic words: *bed, up, boy, run, pretty, hamburger*. Because children entering school know the meanings of those words, there is certainly no need for direct instruction of meanings of these words in school.

The third tier consists of words whose frequency of use is quite low, or which apply to specific domains. This tier might include words such as *isotope, peninsula*, and *legislate*. In general, a rich conceptual knowledge of such words would not be of high utility for most learners. These words are probably best learned when a specific need arises, such as presenting *peninsula* in association with a geography map lesson. Tier 3 words represent new concepts and as such are part of the content being learned in a particular subject area. Thus they are not vocabulary per se in that the main reason they are taught is to build students' content knowledge base rather than to expand students' general language repertoires.

It is Tier 2 that contains words of high frequency for mature language users. They are also words of general utility, not limited to a specific domain. Some examples might be *remarkable, forlorn, cherish, awe*, and *exaggerate*. We have asserted that it is words of this type toward which the most productive instructional efforts can be directed. Because of the role they play in a language user's verbal repertoire, rich knowledge of words in this second tier can have a significant impact on verbal functioning.

The notion that direct instruction be targeted to a constrained corpus of words ameliorates the concern that direct instruction is fruitless because of the great number of words in the English vocabulary. In an attempt to get a rough estimation of how many words would be included in the second tier, we started by using Nagy and Anderson's (1984) analysis of words in printed school English for grades three through nine.

Nagy and Anderson estimate that good readers of this age range may read a million words of text a year. They also estimate that half of the 88,500 word families they calculate to exist in printed school English are so rare that they may be encountered no more than once in an avid reader's lifetime. With these figures in mind, it seems reasonable to consider words—or, rather, word families—that would be encountered once in 10 years, namely, those that occur once or more in 10 million running words of text, as comprising Tiers 1 and 2. That translates into about 15,000 word families, according to Nagy and Anderson's (1984) estimates.

Our best estimate of Tier 1, the most familiar words that need no instruction, is 8,000 word families. We have chosen this figure because Nagy and Anderson state that it may be reasonable to assume that a third-grader already knows 8,000 words. That gives us about 7,000 word families for Tier 2, which we want to focus on. Based on our third study described earlier, which presented 12 encounters as the high-frequency condition, we estimate that the number of words that could be taught, in a rich way, per school year is about 400. Teaching 400 words per year over grades three to nine would provide rich knowledge for 40% of the word families that make up Tier 2. Additionally we now suggest teaching approximately 200 words in kindergarten, first, and second grade, which would increase the total of words taught to nearly 50% of the estimated 7,000 word families that would be taught for Tier 2.

Our estimate needs to be viewed cautiously as it is only an attempt to get a handle on a possible figure for the words we would focus on. Yet it is useful for making two important points. First, nowhere near all the words that are available in print or oral contexts are good candidates for the kind of instruction we used in our vocabulary studies. Second, providing rich conceptual networks for a portion of words that would be good candidates—approximately 40–50% of them—is a significant contribution to the verbal functioning of an individual.

The significance of this contribution is particularly apparent in light of another factor to be considered in developing vocabulary instruction: the target population of learners. The kind of instruction we describe as rich is particularly essential for those children in the lower half of the distribution in both reading skill and socioeconomic status. For example, in our original vocabulary study, the subjects were fourth graders from an urban school, and 79% of them were below the 50th percentile on standardized tests in reading comprehension and vocabulary. In our recent kindergarten and first-grade studies, the children came from schools in which free- and reduced-lunch demographics were about 80%. Children from these backgrounds have been shown to be less likely to acquire, and become proficient in using, rich conceptual networks of Tier 2 words independently. We base this statement on some evidence. One source of evidence is the Curtis (1987) finding, noted at the beginning of this chapter, that students with limited vocabulary knowledge knew not only fewer words, but had more narrow knowledge of those words with which they were familiar.

The other evidence has to do with how acquisition and proficient knowledge of Tier 2 words might develop without direct in-school attention. The chief way is through extensive reading, where unfamiliar words are encountered in new and varied contexts and each new context presents a potential facet of that word's network. However, the children with whom we are concerned here are the less able readers. Not only are these children less likely to read extensively, but evidence shows that they are not particularly facile in deriving word-meaning information from context. Specifically, McKeown (1985) found that less-skilled fifth graders were less able to identify concepts from context that constrained the meaning of an unfamiliar word, less able to evaluate the meaning of a word even when correct constraints were identified, less able to take advantage of multiple contexts that used the unknown word, and less able to identify the meaning of the word after a series of context clues had been presented. In addition, even after the meaning of a word was identified or presented, less-skilled children were less able to identify correct use of the word in subsequent contexts. Thus the power of increasing vocabulary through reading is significantly diminished for less able readers.

In addition to extensive reading, the development of rich networks might be encouraged through accumulated experiences of hearing and using new words in oral contexts. But the use of and encouragement to use a more sophisticated vocabulary does not commonly characterize the informal verbal environment of our target children.

In terms of which words to teach and the kind of instruction to focus on, the foregoing notions were where we started 20 years ago. As noted, the three tiers were initially presented as a way to suggest that direct vocabulary instruction could play a significant role. It wasn't until later that the concept was offered as a heuristic for selecting words. As a heuristic, it is an initial sorting device, and one that seems useful, as our experience indicates that it is readily grasped by teachers. Even if disagreements ensue as to which tier in which to place a particular word, such interaction indicates a reflective stance toward vocabulary, which we see as a positive development on the part of teachers. Indeed, discussion of issues and developing a rationale for choices made may be more important than identifying to which tier a word belongs. Agreement about which words in which tiers is of less consequence than thoughtfulness about why given words are being selected for instruction. A thoughtful stance toward identifying which words to teach on the part of developers and teachers is itself an important step in the right direction.

A Demonstration of the Word Selection Process

The task of selecting words to teach most naturally occurs in association with a text that students will read or that teachers will read to children. Thus in addition to belonging to Tier 2, the role of a word in the text at hand is another important criterion for choosing words.

In our work with teachers we have suggested the following sequence for identifying words in a text selection:

- List all the words that have meanings that are likely to be unfamiliar to your students.
- Which words can be categorized as Tier 2 words?
- Which of the Tier 2 words are most necessary for comprehension? At what level of comprehension, plot or local?
- Are there other words needed for comprehension? Which ones?

As an illustration, we analyzed the first 100 unique words in *Brave Irene* (Steig, 1986), a popular read-aloud, which we have used in first grade. We intentionally chose *Brave Irene* as an example here because it has many words that are potentially unfamiliar to young children. The story is about the young daughter of a dressmaker who undertakes the delivery of a ball gown to the duchess because her mother has become ill. The daughter overcomes many obstacles and gets the gown to the palace on time for the ball. The first 100 unique words take the story from the dressmaker completing the gown, feeling too ill to deliver it, Irene talking her mother into allowing her to deliver the package despite the signs of snow and the distance to the palace, to Irene's packing the gown.

Table 10.1 presents 16 words within the first 100 unique words that several teachers judged might be unfamiliar to young children. We then categorized those words in relationship to their role in the story and tiers.

As indicated in the first column of the table, we have identified four categories of relationships between comprehension of the story and the 16 words judged potentially unfamiliar to target students. It would not be appropriate to teach all 16 words, given that they occur in the first three pages of a 27-page book in which there are a multitude of additional potential words. Nor is it necessary to teach all potentially unknown words, as it is the case that a comprehender can tolerate not knowing the meanings of at least some and perhaps many words in a text (Anderson & Freebody, 1983). Clearly some words have priority over others.

The eight words in the top row are the ones that should have instructional priority over the remaining words given that they are most important to story comprehension. It is of interest that in the top row the nature of the three words in Tier 2 and the five words in Tier 3 are quite different. The Tier 3 words in this story happen to be nouns associated with young children's fiction (at least all but *dressmaker*). These words are part of a fairytale schema and can be explained easily. A *gown* is a beautiful long dress that women wear to special parties. A *duchess* is someone like a queen or princess who lives in a palace. A *palace* is a

TABLE 10.1. Potentially Unfamiliar Words from *Brave Irene*, Categorized by Role in Story and Tier 2 and Tier 3

Role of word	Tier 2	Tier 3
Useful for story comprehension: related to the theme/plot, a key character trait that drives story events or outcome	*huge* *coaxed* *insisted*	*dressmaker* *gown* *duchess* *palace* *ball* (party)
Useful for local context (i.e., understanding a sentence) and a generally useful word.	*managed*	
Not important to story, but a generally useful word.	*admitted* *splendid* *strength* *package*	
Not important to story and not that generally useful.	*tucked* *snugly*	*stitches*

very big, fancy, beautiful place to live in. A *ball* is a special party that takes place in a palace. And a *dressmaker* is someone who makes clothes for people.

In contrast, the first word in Tier 2 in the top row is an adjective and the other two are verbs. These three words play different roles in comprehension than the Tier 3 words. *Huge* is important because the gown is packed in a huge box and is part of the difficulty Irene has trudging through the snow and wind to deliver the gown. *Coaxed* and *insisted* are related to Irene's personality and motives. She wants to take care of her ill mother and *coaxes* her into bed and she *insists* that she can manage the huge box and the bad weather and get the gown to the palace. As such, the essence of Irene's character as a caring and take-charge person is reflected in those verbs. Beyond their role in the story, the three words have broad utility.

Notice that of the remaining eight words all but one, *managed*, have been judged not to be important to comprehension, but the table suggests that four of the words are considered as generally useful words. Which words will need only brief attention and which will need more elaborate attention?

Up to this point we have been implying that all words do not need to be treated equally. Different kinds of words are taught for different reasons and require different levels of attention. Instructional time needs to be allocated in accordance with difficulty and the payoff associated with the word.

Simple, brief instructional treatment of the traditional sort, such as providing a brief explanation of a word as suggested for the nouns in the top row in Tier 3, is probably sufficient for concrete nouns and less abstract words. We also surmise that simple explanations are likely adequate for teaching a number of words that Biemiller suggests would fall between the 20th and the 70th percentages of words known by third graders.

We assert, however, that brief explanations of the words in Tier 2 are not likely to be adequate to acquire a working knowledge of *coaxed* and *insisted* (perhaps this is not the case for *huge*), let alone rich semantic connections and relationships. After story reading, these words would need to be decontextualized and their uses in a variety of other contexts provided. For example, children might be invited to respond to questions such as "Why might you coax your dog to come into the house?" and "When you are a mother or father, what would you insist that your child do before going to bed?"

The issues associated with choosing words to teach are complex. Without acknowledging this complexity, there is always the possibility of turning to superficial and quick solutions. The vocabulary research, development, and instructional communities need to consider the issues and develop criteria that incorporate some of the complexities about which words to teach, yet make the task manageable for teachers and those who develop materials.

Our motive in writing this chapter was to bring attention to different goals in vocabulary and the different types of instructional attention that they entail. Higher verbal goals require deliberately building connections to words and experiences that children already have in their knowledge base in order to make the new words easily accessible when needed for comprehension. Such goals also require building flexibility of word knowledge so that when children meet words in new contexts they are able to bring to bear what they already know about the words and integrate their prior knowledge into the context to make sense of the novel context.

REFERENCES

Anderson, R. C., & Davison, A. (1988). Conceptual and empirical bases of readability formulas. In A. Davison & G. Green (Eds.), *Linguistic complexity and text comprehension* (pp. 23–53). Hillsdale, NJ: Erlbaum.

Anderson, R. C., & Freebody, P. (1983). Reading comprehension and the assessment and acquisition of word knowledge. In B. Hutton (Ed.), *Advances in reading/language research: A research annual* (pp. 231–256). Greenwich, CT: JAI Press.

Beck, I. L., & Carpenter, P. A. (1986). Cognitive approaches to understanding reading: Implications for instructional practice. *American Psychologist, 41*(10), 1098–1105.

Beck, I. L., & McKeown, M. G. (1986). Instructional research in reading: A retrospective. In J. Orasanu (Ed.), *Reading comprehension: From research to practice* (pp. 113–134). Hillsdale, NJ: Erlbaum.

Beck, I. L., & McKeown, M. G. (2001). Text talk: Capturing the benefits of read-aloud experiences for young children. *The Reading Teacher, 55*(1), 10–20.

Beck, I. L., & McKeown, M. G. (2004). *Increasing young children's oral vocabulary repertoires through rich and focused instruction.* Manuscript submitted for publication.

Beck, I. L., McKeown, M. G., & Kucan, L. (2002). *Bringing words to life: Robust vocabulary instruction.* New York: Guilford Press.

Beck, I. L., McKeown, M. G., McCaslin, E. S., & Burkes, A. M. (1979). *Instruc-

tional dimensions that may affect reading comprehension: Examples from two commercial reading programs (LRDC Publication 1979/20). Pittsburgh: University of Pittsburgh, Learning Research and Development Center.

Beck, I. L., McKeown, M. G., & Omanson, R. C. (1987). The effects and uses of diverse vocabulary instructional techniques. In M. G. McKeown & M. E. Curtis (Eds.), *The nature of vocabulary acquisition* (pp. 147–163). Hillsdale, NJ: Erlbaum.

Beck, I. L., Perfetti, C. A., & McKeown, M. G. (1982). Effects of long-term vocabulary instruction on lexical access and reading comprehension. *Journal of Educational Psychology, 74*(4), 506–521.

Biemiller, A. (2005). Addressing developmental patterns in vocabulary: Implications for choosing words for primary grade vocabulary instruction. In E. H. Hiebert & M. L. Kamil (Eds.), *Teaching and learning vocabulary: Bringing research to practice.* Hillsdale, NJ: Erlbaum.

Biemiller, A., & Boote, C. (2004). *An effective method for building vocabulary in primary grades.* Manuscript submitted for publication.

Biemiller, A., & Slonim, N. (2001). Estimating root word vocabulary growth in normative and advantaged populations: Evidence for a common sequence of vocabulary acquisition. *Journal of Educational Psychology, 93*, 498–520.

Carroll, J. B., Davies, P., & Richman, B. (1971). *Word frequency book.* New York: American Heritage.

Clifford, G. J. (1978). Words for schools: The application in education of the vocabulary researches of Edward L. Thorndike. In P. Suppes (Ed.), *Impact of research on education: Some case studies* (pp. 107–198). Washington, DC: National Academy of Education.

Cowley, J. (1999). *Rusty trusty tractor.* Honesdale, PA: Boyds Mills Press.

Coyne, M. D., Simmons, D. C., Kame'enui, E. J., & Stoolmiller, M. (2004). Teaching vocabulary during shared storybook readings: An examination of differential effects. *Exceptionality, 12*, 145–162.

Cronbach, L. J. (1942). An analysis of techniques for systematic vocabulary testing. *Journal of Educational Research, 36*, 206–217.

Curtis, M. E. (1987). Vocabulary testing and vocabulary instruction. In M. G. McKeown & M. E. Curtis (Eds.), *The nature of vocabulary acquisition* (pp. 37–52). Hillsdale, NJ: Erlbaum.

Dale, E. (1965). Vocabulary measurement: Techniques and major findings. *Elementary English, 42*, 895–901.

Davison, A., & Kantor, R. (1982). On the failure of readability formulas to define readable texts: A case study from adaptations. *Reading Research Quarterly, 17*, 187–210.

Duffy, T. M., & Kabance, P. (1981). *Testing a readable writing approach to text revision.* San Diego, CA: Navy Personnel Research and Development Center.

Elley, W. B. (1989). Vocabulary acquisition from listening to stories. *Reading Research Quarterly, 24*, 174–186.

Graves, M. F. (1987). The roles of instruction in fostering vocabulary development. In M. G. McKeown & M. E. Curtis (Eds.), *The nature of vocabulary acquisition* (pp. 165–184). Hillsdale, NJ: Erlbaum.

McKeown, M. G. (1985). The acquisition of word meaning from context by children of high and low ability. *Reading Research Quarterly, 20*(4), 482–496.

McKeown, M. G. (1993). Creating effective definitions for young word learners. *Reading Research Quarterly, 28*, 16–31.

McKeown, M. G., & Beck, I. L. (2003). Taking advantage of read-alouds to help children make sense of decontextualized language. In A. van Kleeck, S. A. Stahl, & E. B. Bauer (Eds.), *Storybook reading* (pp. 159–176). Mahwah, NJ: Erlbaum.

McKeown, M. G., Beck, I. L., Omanson, R. C., & Perfetti, C. A. (1983). The effects of long-term vocabulary instruction on reading comprehension: A replication. *Journal of Reading Behavior, 15*(1), 3–18.

McKeown, M. G., Beck, I. L., Omanson, R. C., & Pople, M. T. (1985). Some effects of the nature and frequency of vocabulary instruction on the knowledge and use of words. *Reading Research Quarterly, 20*(5), 522–535.

Mezynski, K. (1983). Issues concerning the acquisition of knowledge: Effects of vocabulary training on reading comprehension. *Review of Educational Research, 53*, 253–279.

Miller, G. A., & Gildea, P. M. (1985). How to misread a dictionary. *AILA Bulletin.*

Nagy, W. E., & Anderson, R. C. (1984). How many words are there in printed school English? *Reading Research Quarterly, 19*, 304–330.

Nagy, W. E., & Herman, P. A. (1987). Breadth and depth of vocabulary knowledge: Implications for acquisition and instruction. In M. G. McKeown & M. E. Curtis (Eds.), *The nature of vocabulary acquisition* (pp. 19–36). Hillsdale, NJ: Erlbaum.

Nicholson, T., & Whyte, B. (1992). Matthew effects in learning new words while listening to stories. In *Literacy research, theory, and practice: Views from many perspectives* (Forty-first yearbook, National Reading Conference, pp. 499–503). Chicago: National Reading Conference.

Penno, J. F., Wilkinson, I. A. G., & Moore, D. W. (2002). Vocabulary acquisition from teacher explanation and repeated listening to stories: Do they overcome the Matthew effect? *Journal of Educational Psychology, 94*(1), 23–33.

Perfetti, C. A. (1985). *Reading ability.* New York: Oxford University Press.

Robbins, C., & Ehri, L. C. (1994). Reading storybooks to kindergartners helps them learn new vocabulary words. *Journal of Educational Psychology, 86*, 54–64.

Rubin, A. (1985). How useful are readability formulas? In J. Osborn, P. T. Wilson, & R. C. Anderson (Eds.), *Reading education: Foundations of a literate America* (pp. 61–77). Lexington, MA: Lexington Books.

Scott, J., & Nagy, W. E. (1989, December). *Fourth graders' knowledge of definitions and how they work.* Paper presented at the annual meeting of the National Reading Conference, Austin, TX.

Sénéchal, M., Thomas, E., & Monker, J. A. (1995). Individual differences in four-year-olds' ability to learn new vocabulary. *Journal of Educational Psychology, 87,* 218–229.

Stahl, S. A., & Fairbanks, M. M. (1986). The effects of vocabulary instruction: A model-based meta-analysis. *Review of Educational Research, 56,* 72–110.

Steig, W. (1986). *Brave Irene.* New York: Farrar, Straus and Giroux.

Thorndike, E. L. (1921). *The teacher's word book.* New York: Teachers College.

Werner, H., & Kaplan, E. (1952). The acquisition of word meanings: A developmental study. *Monographs of the Society for Research in Child Development, 15*(1, Serial No. 51).

CHAPTER 11

Landmark Vocabulary Instructional Research and the Vocabulary Instructional Research That Makes Sense Now

MICHAEL PRESSLEY
LAUREL DISNEY
KENDRA ANDERSON

We understood our assignment as follows: We were to identify research directions on vocabulary teaching and learning in school that make sense to pursue in the foreseeable future. As scholars who are always evidence-driven, we came to our recommendations by reflecting on the existing scholarship on vocabulary teaching and learning, most of which has been generated in the past quarter century. We showcase in the first section of this chapter what seemed to us to be important theoretical and empirical advances in vocabulary teaching and learning research, concluding the first section with a discussion of research that should be conducted as follow-up to the existing studies. In the second and concluding section of the chapter, we make a more ambitious research proposal. We propose that substantial impact vocabulary instruction in classrooms may be possible by teaching teachers to articulate the wide variety of approaches suggested in the individual theoretical analyses and studies of vocabulary teaching and acquisitions of the past 25 years.

Although we heavily favor instructional experiments in this chapter, instruction and natural development of vocabulary interact and intertwine, and, thus there is going to be some mixing of evidence across diverse types of research. In particular, there will be prominent discussion of work done in the developmental psycholinguistic tradition. There have been some important discoveries by those interested in the development of child language in home settings that should be reflected on seriously by educational researchers who are trying to improve lexical development of children and adolescents in school.

THE MUST-READ SCHOLARSHIP
ON VOCABULARY ACQUISITION

Rather than attempt to review all of the literature on vocabulary teaching and learning, we reviewed selectively, focusing, for the most part, on studies and chapters that are cited again and again in the vocabulary teaching and learning literature. We complement those classic papers with commentary on a few other studies that we found particularly compelling and believe deserve serious reflection by anyone contemplating new research or curriculum design in the area of vocabulary teaching and learning.

Carey and Bartlett (1978)

Carey and Bartlett (1978) asked some preschoolers to do them a favor: "Bring me the chromium tray. Not the blue one, the chromium one." This request was made in the context of two trays, one blue and the other olive. One week and 6 weeks later, some of the children receiving this request knew that chromium was a color (i.e., when given a group of names and asked to identify the colors, *chromium* was identified as a color), and others even knew it was olive. They had learned something about the meaning of the word through one incidental learning opportunity. Carey and Bartlett (1978) referred to such learning as *fast mapping*.

Fast mapping produces long-term retention of more than just color terms (e.g., it works for names of objects) and for more than just 3- and 4-year-olds, with adults also learning the meanings of novel words from a brief exposure (Markson & Bloom, 1997). When preschoolers learn a new term via fast mapping, they generalize the term—that is, they recognize another instance of the object, even if it differs in irrelevant features (e.g., size; Behrend, Scofield, & Kleinknecht, 2001; Kleinknecht, Behrend, & Scofield, 1999; Waxman & Booth, 2000). But perhaps the most dramatic demonstrations have been made with 2-year-olds (Heibeck & Markman, 1987; Markson, 1999). Even the very earliest language acquisition involves some fast mapping.

Although there is far from complete understanding of fast mapping (Bloom, 2000, Chap. 2), that fast mapping occurs makes obvious that incidental learning can be a powerful mechanism in vocabulary development. For incidental learning of vocabulary to occur, however, there has to be incidental mention of vocabulary words. That is, children must experience a lexically rich environment. If they do, there is solid reason to believe they can acquire many vocabulary words from early in life.

Hart and Risley's (1995) Meaningful Differences

Without a doubt, in recent years, the most talked about correlational study having anything to do with vocabulary acquisition was Hart and Risley's (1995) *Meaningful Differences in the Everyday Experiences of Young American Children.* The authors observed 42 families for over 2 years, beginning when each participating child was 6–9 months old. The sample included families from upper, middle, and lower socioeconomic classes. A major interest was the language the children experienced at home, with the most prominent finding in the book being that it varied dramatically as a function of social class. The less affluent the family, the less that was said to the child. The less affluent the family, the less complex was the language directed at the child. The less affluent the family, the more discouraging were the messages the child received (e.g., lower class children heard a high proportion of prohibitions relative to more socioeconomically advantaged children). At 3 years of age, there were huge differences in the vocabulary of the upper-class children compared to the middle- and lower-class children. The upper-class child with the smallest vocabulary knew more words than the lower-class child with the best developed vocabulary. Who was reading well 6 years later? The children who experienced the most language in the first 3 years of life were, with the parent's language interactive style the very strongest predictor of later reading achievement (i.e., accounting for 59% of the variance).

There are strong correlations between amount and quality of language experienced early in life and language development in general as well as vocabulary development in particular (see also Huttenlocher, Vasilyeva, Cymerman, & Levine, 2001; Naigles & Hoff-Ginsberg, 1995; Pearson, Fernandez, Lewedeg, & Oller, 1997). A reasonable hypothesis is that early language interactions are causally important in vocabulary development and subsequent reading achievement. From 2 to 3 years of age, children can import words into their language if they experience them, with incidental learning more likely to occur when children experience a word multiple times and over several days (Schwartz & Terrell, 1983). Such repetition only occurs when children engage in consistent, extensive, and rich verbal interactions with more linguistically mature people.

What if lower-class children received consistently rich verbal input from their parents? Would their language attain the same level as upper- or middle-class children? We do not know, but we do have some well-controlled evaluations that indicate that preschool interventions aimed at increasing cognitive development largely through language stimulation do, in fact, impact children's language development positively (for reviews, see Barnett, 2001, and Gorey, 2001).

One aspect of preschool language interaction that has received substantial attention from scholars is picture-book reading. The more that parents interact with children over books, the better developed is children's language (e.g., Ninio, 1980; Payne, Whitehurst, & Angell, 1994; for reviews, see Bus, van IJzendoorn, & Pelligrini, 1995, and Scarborough & Dobrich, 1994). Most impressive, there are some very well-controlled experimental evaluations that parents and teachers of low-income preschool and primary-grades children can be taught to interact with children over picture books in ways that increase their emergent language skills, including vocabulary development (e.g., Arnold, Lonigan, Whitehurst, & Epstein, 1994; Lonigan & Whitehurst, 1998; Valdez-Menchaca & Whitehurst, 1992; Whitehurst et al., 1988, 1994a, 1994b, 1999; Zevenbergen, Whitehurst, & Zevenbergen, 2003). In short, there is converging evidence that enriching children's verbal interactions during the preschool and primary-grades years is, at a minimum, associated with more advanced language and vocabulary development, and, at least some of the time, causes increases in children's language competence.

Lois Bloom's Work on Child Intentionality in Language Learning

It is easy to read Hart and Risley (1995), as well as some of the other studies covered thus far in this chapter, and conclude that language happens to the child, with language proceeding from caregiver to child. The child is a receiver of input who learns from it. In contrast, Lois Bloom and her colleagues have provided evidence that children very much are determinants of what gets talked about when young word learners and adults interact. Caregivers tend to name and talk about objects that children are attending to, with the children definitely making clear to caregivers what it is in the environment that interests them and commands their attention. That is, they let adults know what they want to talk about. In turn, what caregivers talk about impacts the words that children learn (Bloom, Margulis, Tinker, & Fujita, 1996; Bloom & Tinker, 2001). For a review of all the evidence that children are very much active players in their own vocabulary development, see Bloom (2000).

A pedagogical turn on this is for adults intentionally to talk about what children are interested in. Valdez-Menchaca and Whitehurst (1988) studied this topic in a second-language learning situation, with English-speaking children learning Spanish. In the experimental situation, adults labeled a toy in Spanish when the child expressed interest in it. Controls heard the same labels, but not at a time when they seemed to be intrigued by a toy. The children who heard the labels when they were interested in particular toys were more likely to use the words in their later speech, although both groups of children learned the meanings of the words. In matters of vocabulary acquisition, as in many aspects of learning, children's interest matters, with learning more certain when teachers teach to children's interests (Hidi, 1990). There are a few other tactics teachers can take to make vocabulary learning more certain, with teaching well informed by a variety of studies that follow in this section.

Pany, Jenkins, and Schreck (1982)

When Pressley first read the Pany et al. (1982) study, his reaction was that it had the most undemanding control condition he had ever encountered in a vocabulary-learning experiment. The task was to learn the meanings of vocabulary words, with the words presented and then tested a few minutes later, with several types of measures of word learning (i.e., recall of the word meaning, recognition of synonyms in a multiple-choice format, determining whether target vocabulary were used correctly in sentences).

Across three experiments, a range of 10- to 11-year-old children participated, some of whom were average grade-four students, some of whom were students in grades four and five described as learning-disabled, and some of whom were grade-four students who were considered at risk because of low economic status. The key independent variable was how the vocabulary words were presented. In the *meanings from context* condition, the vocabulary appeared in a two-sentence context from which the meaning of the target word could be inferred. In the *meanings given* condition, the student read a sentence containing the word, and then the experimenter told the student the meaning of the word and provided another sentence example in which the word was used. In the *meanings practiced* condition, the experimenter provided a synonym for the target word and the students repeated the synonyms twice.

But what about that undemanding control condition? Participants in the control condition were presented the vocabulary words but were not provided the meanings of the words during study. As undemanding as it was, that control condition permitted an important conclusion. Performances in both the *meanings given* and the *meanings practiced* conditions were much better than in the control condition. In other words, just providing a definition of a word improves children's learning.

Another very important finding, however, was that performances in the *meanings from context* condition were generally not much better than in the no meaning exposure control condition. That was despite the fact that the contexts were rigged so that inferring the meanings should have been easy (i.e., the first sentence contained the target vocabulary word and the second sentence contained an explicit synonym). Even though children sometimes learn word meanings from context, as they seem to do when they fast-map, such learning was not as certain or as great as when the meaning was provided in the Pany et al. (1982) study.

Since Pany et al. (1982), there has been plenty of research making clear that when readers attempt to derive the meanings of words that are encountered in context (i.e., in sentences, paragraphs, stories), they often get them wrong (for a review, see Fukkink & de Glopper, 1998). Often, verbal contexts are not exactly flush with clues about the meanings of particular words. Sometimes the reader lacks the prior knowledge to make sense of the clues that are in the text. It really is not very surprising that people sometimes cannot guess the meanings of words from context, even if they try hard to do so.

A final finding in Pany et al. (1982) that deserves mention is that if practicing the word and its meaning did not make learning perfect, it made it better compared to the condition where the meaning was simply presented. Thorndike's (1911) views on repetition are valid with respect to learning vocabulary meanings, a task with a strong associative component.

As we leave this discussion of Pany et al. (1982), we note that it made very clear the power of giving students definitions, which definitely increases vocabulary learning. That said, providing definitions to students does not guarantee that they will really understand completely the meaning of the words defined.

Miller and Gildea (1987): Concerns about Learning Vocabulary Words from Definitions

As long as there have been dictionaries, teachers have been sending their students to dictionaries to look up the meanings of words they do not know. Confidence that this practice produces understanding of the words looked up was shattered by Miller and Gildea's (1987) article. They asked children in grades five and six to read dictionary definitions for words they did not know and then write meaningful sentences containing the words. The children wrote many sentences that those authors referred to as "mystifying," including the following examples (Miller & Gildea, 1987, p. 98):

Me and my parents *correlate*, because without them, I wouldn't be here.
I was *meticulous* about falling off the cliff.
The *redress* for getting well when you're sick is to stay in bed.
I *relegated* my pen pal's letter to her house.
That news is very *tenet*.

Moreover, it did not help if the definition was accompanied by a model sentence. Consider *usurp*, which means take, accompanied by the illustrative sentence "The king's brother tried to *usurp* the throne." Children's own sentences for *usurp* still missed the meaning, however. In all of the following children-generated sentences, the word *take* or a variation of it would make sense, but not the word *usurp*:

The blue chair was *usurped* from the room.
Don't try to *usurp* the tape from the store.
The thief tried to *usurp* the money from the safe.

Yes, like the participants in Pany et al. (1982) who were provided the definitions of new words, Miller and Gildea's (1987) participants got something out of that information. But the bottom line from Miller and Gildea (1987) was that providing definitions alone or with examples of words used in context is a teaching strategy fraught with difficulties.

There are better and worse dictionary definitions (i.e., clearer and more complete definitions vs. more vague and incomplete definitions). Verbal contexts surrounding vocabulary words can be rich in clues to meaning or sparse in them. Such differences make a difference in whether people learn the meanings of unfamiliar words and use them sensibly (see Nist & Olejnik, 1995, for a telling empirical analysis). Miller and Gildea's (1987) warnings about learning from dictionary definitions and verbal contexts were important then and remain so now.

The Keyword Method Studies

In the late 1970s and early 1980s, Pressley, Levin, and their colleagues did a series of studies on the keyword method of vocabulary learning. Basically, when using the keyword method, learners identify a part of a to-be-learned word that sounds like a word they already know. For example, for the word *loggia*, which means balcony, a keyword might be *log*. The learner then forms an interactive image that includes the word's meaning referent and the keyword referent (e.g., a pile of fire logs on a balcony). Later, when asked for the meaning of *loggia*, the learner recalls the image with the logs and remembers that *loggia* means balcony. Although the keyword method was studied most extensively with foreign vocabulary, there were enough experiments with English vocabulary to be certain of its effectiveness when English first-language students are acquiring native language words. The keyword method produces hugely positive effects with respect to immediate learning, although the evidence is more mixed with respect to whether it produces advantages with respect to long-term retention of meanings (McDaniel, Pressley, & Dunay, 1987; Thomas & Wang, 1996; Wang & Thomas, 1995; Zhang & Schumm, 2000).

Despite the generally positive appraisal of the keyword method (see Pressley, Levin, & Delaney, 1982), one point we emphasize here is that, as far as we can tell, the keyword method has had no impact on educational practice. The method requires a lot of cognitive effort (Pressley & Levin, 1978) and probably seems unnatural to many teachers (Levin & Pressley, 1985). More is required than huge effect sizes relative to other intervention or control conditions for a vocabulary instructional intervention to be deployed in schools!! It must be acceptable to educators (Pressley & Harris, 1994).

Robert Sternberg's (1987) Theory of Learning Words from Context

Robert Sternberg (1987) made a strong case that most vocabulary had to be learned from context. His 1987 chapter has received substantial attention from vocabulary researchers. According to Sternberg's analysis, there are two ways vocabulary learning from context can occur: incidentally or through learners' intentional efforts.

Incidental Learning

By early adulthood, individuals have learned tens of thousands of words. Given that only a few hundred words a year seem to be taught directly in school, the only way to explain the learning of so many words is that people acquire them by interacting with others, listening to radio and television, and reading—that is, by acquiring words incidental to other tasks.

When Sternberg (1987) offered his analysis, there were definitely indications in the literature that learning from semantic contexts was anything but certain. For example, it was known that often learners failed to infer correctly the meanings of novel words encountered in texts (e.g., Daalen-Kapteijns & Elshout-Mohr, 1981; McKeown, 1985; Schatz & Baldwin, 1986). Even so, Sternberg (1987) inspired additional evaluations of incidental vocabulary learning from context. Swanburn and de Glopper (1999) reviewed these evaluations and concluded that readers often do learn vocabulary from context, but such learning is anything but certain. They estimated that about 15% of novel vocabulary words encountered in text are learned to some extent. Maybe the reader does not get the whole meaning, but he or she gets at least some of it, just like fast-mapping preschoolers do not get the whole meaning of words they hear one or two times, but do fast-map some of the meaning (Carey & Bartlett, 1978).

Teaching Students to Make Intentional Contextual Analyses

Sternberg and his colleagues recognized two types of contextual clues that could facilitate vocabulary learning that learners could be taught to analyze. One was external context cues (i.e., meaning cues in the text surrounding a new vocabulary word; Sternberg, 1987). The second was internal context clues: prefixes, suffixes, and stems (Sternberg,

Powell, & Kaye, 1983; Sternberg & Powell, 1983). Although the various Sternberg papers described preliminary data about efforts to train context analyses strategies, to our knowledge this work was never published.

More positively, Sternberg stimulated researchers to study such teaching. In 1998, Kuhn and Stahl identified 14 studies in which students had been taught to use external semantic context clues, and found clear evidence that compared to no-instruction controls, students taught to use external semantic contexts, became better at figuring out the definitions of words. (See Fukkink & de Glopper, 1998, who, after meta-analyzing studies in which students were taught to use context clues, concluded that such instruction had a moderate impact on students' abilities to figure out meanings.) That said, Kuhn and Stahl (1998) detected an interesting twist that is very important. In four of the studies, control participants simply practiced figuring out the meanings of words in text in the absence of instruction. They improved as much as participants who were taught specific context analysis strategies. Just being prompted to figure out the meanings of words in context and given a little practice at it is as powerful as much more elaborate instruction (i.e., instruction providing detailed information about the various types of semantic context cues).

What about analysis of internal context clues (i.e., word parts)? The clearly interpretable database on the value of teaching internal cue analysis is thin and equivocal (see Baumann, Kame'enui, & Ash, 2003, for a review). That said, Levin, Carney, and Pressley (1988) demonstrated that if undergraduates are taught word components (i.e., the meanings of prefixes, suffixes, and stems), they can use them to figure out the meanings of previously unknown words. The effects in that study were clear and large, although the conditions in the study were such that it was saliently obvious to apply the root word knowledge that was just taught. Graves and Hammond (1980) reported a similar finding with grade-seven students, demonstrating that seventh graders could generalize knowledge of prefixes taught in the context of one set of vocabulary words to new vocabulary words that included the prefixes. Wysocki and Jenkins (1987) found that fourth-, sixth-, and eighth-grade students could transfer knowledge of suffixes to new lists, although the effects were only large with generously liberal scoring of the inferred definitions by the students. In short, there is at least some evidence that teaching morphemes can improve children and adults' skill at inferring the meanings of words. That said, we have yet to see a study where this effect is robust —for example, it is obtained in a situation where it is not fairly obvious that what was previously learned could and should be used to infer the meanings of new words.

Summary

Although there is some evidence of incidental learning from context and some evidence that intentional contextual analysis strategies can be taught profitably, learning from context is neither certain nor are the effects typically large. Even so, contextual analysis continues to receive the attention of researchers interested in vocabulary learning because many are convinced that Sternberg (1987) was right: most vocabulary words are acquired from context.

Carlisle, Fleming, and Gudbrandsen's (2000) Study of Incidental Learning of Vocabulary during Constructivist Science Units

One recent study of incidental learning of vocabulary especially caught our attention as we reviewed the literature to write this chapter. Carlisle, Fleming, and Gudbrandsen (2000) assessed the vocabulary learning of fourth- and eighth-grade students as a function of participating in a month-long science unit. Since learning vocabulary was not the focus of the science lessons, vocabulary acquisition was incidental. Carlisle et al. (2000), in fact, found some incidental acquisition of words covered in the unit. (There were control conditions to assess whether learning of words pertaining to the science unit exceeded acquisition of new words in general over a month, which it did.) Even so, there was certainly room for more learning, with knowledge of the vocabulary in the unit far from perfect at the end of the unit of study.

Carlisle et al. (2000) included lots of interesting additional assessments, for instance, establishing that students who began the unit with greater understanding of vocabulary pertaining to the topic of the unit learned more vocabulary incidentally during instruction than students who started the unit with little prior knowledge. What vocabulary a student learns incidentally during content instruction depends both on exposure to vocabulary and the student's previous knowledge about the topic of instruction.

More about Teaching Intentional Contextual Analyses: Baumann and Associates' Instructional Studies of Morphemic and Semantic Contextual Analyses

One set of recent investigations of intentional contextual analyses also caught our attention more than others as we reviewed this literature. Baumann and his associates (Baumann et al., 2002; Baumann, Edwards, Boland, Olejnik, & Kame'enui, 2003) studied the effects of teaching morphemic and semantic contextual analyses to fifth-grade students. In one study, instruction occurred over 2 months, in the other over 12 50-minute lessons. In the most ambitious instructional conditions of the experiments, students were taught to use both the morphemic analysis procedures and semantic contextual analysis procedures. The morphemic lessons focused on teaching students to use root words, prefixes, and suffixes to learn the meanings of new vocabulary words encountered in readings, with 15 specific prefixes and five specific suffixes taught. The semantic context instruction emphasized carefully reading the sentences around a novel word to determine the word's meaning, with instruction about how context sometimes includes definitional clues, actual synonyms for novel words, information about the opposite meaning of the word, and examples if the novel word is a general concept. The participants were taught that clues to meaning are often spread over several surrounding sentences.

In general, the lessons were well planned, including a lot of practice in using the morphemic and semantic context strategies. The participants were also provided an overarching scheme for applying the morphemic and semantic context strategies they had learned, one emphasizing the critical metacognitive information about when and where the morphemic and semantic context strategies should be used. The fifth graders were explicitly instructed to do as follows:

> When you come to a word, and you don't know what it means, use:
> 1. CONTEXT CLUES: Read the sentences around the word to see if there are clues to its meaning. 2. WORD-PART CLUES: See if you can break the word into a root word, prefix, or suffix to help figure out its meaning. 3. CONTEXT CLUES: Read the sentences around the word again to see if you have figured out its meaning. (Edwards, Font, Baumann, & Boland, 2004, p. 170)

There were some clear effects among the specific findings in these studies. Teaching the morphemic and semantic context strategies promoted learning of the words in the texts that were read by the students during the study. Also, there was some evidence that the fifth graders were able to transfer the skills they learned to determine the meanings of words in novel texts, although the effects were moderate-sized at best and more often small to nonexistent. There was no evidence, however, that teaching these skills increased comprehension of what was read.

This is the latest, visible research making the point that short-term vocabulary-focused interventions can have specific impacts on vocabulary learning without having much general impact. This is a point that has been made prominently in the research literature, including in the work reviewed next.

Beck and McKeown's Studies of Rich Vocabulary Instruction

Beck, Perfetti, and McKeown (1982) and McKeown, Beck, Omanson, and Perfetti (1983) taught about 100 vocabulary words to elementary-school students over a semester. These words were taught using what Beck and her colleagues refer to as a "rich instructional approach" (see Beck, McKeown, & Omanson, 1987; McKeown & Beck, 2004). This approach requires learners to use and think about the words to-be-learned in many ways, for example, by making decisions about whether and when a word is used in a context correctly and making distinctions concerning subsets of the words that were related in meaning. There were many encounters with each taught word over the months of instruction, with McKeown, Beck, Omanson, and Pople (1985) providing a very analytical demonstration that more frequent encounters with a vocabulary word as part of rich instruction definitely make a difference in how well it is learned. (The general point that frequency of exposure to specific vocabulary increased learning of words was definitely clear by the mid-1980s; see Stahl & Fairbanks, 1986.) Also, as part of the Beck and McKeown approach, students often were required to explain their thinking as they worked with the words they were learning. In short, Beck and McKeown emphasized long-term instruction of vocabulary that stimulated student thoughtfulness.

Beck, McKeown, and their associates provided the most visible studies confirming the theory that teaching vocabulary increases comprehension of text containing taught vocabulary, with smaller, more general effects on comprehension (for a review, see Stahl & Fairbanks, 1986). Their work permitted an optimist to see the glass as half-full—at least comprehension improved if the texts contained the words taught—or a pessimist to see the glass as half-empty—comprehension did not improve much more generally from teaching vocabulary words, most emphatically, on standardized assessments of comprehension. In the two decades since Beck's research, we are aware of no work that changes that two-edged conclusion.

One tactic to take, given the classic Beck and McKeown outcome, is to teach words that students will encounter in text. Given that only a few hundred vocabulary words can be taught in school each year, the question arises—Which words should be taught? Beck, McKeown, and Kucan (2002) have proposed an intriguing hypothesis that takes into account the theory that children should be taught words they will encounter and the practical fact that the number of words they can be taught is limited. First, they advise, do not worry about teaching the words that children know already as a function of living in the world. Also, do not bother teaching words that are very low frequency in the language, perhaps because they are very domain-specific (e.g., *isotope*, unless, of course, you are teaching chemistry). What should be taught are high-frequency words that occur across a number of domains but are not known by many students (e.g., at the elementary level, teach *coincidence, absurd, industrious, fortunate*). Beck et al. (2002) classify these as Tier 2 words, referring to well-known words as Tier 1 and to low-frequency words as Tier 3. As far as we know, however, Beck et al.'s (2002) position is an untested hypothesis, although one that seems testable to us and one that should be tested.

Landmark Research Summaries

During this quarter century of progress in vocabulary teaching and learning research in classrooms, there have been two important volumes that have summarized the state of the field and its thinking. One was McKeown and Curtis's (1987) *The Nature of Vocabulary Acquisition* and the other was Baumann and Kame'enui's (2004) *Vocabulary Instruction: Research to Practice*. There also have been a number of review chapters and articles (Fukkink & de Glopper, 1998; Stahl & Fairbanks, 1986; Swanburn & de Glopper, 1999), with the most up-to-date one now being Baumann et al. (2003). McKeown and Curtis (1987), Baumann and Kame'enui (2004), and Baumann et al. (2003) are must reads for anyone wanting or needing to develop expertise on the scientific evidence pertaining to vocabulary teaching and learning in classrooms.

Summing Up: What Do We Know about Vocabulary Learning and Instruction? What Do We Still Need to Know?

Based on extant research, most of which was produced in the past quarter century, we know plenty about how to teach vocabulary. First, children do learn much of their vocabulary incidentally. For that to happen, children need to be in a vocabulary-rich environment, one that is responsive to their curiosities. That parents of preschoolers can learn how to interact with children over books to increase their vocabulary learning is very heartening, although the preschooler and school-age child's life involves more than interactive book reading. There is an urgent need for much more work on how to enrich children's language environments to maximize their language exposure and development.

Repetition matters with respect to incidental learning of vocabulary, which occurs best over days and weeks. Much of vocabulary learning is associative learning, which is facilitated by rich verbal interactions in the world.

By filling lessons with worthwhile readings, teachers go far in stimulating worthwhile talk and set the stage for a test of the hypothesis advanced by Beck et al. (2002): Can teachers determine which words encountered in text and elsewhere are important for students to know, and then teach those words? In addition, Carlisle et al.'s (2000) demonstration that vocabulary can be learned from high-quality units deserves serious reflection. What difference would it make if students spent every day in high-quality lessons, involving discussion and reflection filled with the vocabulary that science-, mathematics-, and social studies-literate people need to know?

There are some paradoxes in the vocabulary-teaching and vocabulary-learning literature. Although furnishing students with vocabulary definitions provides a big boost in learning, students definitely do not fully understand the meanings of words from definitions alone. The rich vocabulary instruction advocated by Beck and McKeown and their associates, which involves using words in a variety of ways over an extended period of time, makes a great deal of sense. During such instruction, there should be plenty of opportunity to elaborate and refine understanding of to-be-learned vocabulary.

In reflecting on the vocabulary-teaching and vocabulary-learning data, it is absolutely essential to keep in mind that often the effects of vocabulary instruction have been modest, with many more words not learned than learned incidentally, with sensible-seeming strategies like semantic context analysis producing variable and often small effects, and with increased learning of vocabulary translating into modest and quite specific comprehension gains, when there have been any comprehension gains at all (i.e., increasing comprehension of texts containing the taught vocabulary words but not more generally impacting comprehension).

In short, this is generally a modest-effects literature, consistent with other specific, modest effects in the reading instructional literature, such as the modest effects of teaching phonemic awareness on reading (Bus & van IJdendoorn, 1999; National Reading Panel, 2000) or the modest effects of phonics instruction (National Reading Panel, 2000). We point out, in particular, given that the goal of teaching vocabulary is increased comprehension, that there is nothing in this vocabulary instruction literature that suggests effects comparable to the substantial effects on comprehension produced by well-taught, well-thought-out repertoires of comprehension strategies. If you need convincing, look at the large effects, including on standardized tests, in well-controlled studies of comprehension strategies instruction like those offered by Anderson (1992), Brown, Pressley, Van Meter, and Schuder (1996), or Collins (1991).

Indeed, the only large effect of vocabulary instruction on comprehension seems to take place when students are taught vocabulary that occurs in subsequently tested texts. Rather than discounting this as merely "teaching to the test," we think it deserves a lot of attention and reflection. Perhaps we *should* be teaching students the vocabulary they are likely to encounter in text. Of course, educators have known for years that it makes sense to preteach vocabulary before students read a selection (Stahl & Fairbanks, 1986). But we think teachers need to do this on a grand scale. Schools should be teaching students the words they most need to know to be literate in the world. The problem is that we do not know what those words are.

It is time to get serious about identifying the vocabulary words that literate adults should know and be able to use. How might this be accomplished? We need contemporary analyses of texts to determine just what words young people are likely to encounter when they read. Given current technology, that should be easy. Next, the vocabulary so identified must be communicated to the K–12 education community broadly defined (e.g., teachers, materials developers and publishers, education policymakers). A mature vocabulary is an essential part of cultural knowledge, one that we have not reflected on well enough to know what children need to know. For example, one of us (Pressley) recently chaired the language arts expectations committee for Michigan. One of the most frustrating aspects of the task was that it proved impossible to identify vocabulary words that kindergarten through grade-eight students should know and be held accountable for. There needs to be some very, very serious work on this problem, resulting in sets of words that students need to know that teachers can teach over the course of the year connected to the topics that need to be covered well in the elementary curriculum.[1]

Given the interest of several contributors to this volume in morphological aspects of vocabulary learning, we cannot resist making the point that it is surprising how little research has been conducted on the impact of teaching students common parts of words (prefixes, suffixes, root words). It makes sense to get very serious about building students' morphological analysis skills to determine how much such knowledge can improve vocabulary learning. We suspect that long-term teaching aimed at developing such knowledge to the point that encountering word parts would automatically activate their meanings might go far in improving the acquisition of new words and the understanding of novel words encountered in context. This is one of those really obvious hypotheses that just has not gotten the test it deserves.

Equally surprising is that the vocabulary-learning acquisition literature is not very analytical about what is learned when a student acquires vocabulary knowledge. At a minimum, students need to learn the word as a stimulus (e.g., most students will not be able to remember the whole word *anthropomorphism* following a single exposure). Then the learner has to learn the definition, which can include substantial conceptual development (e.g., learning the word *diaspora* requires understanding the concept of population spread). The lack of attention to this dimension of vocabulary learning is particularly surprising given the substantial interest in children's conceptual development during the past quarter century (see Murphy, 2002). There also is an associative component, that is, learning the association between the word and its meaning (e.g., remembering that *anthropomorphism* refers to a characteristics of a god and *diaspora* is about spreading population). Each of these components has the potential to be challenging to child learners. Really analytical work on vocabulary acquisition might document how these challenges interact with each other and with characteristics of the learner. For ex-

---

[1]As this chapter was being drafted, we learned of ongoing work by Professor Andrew Biemiller of the University of Toronto, who is attempting to develop lists of vocabulary words that are appropriate to teach in K–12 education.

ample, for a child with good prior knowledge of morphemes, recognizing the morphemes in a word like *anthropomorphism* might help with learning the word *per se*, understanding the concept it refers to, and associating the word with the concept. There is room for much more analytical work on vocabulary learning than has been reported to date.

We close this section with three warnings. First, do not believe for a minute that developing powerful vocabulary-teaching and vocabulary-learning procedures will result in their embrace by teachers. The keyword studies are telling on this point. Often, the keyword method produced very large effects on vocabulary learning. Yet, we have never seen the method widely used in schools. Like all instructional procedures that make it into school, vocabulary-learning and vocabulary-teaching procedures must make sense to teachers and kids (Pressley & Harris, 1994)! The keyword method has never passed that test.

Second, although the correlations between vocabulary knowledge and comprehension have been recognized for a long time (Cunningham & Stanovich, 1997; Davis, 1944, 1968; Singer, 1965; Spearitt, 1972; Thurstone, 1946), do not be seduced into believing that increasing vocabulary knowledge will automatically increase comprehension ability. The obvious potential intervening variable is general intelligence.

Third, this obsession with vocabulary effects on comprehension ignores the fact that vocabulary serves other purposes. Might writing or oral communications improve with increased vocabulary knowledge because of such knowledge? After all, productive expression depends greatly on lexical precision. We are struck by the reality that no one seems to care much about such relationships compared to the vocabulary–comprehension link. We advise that as vocabulary research proceeds, it is essential for researchers to be more attentive to a fuller array of potential impacts produced by interventions that increase vocabulary knowledge. Even if increasing vocabulary only causes small improvements in comprehension, it seems to us that it has the potential to impact other literacy competencies, such as writing and oral communications, that are every bit as important as understanding text.

THE BIG HYPOTHESIS

The Pressley group has put forward a great deal of data in the past decade about the nature of effective primary-grades instruction (e.g., Bogner, Raphael, & Pressley, 2002; Dolezal, Welsh, Pressley, & Vincent, 2003;

Morrow, Tracey, Woo, & Pressley, 1999; Pressley, Allington, Wharton-McDonald, Block, & Morrow, 2001; Pressley, Dolezal, et al., 2003; Pressley, Roehrig, et al., 2003; Pressley, Allington, et al., 2001; Pressley, Wharton-McDonald, et al., 2001; Pressley, Wharton-McDonald, & Mistretta, 1998; Wharton-McDonald, Pressley, & Hampston, 1998). A main finding in those studies is that good teachers use a repertoire of effective strategies to develop literacy skills in their students. Basically, they articulate a number of teaching elements, each of which works at least in some small way with at least some students. Good teaching makes consistent, intelligent use of procedures, which each have some impact. So, the excellent grade-one teacher does phonics lessons, which has a small to moderate impact on reading. She has her students compose within the context of a plan–draft–revise model, with the essays getting a little better every week and month of the school year. She begins comprehension instruction, which, over the course of a school year, can substantially increase students' active processing of texts they hear and read. The field notes generated in the studies conducted by the Pressley group revealed that effective teachers, in fact, do teach vocabulary. The universal approach is to teach words as they are encountered in lessons, with much of the teaching aimed at increasing incidental learning (e.g., there is brief discussion of an unfamiliar word, with no subsequent assessment of whether the children know the word). Based on the review of the vocabulary-teaching and vocabulary-learning research just presented, it seems there is room for improvement with respect to vocabulary instruction even in effective classrooms.

Based on the vocabulary-learning theoretical and empirical literature, the following could be justified in any elementary or secondary classroom:

1. Immersing children in rich verbal interactions, especially meaningful and interesting conversations around worthwhile content and experiences (e.g., hands-on science experiences, deeply connected social studies units on topics that appeal to students).
2. Promoting extensive reading of worthwhile texts that are filled with mature vocabulary.
3. Attending responsively to students' vocabulary needs—for example, monitoring when students are struggling to identify a word to put into writing or an oral presentation and helping students with it; monitoring when students are intrigued by any content that includes objects that could be identified by vocabulary students should know (e.g., when students are intrigued by *concave*

and *convex* lenses as part of an experiment on light, make certain they know the difference between *concave* and *convex*); and being sensitive to unfamiliar words in read-alouds, making certain that potential teachable moments around such words results in teaching of the words.

4. Finding ways to provide definitions to students of potentially unfamiliar words, including making certain that students use dictionaries. The dictionaries available to students should be excellent ones that do a good job of explaining the meanings of words. Students can also be taught to use Internet dictionaries and hypertext options to access the meanings of words.

5. Rich teaching of vocabulary words, involving extensive use of and experience with them over long periods of time, makes a good deal of sense.

6. Teaching children that the meanings of words often can be inferred from context clues, that is, from information in the sentences surrounding unfamiliar words. Encourage students to look for clues to the meanings of novel words.

7. Teaching children the meanings of common word parts (i.e., prefixes, suffixes, roots) and providing substantial practice in applying this knowledge to understanding unfamiliar words, practice that encourages students to internalize morphological analysis (i.e., automatically relate what they know about word parts when they encounter a new word).

8. Provide rich vocabulary instruction, for example, as in the Beck et al. (1982) study.

We note that effective teaching is not accomplished in the short term, but rather occurs over years. Thus, from our perspective, what makes a great deal of sense at this juncture are experiments where teachers are taught to use the diverse range of vocabulary-enhancing techniques just listed over at least a school year, with the reading achievement of students taught by such teachers compared with the reading achievement of students taught by teachers not immersing their students in vocabulary-learning opportunities.

In specifying "at least a year," we are reflecting a reality of educational experiments in the United States. We cannot locate a single educational experiment that held its randomization samples for longer than a school year. Even with outstanding school district cooperation, there will be attrition from the study with every passing year and cross-condition contaminations (e.g., students in vocabulary-immersion classrooms in year 1 will end up in control classrooms in subsequent years because of local decisions sensitive to needs other than maintaining the randomization; control teachers will find out the vocabulary instructional techniques and begin to use them in their classrooms).

Will such vocabulary instruction flooding impact vocabulary acquisition? That seems almost certain given the track record of individual vocabulary interventions increasing vocabulary learning. Will it impact literacy more broadly in such areas as comprehension, writing, and oral communications? That is harder to know, but we believe that massive intervention over a long term has a better chance of producing discernible, more general effects than the shorter term studies of the past.

A reasonable question is whether real teachers can learn to immerse their students in vocabulary instruction. The only way to know is to try. It would make sense to do some qualitative, intervention development research in advance of the true experiments just proposed. Such work not only would provide information about whether such instruction can be developed but how it might be developed well.

We warn that such instruction is most likely to happen in the classrooms of teachers who are already pretty good. Consider some work now being carried out by Pressley and Katie Hilden. They are studying two middle schools that are trying to jump-start comprehension strategies instruction. The teachers who are already pretty good teachers are doing better at incorporating the comprehension strategies into their classrooms than are other teachers. Why? The overarching conclusion of the Pressley group in the past decade is that excellent teaching is not just teaching content, it also involves flooding the classroom with motivation and managing the classroom well. Teachers who are already doing that can devote their energies and attention to new elements of instruction, whereas teachers who are not doing that must attend to managing substantial student off-task behavior and other misbehaviors. Thus it might make sense for a first test of the vocabulary instructional flooding hypothesis to take place in classrooms that are already pretty good.

It might seem strange that we would advocate making vocabulary instructional flooding a research priority over additional research on the individual mechanisms of vocabulary teaching and learning. However, we think there is enough data already to decide what makes sense to try as part of instructional flooding. It is very rare for there to be dozens of experiments on particular instructional mechanisms. Researchers, practitioners, and policymakers need to recognize that evidence-based decisions on particular instructional techniques usually will be informed by a very few true experiments (Cook, 2002). Engaging teaching and learning is an articulation of a variety of mechanisms and never the mindless repetition of single mechanisms (e.g., Pressley, Dolezal, et al., 2003), just like real learning is an articulation of thinking processes rather than a single process (e.g., Pressley & Afflerbach, 1995). In short, as we reflected on the vocabulary-teaching and vocabulary-learning research of the past, we think it is time to move beyond the study of individual mechanisms and toward asking whether evidence-based vocabulary instruction and curriculum packages can be developed that will make a difference in real classrooms. Such instruction will be multicomponential and longer term than any of the vocabulary instruction addressed in experiments to date.

REFERENCES

Anderson, V. (1992). A teacher development project in transactional strategy instruction for teachers of severely reading-disabled adolescents. *Teaching and Teacher Education, 8*, 391–403.

Arnold, D. H., Lonigan, C. J., Whitehurst, G. J., & Epstein, J. N. (1994). Accelerating language development through picture book reading: Replication and extension to a videotape training format. *Journal of Educational Psychology, 86*, 235–243.

Barnett, W. S. (2001). Preschool education for economically disadvantaged children: Effects on reading achievement and related outcomes. In S. B. Neuman & D. K. Dickinson (Eds.), *Handbook of early literacy research* (Vol. 1, pp. 421–443). New York: Guilford Press.

Baumann, J. F., Edwards, E. C., Boland, E. M., Olejnik, S., & Kame'enui, E. J. (2003). Vocabulary tricks: Effects of instruction in morphology on fifth-grade students' ability to derive and infer word meanings. *American Educational Research Journal, 40*, 447–494.

Baumann, J. F., Edwards, E. C., Font, G., Tereshinski, C. A., Kame'enui, E. J., & Olejnik, S. F. (2002). Teaching morphemic and contextual analysis to fifth-grade students. *Reading Research Quarterly, 37*, 150–176.

Baumann, J. F., & Kame'enui, E. J. (Eds.). (2004). *Vocabulary instruction: Research to practice.* New York: Guilford Press.

Baumann, J. F., Kame'enui, E. J., & Ash, G. E. (2003). Research on vocabulary instruction: Voltaire redux. In J. Flood, D. Lapp, J. R. Squire, & J. M. Jensen (Eds.), *Handbook of research on teaching the English language arts* (pp. 752–785). Mahwah, NJ: Erlbaum.

Beck, I. L., McKeown, M. G., & Kucan, L. (2002). *Bringing words to life: Robust vocabulary instruction.* New York: Guilford Press.

Beck, I. L., McKeown, M. G., & Omanson, R. C. (1987). The effects and uses of diverse vocabulary instructional techniques. In M. G. McKeown & M. E. Curtis (Eds.), *The nature of vocabulary acquisition* (pp. 147–163). Englewood Cliffs, NJ: Erlbaum.

Beck, I. L., Perfetti, C. A., & McKeown, M. G. (1982). Effects of long-term vocabulary instruction on lexical access and reading comprehension. *Journal of Educational Psychology, 74,* 506–521.

Behrend, D. A., Scofield, J., & Kleinknecht, E. E. (2001). Beyond fast mapping: Young children's extensions of novel words and novel facts. *Developmental Psychology, 37,* 698–705.

Bloom, L. (2000). The intentionality model of word learning: How to learn a word, any word. In R. M. Golinkoff, K. Hirsh-Pasek, L. Bloom, L. B. Smith, A. L. Woodward, N. Akhtar, et al. (Eds.), *Becoming a word learner: A debate on lexical acquisition* (pp. 19–50). New York: Oxford University Press.

Bloom, L., Margulis, C., Tinker, E., & Fujita, N. (1996). Early conversations and word learning: Contributions from child and adult. *Child Development, 67,* 3154–3175.

Bloom, L., & Tinker, E. (2001). The intentionality model and language acquisition. *Monographs of the Society for Research in Child Development, 66* (Serial No. 267), i–viii, 191.

Bloom, P. (2000). *How children learn the meanings of words.* Cambridge MA: MIT Press.

Bogner, K., Raphael, L. M., & Pressley, M. (2002). How grade-1 teachers motivate literate activity by their students. *Scientific Studies of Reading, 6,* 135–165.

Brown, R., Pressley, M., Van Meter, P., & Schuder, T. (1996). A quasi-experimental validation of transactional strategies instruction with low-achieving second grade readers. *Journal of Educational Psychology, 88,* 18–37.

Bus, A. G., & van IJzendoorn, M. H. (1999). Phonological awareness and early reading: A meta-analysis of experimental training studies. *Journal of Educational Psychology, 91,* 403–414.

Bus, A. G., van IJzendoorn, M. H., & Pellegrini, A. D. (1995). Joint book reading makes for success in learning to read: A meta-analysis on intergenerational transmission of literacy. *Review of Educational Research, 65,* 1–21.

Carey, S., & Bartlett, E. (1978). Acquiring a single new word. *Papers and Reports on Child Language Development, 15,* 17–29.

Carlisle, J. F., Fleming, J. E., & Gudbrandsen, B. (2000). Incidental word learning in science classes. *Contemporary Educational Psychology, 25,* 184–211.

Collins, C. (1991). Reading instruction that increases thinking abilities. *Journal of Reading, 34,* 510–516.

Cook, T. D. (2002). Randomized experiments in educational policy research: A critical examination of the reasons the educational evaluation community has offered for not doing them. *Educational Evaluation and Policy Analysis, 24*, 175–199.

Cunningham, A. E., & Stanovich, K. E. (1997). Early reading acquisition and its relation to reading experience and ability 10 years later. *Developmental Psychology, 33*, 934–945.

Daalen-Kapteijns, M. M., & Elshout-Mohr, M. (1981). The acquisition of word meanings as a cognitive verbal process. *Journal of Verbal Learning and Verbal Behavior, 20*, 386–399.

Davis, F. B. (1944). Fundamental factors in reading comprehension. *Psychometrica, 9*, 185–197.

Davis, F. B. (1968). Research in comprehension in reading. *Reading Research Quarterly, 3*, 499–545.

Dolezal, S. E., Welsh, L. M., Pressley, M., & Vincent, M. (2003). How nine third-grade teachers motivate student academic engagement. *Elementary School Journal, 103*, 239–267.

Edwards, E. C., Font, G., Baumann, J. F., & Boland, E. (2004). Unlocking word meanings: Strategies and guidelines for teaching morphemic and contextual analysis. In J. F. Baumann & E. J. Kame'enui (Eds.), *Vocabulary instruction: Research to practice* (pp. 159–176). New York: Guilford Press.

Fukkink, R. G., & de Glopper, K. (1998). Effects of instruction in deriving word meaning from context: A meta-analysis. *Review of Educational Research, 68*, 450–469.

Gorey, K. M. (2001). Early childhood education: A meta-analytic affirmation of the short- and long-term benefits of educational opportunity. *School Psychology Quarterly, 16*, 9–30.

Graves, M. F., & Hammond, H. K. (1980). A validated procedure for teaching prefixes and its effect on students' ability to assign meaning to novel words. In M. L. Kamil & J. Moe (Eds.), *Perspective on reading research and instruction: Twenty-ninth yearbook of the National Reading Conference* (Vol. 29, pp. 184–188). Washington, DC: National Reading Conference.

Hart, B., & Risley, T. R. (1995). *Meaningful differences in the everyday experience of young American children.* Baltimore: Brookes.

Heibeck, T. H., & Markman, E. M. (1987). Word learning in children: An examination of fast mapping. *Child Development, 58*, 1021–1034.

Hidi, S. (1990). Interest and its contribution as a mental resource for learning. *Review of Educational Research, 60*, 549–571.

Huttenlocher, J., Vasilyeva, M., Cymerman, E., & Levine, S. (2001). Language input and child syntax. *Cognitive Psychology, 45*, 337–374.

Kleinknecht, E. E., Behrend, D. A., & Scofield, J. M. (1999, March). *What's so special about word learning, anyway?* Paper presented at the biennial meetings of the Society for Research in Child Development, Albuquerque, NM.

Kuhn, M. R., & Stahl, S. A. (1998). Teaching children to learn word meanings from context: A synthesis and some questions. *Journal of Literacy Research, 30*, 119–138.

Levin, J. R., Carney, R. N., & Pressley, M. (1988). Facilitating vocabulary infer- ring through root word instruction. *Contemporary Educational Psychology, 13*, 316–322.

Levin, J. R., & Pressley, M. (1985). Mnemonic vocabulary instruction: What's fact, what's fiction? In R. F. Dillon (Ed.), *Individual differences in cognition* (Vol. 2, pp. 145–172). Orlando, FL: Academic Press.

Lonigan, C. J., & Whitehurst, G. J. (1998). Relative efficacy of parent and teacher involvement in a shared-reading intervention for preschool children from low-income backgrounds. *Early Childhood Research Quarterly, 13*, 263– 290.

Markson, L. (1999). *Mechanisms of word learning in children: Insights from fast mapping.* Unpublished doctoral dissertation, University of Arizona.

Markson, L., & Bloom, P. (1997). Evidence against a dedicated system for word learning in children. *Nature, 385*, 813–815.

McDaniel, M. A., Pressley, M., & Dunay, P. K. (1987). Long-term retention of vocabulary after keyword and context learning. *Journal of Educational Psychology, 79*, 87–89.

McKeown, M. G. (1985). The acquisition of word meaning from context by chil- dren of high and low ability. *Reading Research Quarterly, 20*, 482–496.

McKeown, M. G., & Beck, I. L. (2004). Direct and rich vocabulary instruction. In J. F. Baumann & E. J. Kame'enui (Eds.), *Vocabulary instruction: Research to practice* (pp. 13–27). New York: Guilford Press.

McKeown, M. G., Beck, I. L., Omanson, R. C., & Pople, M. T. (1985). Some ef- fects on the nature and frequency of vocabulary instruction on the knowl- edge and use of words. *Reading Research Quarterly, 20*, 522–535.

McKeown, M. G., Beck, I. L., Omanson, R. C., & Perfetti, C. A. (1983). The ef- fects of long-term vocabulary instruction on reading comprehension: A replication. *Journal of Reading Behavior, 15*, 3–18.

McKeown, M. G., & Curtis, M. E. (Eds.). (1987). *The nature of vocabulary ac- quisition.* Hillsdale, NJ: Erlbaum.

Miller, G. A., & Gildea, P. M. (1987). How children learn words. *Scientific Ameri- can, 252*(3), 94–99.

Morrow, L. M., Tracey, D. H., Woo, D. G., & Pressley, M. (1999). Characteristics of exemplary first-grade literacy instruction. *The Reading Teacher, 52*, 462–476.

Murphy, G. L. (2002). *The big book of concepts.* Cambridge, MA: MIT Press.

Naigles, L., & Hoff-Ginsberg, E. (1995). Input to verb learning: Evidence for the plausibility of syntactic bootstrapping. *Developmental Psychology, 5*, 827– 837.

National Reading Panel. (2000). *Report of the National Reading Panel: Teaching children to read: An evidence-based assessment of the scientific research literature on reading and its implications for reading instruction: Reports of the subgroups.* Washington, DC: National Institutes of Health, National Institute of Child Health and Human Development

Ninio, A. (1980). Picture-book reading in mother–infant dyads belonging to two subgroups in Israel. *Child Development, 51*, 587–590.

Nist, S. L., & Olejnik, S. (1995). The role of context and dictionary definitions on varying levels of word knowledge. *Reading Research Quarterly, 30,* 172–193.

Pany, D., Jenkins, J. R., & Schreck, J. (1982). Vocabulary instruction: Effects on word knowledge and reading comprehension. *Learning Disability Quarterly, 5,* 202–215.

Payne, A. C., Whitehurst, G. J., & Angell, A. L. (1994). The role of home literacy environment in the development of language ability in preschool children from low-income families. *Early Childhood Research Quarterly, 9,* 427–440.

Pearson, B. Z., Fernandez, S. C., Lewedeg, V., & Oller, D. K. (1997). The relation of input factors to lexical learning by bilingual infants. *Applied Psycholinguistics, 18,* 41–58.

Pressley, M., & Afflerbach, P. (1995). *Verbal protocols of reading: The nature of constructively responsive reading.* Hillsdale, NJ: Erlbaum.

Pressley, M., Allington, R., Wharton-McDonald, R., Block, C. C., & Morrow, L. M. (2001). *Learning to read: Lessons from exemplary first grades.* New York: Guilford Press.

Pressley, M., Dolezal, S. E., Raphael, L. M., Welsh, L. M., Roehrig, A. D., & Bogner, K. (2003). *Motivating primary-grade students.* New York: Guilford Press.

Pressley, M., & Harris, K. R. (1994). Increasing the quality of educational intervention research. *Educational Psychology Review, 6,* 191–214.

Pressley, M., & Levin, J. R. (1978). Developmental constraints associated with children's use of the keyword method of foreign language vocabulary learning. *Journal of Experimental Child Psychology, 26,* 359–372.

Pressley, M., Levin, J. R., & Delaney, H. D. (1982). The mnemonic keyword method. *Review of Educational Research, 52,* 61–92.

Pressley, M., Roehrig, A., Raphael, L., Dolezal, S., Bohn, K., Mohan, L., et al. (2003). Teaching processes in elementary and secondary education. In W. M. Reynolds & G. E. Miller (Eds.), *Comprehensive handbook of psychology, Volume 7: Educational psychology* (pp. 153–175). New York: Wiley.

Pressley, M., Wharton-McDonald, R., Allington, R., Block, C. C., Morrow, L., Tracey, D., et al.. (2001). A study of effective grade-1 literacy instruction. *Scientific Studies of Reading, 5,* 35–58.

Pressley, M., Wharton-McDonald, R., & Mistretta, J. (1998). Effective beginning literacy instruction: Dialectical, scaffolded, and contextualized. In J. L. Metsala & L. C. Ehri (Eds.), *Word recognition in beginning literacy* (pp. 357–373). Mahwah, NJ: Erlbaum.

Scarborough, H. S., & Dobrich, W. (1994). On the efficiency of reading to preschoolers. *Developmental Review, 14,* 245–302.

Schatz, E. K., & Baldwin, R. S. (1986). Context clues are unreliable predictors of word meanings. *Reading Research Quarterly, 21,* 439–453.

Schwartz, R. G., & Terrell, B. Y. (1983). The role of input frequency in lexical acquisition. *Journal of Child Language, 10,* 57–64.

Singer, H. A. (1965). A developmental model of speed of reading in grades 3 through 6. *Reading Research Quarterly, 1,* 29–49.

Spearitt, D. (1972). Identification of subskills of reading comprehension by maximum likelihood factor analysis. *Reading Research Quarterly, 8,* 92–111.

Stahl, S. A., & Fairbanks, M. M. (1986) The effects of vocabulary instruction: A model-based meta-analysis. *Review of Educational Research, 56,* 72–110.

Sternberg, R. J. (1987). Most vocabulary is learned from context. In M. G. McKeown & M. E. Curtis (Eds.), *The nature of vocabulary acquisition.* Hillsdale, NJ: Erlbaum.

Sternberg R. J., & Powell J. S. (1983). Comprehending verbal comprehension. *American Psychologist, 38,* 878–893.

Sternberg, R. J., Powell, J. S., & Kaye, D. B. (1983). Teaching vocabulary-building skills: A contextual approach. In A. C. Wilkinson (Ed.), *Classroom computers and cognitive science* (pp. 121–143). New York: Academic Press.

Swanburn, M. S. L., & de Glopper, K. (1999). Incidental word learning while reading: A meta-analysis. *Review of Educational Research, 69,* 261–285.

Thomas, M. H., & Wang, A. Y. (1996). Learning by the keyword mnemonic: Looking for long-term benefits. *Journal of Experimental Psychology: Applied, 2,* 330–342.

Thorndike, E. L. (1911). *Animal intelligence.* New York: Macmillan.

Thurstone, L. L. (1946). A note on a reanalysis of Davis' reading texts. *Psychometrica, 11,* 185–188.

Valdez-Menchaca, M. C., & Whitehurst, G. J. (1988). The effects of incidental teaching on vocabulary acquisition by young children. *Child Development, 59,* 1451–1459.

Valdez-Menchaca, M. C., & Whitehurst, G. J. (1992). Accelerating language development through picture book reading: A systematic extension to Mexican day care. *Developmental Psychology, 28,* 1106–1114.

Wang, A. Y., & Thomas, M. H. (1995). Effects of keyword on long-term retention: Help or hindrance? *Journal of Educational Psychology, 87,* 468–475.

Waxman, S. R., & Booth, A. E. (2000). Principles that are invoked in the acquisition of words, but not facts. *Cognition, 77,* B33–B43.

Wharton-McDonald, R., Pressley, M., & Hampston, J. M. (1998). Literacy instruction in nine first-grade classrooms: Teacher characteristics and student achievement. *Elementary School Journal, 99,* 101–128.

Whitehurst, G. J., Arnold, D. S., Epstein, J. N., Angel, A. L., Smith, M., & Fischel, J. E. (1994a). A picture book reading intervention in day care and home for children from low-income families. *Developmental Psychology, 30,* 679–689.

Whitehurst, G. J., Epstein, J. N., Angel, A. L., Payne, A. C., Crone, D. A., & Fischel, J. E. (1994b). Outcomes of an emergent literacy intervention in Head Start. *Journal of Educational Psychology, 86,* 542–555.

Whitehurst, G. J., Falco, F. L., Lonigan, C. J., Fischel, J. E., DeBaryshe, B. D., Valdez-Menchaca, M. C., et al. (1988). Accelerating language development through picture book reading. *Developmental Psychology, 24,* 552–559.

Whitehurst, G. J., Zevenbergen, A. A., Crone, D. A., Schultz, M. D., Velting,

O. N., & Fischel, J. E. (1999). Outcomes of an emergent literacy intervention from Head Start through second grade. *Journal of Educational Psychology, 91*, 261–272.

Wysocki, K., & Jenkins, J. R. (1987). Deriving word meanings through morphological generalization. *Reading Research Quarterly, 22*, 66–81.

Zevenbergen, A. A., Whitehurst, G. J., & Zevenbergen, J. A. (2003). Effects of a shared-reading intervention on the inclusion of evaluative devices in narratives of children from low-income families. *Journal of Applied Developmental Psychology, 24*, 115.

Zhang, Z., & Schumm, J. S. (2000). Exploring effects of the keyword method on limited English proficient students' vocabulary recall and comprehension. *Reading Research and Instruction, 39*, 202–221.

CHAPTER 12

Working Memory
A System for Learning

SUSAN E. GATHERCOLE

This chapter draws together recent findings and ideas concerning the nature and function of short-term memory during childhood. Why is it useful for humans to have short-term memory, a system whose time span is limited to mere seconds, and whose operation is highly vulnerable to disruption and information loss? The hypothesis evaluated in this chapter is that the primary function of this fragile but invaluable system is to support learning—probably across the lifespan, and certainly during the childhood years when so much knowledge and so many complex skills are acquired in a relatively short period of time.

WORKING MEMORY AS A MENTAL WORKSPACE

The theoretical account of short-term memory that has guided the work reviewed here is the "working memory" model originally advanced by Baddeley and Hitch in 1974. At the heart of the model is the *central executive*, a limited-capacity system with high-level functions that include coordinating the flow of information both within working memory and with other more permanent memory systems, the attentional control of action, shifting between cognitive activities, and updating the contents of working memory (e.g., Baddeley, 1986, 1996; Miyake, Friedman, Emerson, Witzki, & Howerter, 2000). The central executive is linked with three other components of working memory: the *phonological loop*,

233

specialized for the maintenance of material that can be represented in phonological form (Baddeley, 1986); the *visuospatial sketchpad,* which processes and stores nonverbal material; and the *episodic buffer,* which is responsible for the integration of cognitive events across different representation domains (Baddeley, 2000).

Baddeley and Hitch's (1974) article was also ground-breaking in its conceptualization of the role of short-term memory. In contrast to the traditional interpretation of short-term memory as a relatively passive and highly specialized storage device, these authors proposed that the short-term memory system plays an active and very flexible role in supporting complex cognitive processing in everyday life, and should therefore be viewed as a "working" memory. This concept of short-term memory as a workspace capable of storing and processing information in the course of ongoing cognitive activities is now widely accepted (Case, Kurland, & Goldberg, 1982; Daneman & Carpenter, 1980; Engle, Kane, & Tuholski, 1999; Just & Carpenter, 1992).

DEVELOPMENT AND VARIATION IN WORKING MEMORY

Many insights into the role of working memory in supporting learning have been gained by investigating the substantial degree of individual variation in working memory function in the general population. Working memory capacity increases steadily from about 4 years of age (the youngest point at which it can probably be reliably assessed) to about 14 years of age (Gathercole, Pickering, Ambridge, & Wearing, 2004), at which time performance is close to adult levels.

The substantial degree of individual variation is illustrated in Figure 12.1, based on data from the Working Memory Test Battery for Children (Pickering & Gathercole, 2001). The figure shows the mean scores and both 10th and 90th centile points between ages 5 and 14 years on memory span measures associated with the central executive. Within each age, individual differences are so great that in a regular class of schoolchildren, age-appropriate levels of working memory performance will vary by several years.

The scores in Figure 12.1 are derived from scores on three complex memory span tasks. Each task imposes simultaneous processing and storage demands. For example, one task is listening recall, in which the child listens to a series of spoken sentences, decides whether each one is true or false, and then at the end of the sequence of sentences at-

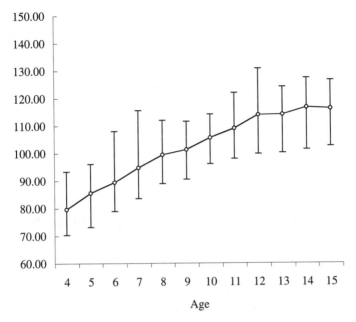

FIGURE 12.1. Composite working memory span scores from the Working Memory Test Battery for Children (Pickering & Gathercole, 2001) as a function of age. Values shown are means, 10th and 90th percentile points. Scores are standardized across the entire sample, with a mean of 100 and a standard deviation of 15.

tempts to recall the final word from each sentence in order. The task therefore involves both storage (of the final sentence words) and processing (of the meaning of each sentence). The processing and coordination element of this and other verbal complex span tasks such as backward digit recall and counting recall taps the central executive, whereas the phonological loop supports the verbal storage component of the task (Baddeley & Logie, 1999).

There are several theoretical accounts of developmental changes and individual variation in performance on complex span tasks. According to one influential view, both processing and storage are supported by a single limited resource. As the efficiency of processing increases with age, more of this resource is available to support storage, leading to improvements in task scores. An alternative view is that developmental increases in complex memory span result from faster processing times that in turn reduce time-based forgetting in the course of switching between the processing and storage elements of the tasks (e.g., Towse &

Hitch, 1995; Towse, Hitch, & Hutton, 1998). More recent evidence suggests that the developmental function arises from a complex interplay of factors that include time-based forgetting, intrinsic memory loads, and attentional processes (Barrouillet & Camos, 2001; Conlin, Gathercole, & Adams, 2003; Towse, Hitch, & Hutton, 2002).

This chapter appraises the relationship between working memory and successful learning in a number of different populations: in unselected samples, in children with special educational needs, and in children with specific difficulties with language. In each case, failure to show normal rates of learning is accompanied by poor working memory function.

WORKING MEMORY AND ACADEMIC ACHIEVEMENT

National assessments of children's achievements at particular points in their school careers (termed "key stages") were introduced following the implementation of a National Curriculum for state schools in England. Key stage 1 assessments take place at 6/7 years, key stage 2 assessments at 10/11 years, and key stage 3 assessments at 13/14 years. At each stage, the performance of each child is evaluated against expectations of normal levels of attainment at each age, with expected levels being 2 at key stage 1, 4 at key stage 2, and 5 or 6 at key stage 3. There are three areas of assessment: English (including literacy), mathematics, and science. Levels of achievement are based on measures ranging from teacher-based assessments to standardized tests.

Across a series of studies, we have evaluated the extent to which children's levels of attainment in these National Curriculum assessments are related to working memory function. In an initial study, we investigated the relationships between working memory function skills and key stage 1 assessments at 6 and 7 years of age (Gathercole & Pickering, 2000). The results were clear. The children who failed to meet the expected levels of achievement in English and mathematics for their age (i.e., obtaining below a level 2) performed more poorly on complex working memory span measures than children obtaining levels 2 and 3.

Subsequent studies have replicated these findings, and extended the relationships between working memory and scholastic attainment to subsequent key stages. Gathercole, Pickering, Knight, and Stegmann (2004) found that at both key stage 1 and key stage 3 (ages 7 and 14 years), scores on complex memory span tests were below average levels for children failing to achieve expected levels for their age in mathematics and science, and above average levels for those children exceeding nationally expected levels. English assessments at age 7, although not at age 14, were also directly related to working memory skill. Importantly, phonological loop skills did not show a comparable linear relationship with National Curriculum scores in either age group, indicating that the crucial constraining influence on learning was the central executive rather than the phonological loop.

A recent study by Jarvis and Gathercole (2003) further illuminated the nature of the relationship between working memory and scholastic attainment. This study included measures of both verbal and visuospatial complex memory, in order to test the possible domain-specificity of central executive resources and their links with learning. At both key stages 2 and 3 (ages 11 and 14, respectively), verbal and visuospatial working memory were both causally and separately linked with attainment levels, as shown in Figure 12.2. A degree of subject-specificity to the associations was found, with unique links between nonverbal working memory scores and both mathematics and science levels (but not English level) at both key stages.

The studies described so far have used cross-sectional designs to establish associations between working memory skills and school-based achievements at particular ages. However, if there is a genuine causal link between working memory and learning, working memory skills early in the child's school career should effectively predict later levels of

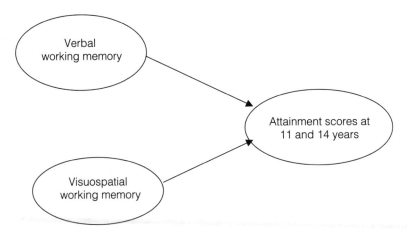

FIGURE 12.2. Schematic model of causal paths between working memory and attainment levels, at ages 11 and 14 years (Jarvis & Gathercole, 2003).

achievement. We tested this prediction in a longitudinal study in which children's verbal working memory abilities were assessed at school entry at 4 years and related to their later attainment levels at key stage 1 (Gathercole, Brown, & Pickering, 2003). Shortly after school entry, the children were also tested on local education authority "baseline assessments" in the areas of language, reading, writing, mathematics, and social skills.

The resulting causal paths between measures at age 4 and attainment levels in English and mathematics at key stage 1 are shown in Figure 12.3. Both the working memory and baseline assessment scores were directly linked to children's later achievements in the English assessments. Mathematics achievements at this stage, in contrast, were uniquely associated only with the school's own baseline assessments.

These findings indicate, first, that working memory measures and baseline assessments tap different underlying constructs; and second, that both constructs contribute significantly to learning in the area of literacy. We have argued that a fundamental distinction between the two types of assessment concerns the extent to which they tap previously acquired knowledge (Gathercole et al., 2003). Baseline assessments largely measure knowledge that the child has already gained in the course of his or her experiences and learning achievements prior to school. Examples of typical test items on baseline scales are whether or not the

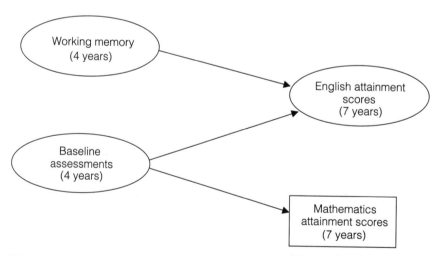

FIGURE 12.3. Schematic model of causal paths between working memory and baseline assessments at age 4 years, and key stage 1 attainment levels at age 7 years (Gathercole, Brown, & Pickering, 2003).

child can write his or her own name or recognize printed letters or digits. These are tasks that the child either can or cannot do, on the basis of previously acquired knowledge. In contrast, it is unlikely that any child has either encountered working memory tasks or the specific stimulus materials they employ before. Thus performance on these measures is constrained by a limited cognitive resource (working memory) rather than by crystallized knowledge. Consistent with this analysis, working memory assessments are relatively independent of general background factors such as socioeconomic status and preschool education (see, e.g., Alloway, Gathercole, Willis, & Adams, 2005a; Dollaghan, Campbell, Needleman, & Dunlosky, 1997), whereas baseline assessments are significantly associated with such factors (see, e.g., Lindsay & Desforges, 1999; Strand, 1999).

WORKING MEMORY AND SPECIAL EDUCATIONAL NEEDS

If poor working memory function does indeed directly constrain the capacity to learn complex skills and acquire new knowledge, children with extreme deficits of working memory should experience significant learning difficulties. The opportunity to test the hypothesis that deficits of working memory may be a direct cause of recognized learning difficulties was provided by the standardization study of the Working Memory Test Battery for Children (Pickering & Gathercole, 2001). Over 700 children between 4 and 15 years of age participated in this study. Of these, approximately 80 children had special educational needs that were identified by their schools. Once the test scores were standardized on the entire sample, we investigated the working memory profiles of the children with special educational needs, grouped according to their areas of learning difficulty (Pickering & Gathercole, 2004). Working memory profiles varied systematically as a function of the nature of the learning difficulties. In the group with learning difficulties in both literacy and mathematics, low scores on both working memory and phonological loop tests were 31 times more common than in the remainder of the standardization sample who had no special educational needs. In a smaller group of children whose learning difficulties were specific to language, this profile was 43 times more common than in the comparison sample. The degree of working memory impairment of these children with recognized learning difficulties was therefore very unusual in the general population. In comparison, children with recognized special educational needs of a noncognitive origin (such as children with behavioral problems) failed to show significantly inflated incidence of working memory deficits.

An important feature of this study is the direct comparison of working memory profiles in children with special needs with those of the larger population from which they were drawn, eliminating many of the usual biases of sampling in studies of special populations. The finding of very poor working memory function in children with difficulties in the areas of both literacy and mathematics has also been replicated in an independent sample of children between 7 and 11 years old (Gathercole, Alloway, Willis, & Adams, 2004; see also Alloway, Gathercole, Adams, & Willis, 2005b).

WORKING MEMORY AND SPECIFIC LANGUAGE IMPAIRMENT

There has been considerable interest in the working memory skills of children with a relatively common developmental pathology known as specific language impairment (SLI). SLI is diagnosed in children whose language development falls significantly below that expected on the basis of age, despite normal general cognitive function, sensory abilities, and other developmental experiences. In an early study, we discovered that children with SLI perform at even lower levels on measures of the phonological loop than on the language measures that form the criterial basis for their clinical diagnosis (Gathercole & Baddeley, 1990; see also Bishop, North, & Donlan, 1996; Dollaghan & Campbell, 1998; Montgomery, 1995).

Children with SLI also perform poorly on verbal complex memory span measures associated with the central executive (Ellis Weismer, Evans, & Hesketh, 1999; Montgomery, 2000). In a recent study, we investigated whether the phonological loop and central executive deficits in SLI co-occur or represent separable deficits (Archibald & Gathercole, in press). The results of this study were striking. Deficits in verbal complex memory span were present in all of the children with SLI, and the majority also showed deficits in phonological short-term memory. The co-occurrence of marked deficits in both the phonological loop and the central executive was rare in the general population, and approximately 50 times more common in the SLI group. This twinning of central executive and phonological loop deficits is also consistent with the working memory profiles of a small group of children with special educational needs that were specific to language (Pickering & Gathercole, 2004).

These findings suggest a core deficit of central executive function in SLI, with an additional impairment of the phonological loop in many of the cases. Despite the verbal storage demands of the complex memory span tasks used in these studies, the data cannot be explained in terms simply of an underlying phonological loop deficit. In a recent study we investigated the language abilities of children selected on the basis of consistently poor performance on phonological loop measures between 5 and 8 years of age (Gathercole, Tiffany, Briscoe, Thorn, & the ALSPAC Team, 2005). The memory deficits of this group were quite specific: their verbal complex memory span scores fell within the normal range. Importantly, their performance on a range of measures of language function—including vocabulary knowledge and language comprehension—was entirely normal. These data establish that a deficit of the phonological loop alone is not a sufficient condition for impaired language development. It should, however, be noted, that the low phonological loop group were impaired in learning of novel phonological forms, consistent with the view that the specific developmental function of the phonological loop is to support vocabulary acquisition (Baddeley, Gathercole, & Papagno, 1998). It therefore appears that by 8 years of age, the low phonological loop children were able to overcome their phonological learning impairment, possibly as a consequence both of the redundancy of language exposure and compensatory contributions of other intact cognitive learning systems.

We suggest that the more profound working memory deficits that characterize SLI cannot be overcome in these ways, and that such children cannot adequately meet the working memory demands of many learning situations. As a consequence, children with SLI fail to develop language and other high-level cognitive skills such as literacy and mathematics at a normal rate. The ability to hold information in mind for brief periods, possibly while carrying out effortful processing at the same time, is crucial to successful learning, and children with poor capacities to do this will not be able to complete many learning activities successfully. More direct evidence that working memory constrains classroom-based learning in this way is provided in the next section.

OBSERVING WORKING MEMORY
CONSTRAINTS ON LEARNING

Although the empirical relationship between working memory abilities and learning achievements across the childhood years is now well established, the ways in which poor working memory capacities constrain successful learning during specific learning activities have not to date been the subject of investigation. We have recently begun to address this issue in a study of children selected on the basis of very low scores on complex memory span measures at school entry at 4 years (Gathercole, Lamont, & Alloway, in press). The children were observed in the course of their regular classroom activities more than 1 year later, when they were 5 or 6 years of age. The observations focused on learning situations in which the working memory demands were judged to be significant, in terms either of the storage load or the combined processing and storage loads.

At the time of the observations, all of the low working memory children were working in the lowest ability groups in the class. Although the children were generally reserved and rarely volunteered information during group activities, their social adjustment was normal in terms of their relationships with teachers and peers. These children were observed failing during many routine classroom activities that imposed significant burdens on working memory. They encountered particular problems in tasks that required both memory storage and effortful processing, and in keeping track of their place in complex task structures. Examples of such activities include writing sentences from memory, carrying out numerical calculations abstracted from questions coached in everyday language, and counting words in sentences. In these situations, children frequently lost track of their place in the complex task structure, resulting in repetitions, place skipping, and task abandonment. The children also had poor memory for instructions given in the classroom, frequently failing to follow more than the first step in multistep commands. This profile of classroom failures was not observed in children with normal working memory function.

WORKING MEMORY AS A BOTTLENECK FOR LEARNING

Our proposal is that because children with low working memory often fail to meet the working memory demands of individual learning episodes, the incremental process of acquiring skill and knowledge over the school years is disrupted (Gathercole et al., in press). In this way, working memory can act as a bottleneck for learning in children with poor working memory skills. If this is the case, what can be done to ameliorate the learning difficulties resulting from impairments of working memory? While the ideal solution would be to remediate these memory impairments directly, there is little evidence that training working memory in children with low working memory skills leads to substantial gains in academic attainments (see, e.g., Turley-Ames & Whitfield, 2003).

We recommend instead an alternative approach to enhancing learning in children with poor working memory that is currently being implemented. The aim of the intervention is to minimize the memory-related failures in classroom-based learning activities frequently experienced by children with working memory impairments. The major focus is on methods for reducing working memory loads in target learning activities and facilitating the child's use of strategies to prevent working memory overload. Schools participating in the study receive guidance materials designed to promote understanding of working memory and its effective management in the classroom, and also participate in training workshops. The principles of the intervention and examples of ways of reducing working memory loads are outlined in our booklet *Understanding Working Memory: A Classroom Guide* (psychology.dur.ac.uk/research/wm/research.htm), and are summarized in Table 12.1.

At the core of the working memory intervention lies the need to reduce working memory loads where necessary. Cognitive theory identifies a number of ways in which this can be achieved. In activities that combine significant processing and storage demands, it may be useful to simplify the processing activity. For example, sentence writing was a source of particular difficulty for all of the children with low working memory that we observed. The processing loads involved in sentence writing can be diminished by reducing the linguistic complexity of the sentence—in terms either of the vocabulary (common vs. lower frequency words) or of the syntactic structures (simple subject–verb–object

---

TABLE 12.1. Principles of the Working Memory Intervention

- Evaluate the working demands of learning activities in lesson planning.
- Recognize the hallmarks of working memory failures: forgetting, losing place in complex tasks, and frequent task abandonment.
- In the case of task failures that are possibly due to excessive working memory loads, reduce working memory loads.
- Be prepared to offer crucial information repeatedly.
- Encourage the child to use appropriate memory aids, and provide the child with training in their use.
- Develop the child's use of memory-relieving strategies.

constructions rather than relative clauses). The planned sentences could also be reduced in length. If the child has to work with lengthy sentences and difficult words, the chances of task failure will increase dramatically, and opportunities for learning will be lost.

The working memory demands of tasks with a complex structure that require accurate place keeping can be reduced by breaking down the tasks into discrete steps, with memory support being made available where possible. External memory aids are in wide usage in classrooms. In our observational study, however, we found that children with poor working memory function often choose not to use such devices in the context of relatively complex tasks, and gravitate instead toward lower level strategies whose processing requirements may be less (such as simple counting) but are also less efficient (e.g., more error-prone and time-consuming). In order to facilitate children's effective use of such devices, it may be useful to give the child regular periods of practice in the use of the aids in the context of simple activities. Relevant spellings also function as useful memory aids in writing activities. Reducing the processing load and opportunity for error in spelling individual words will increase the child's success in completing the sentence as a whole. However, reading off information from such external aids was observed in itself to be a source of error in low memory children in our study, with children commonly losing their place within either the word or the sentence. Making available spellings of key words on the child's own whiteboard placed on his or her desk rather than a distant class board will reduce these errors by making the task of locating key information easier and reducing opportunities for distraction. Methods for marking the child's place in word spellings may also be useful, as loss of position within a word while copying was a frequent source of error and task abandonment.

It is also important to ensure that the child can remember the task that has been set. We observed many occasions in which children with low working memory failed to remember what was required of them. The child's memory for instructions is likely to be enhanced by keeping the instructions as brief and linguistically simple as possible. Instructions should be broken down into smaller constituent parts where possible, which will also have the advantage of reducing task complexity. One effective strategy for improving the child's memory for the task is frequent repetition of instructions. For tasks that take place over an extended period of time, reminding of crucial information rather than repetition of the original instruction is likely to be most useful. Finally, one of the best ways to ensure that the child has not forgotten crucial information is to ask him or her to repeat it back. Our observations indicate that the children themselves have good insight into their working memory failures.

CONCLUSIONS

It has been argued in this chapter that working memory acts as a gateway to learning, and that learning across the school years is severely compromised in children with poor working memory function. Typically, such children have relatively pervasive learning difficulties in the key areas of language, literacy, and mathematics. Our own work indicates that children with working memory impairments often fail to meet the working memory demands of structured learning activities in the classroom, and that this results in lost opportunities for learning that limit the rate and ease with which they reach milestones of scholastic achievement. We have proposed that learning will be most successful under conditions in which children's working memory capacities can match the memory demands of the situation. In a "memory-aware classroom," teaching staff would be sensitive to the working memory loads of learning activities, to the hallmarks of working memory overload, and to means of reducing excess working memory loads. Such a classroom environment would, we predict, be highly effective in enhancing learning outcomes for children with low memory.

ACKNOWLEDGMENTS

The research discussed in this chapter was supported by the Medical Research Council, the Wellcome Trust, and the Economic and Social Research Council.

REFERENCES

Alloway, T. P., Gathercole, S. E., Adams, A. M., & Willis, C. (2005a). Working memory and phonological awareness as predictors of progress towards early learning goals at school entry. *British Journal of Developmental Psychology*, *23*, 417–426.

Alloway, T. P., Gathercole, S. E., Adams, A.-M., & Willis, C. S. (2005b). Working memory abilities in children with special educational needs. *Educational and Child Psychology*, *22*, 56–67.

Archibald, L., & Gathercole, S. E. (in press). Short-term and working memory in specific language impairment. *International Journal of Communication Disorders.*

Baddeley, A. D. (1986). *Working memory.* Oxford, UK: Oxford University Press.

Baddeley, A. D. (1996). Exploring the central executive. *Quarterly Journal of Experimental Psychology, 49A,* 5–28.

Baddeley, A. D. (2000). The episodic buffer: A new component of working memory? *Trends in Cognitive Sciences, 4,* 417–423.

Baddeley, A. D., Gathercole, S. E., & Papagno, C. (1998). The phonological loop as a language learning device. *Psychological Review, 105,* 158–173.

Baddeley, A. D., & Hitch, G. (1974). Working memory. In G. Bower (Ed.), *The psychology of learning and motivation* (pp. 47–90). New York: Academic Press.

Baddeley, A. D., & Logie, R. H. (1999). The multiple-component model. In A. Miyake & P. Shah (Eds.), *Models of working memory: Mechanisms of active maintenance and executive control* (pp. 28–61). New York: Cambridge University Press.

Barrouillet, P., & Camos, V. (2001). Developmental increase in working memory span: Resource sharing or temporal decay? *Journal of Memory and Language, 45,* 1–20.

Bishop, D. V. M., North, T., & Donlan, C. (1996). Nonword repetition as a behavioural marker for inherited language impairment: Evidence from a twin study. *Journal of Child Psychology and Psychiatry, 37,* 391–403.

Case, R., Kurland, D. M., & Goldberg, J. (1982). Operational efficiency and the growth of short-term memory span. *Journal of Experimental Child Psychology, 33,* 386–404.

Conlin, J. A., Gathercole, S. E., & Adams, J. W. (2003). *Children's working memory: Investigating performance limitations in complex span tasks.* Manuscript submitted for publication.

Daneman, M., & Carpenter, P. A. (1980). Individual differences in working memory and reading. *Journal of Verbal Learning and Verbal Behavior, 19,* 450–466.

Dollaghan, C., & Campbell, T. F. (1998). Nonword repetition and child language impairment. *Journal of Speech, Language, and Hearing Research, 41,* 1136–1146.

Ellis Weismer, S., Evans, J., & Hesketh, L. (1999). An examination of working memory capacity in children with specific language impairment. *Journal of Speech, Language, and Hearing Research, 42,* 1249–1260.

Engle, R. W., Kane, M. J., & Tuholski, S. W. (1999). Individual differences in working memory capacity and what they tell us about controlled attention, general fluid intelligence, and functions of the prefrontal cortex. In A. Miyake & P. Shah (Eds.), *Models of working memory: Mechanisms of active maintenance and executive control* (pp. 102–134). New York: Cambridge University Press.

Gathercole, S. E., Alloway, T. P., Willis, C., & Adams, A. M. (2004). *Working memory in children with literacy and mathematical difficulties.* Manuscript submitted for publication.

Gathercole, S. E., & Baddeley, A. D. (1990). Phonological memory deficits in language disordered children: Is there a causal connection? *Journal of Memory and Language, 29,* 336–360.

Gathercole, S. E., Brown, L., & Pickering, S. J. (2003). Working memory assessments at school entry as longitudinal predictors of National Curriculum attainment levels. *Educational and Child Psychology, 20,* 109–122.

Gathercole, S. E., Lamont, E., & Alloway, T. P. (2006). Working memory in the classroom. In S. J. Pickering & G. Phye (Eds.), *Working memory and education.* New York: Academic Press.

Gathercole, S. E., & Pickering, S. J. (2000). Working memory deficits in children with low achievements in the National Curriculum at seven years of age. *British Journal of Educational Psychology, 70,* 177–194.

Gathercole, S. E., Pickering, S. J., Ambridge, B., & Wearing, H. (2004). The structure of working memory from 4 to 15 years of age. *Developmental Psychology, 40,* 177–190.

Gathercole, S. E., Pickering, S. J., Knight, C., & Stegmann, Z. (2004). Working memory skills and educational attainment: Evidence from National Curriculum assessments at 7 and 14 years of age. *Applied Cognitive Psychology, 40,* 1–16.

Gathercole, S. E., Tiffany, C., Briscoe, J., Thorn, A. S. C., & the ALSPAC Team. (2005). Developmental consequences of phonological loop deficits during early childhood: A longitudinal study. *Journal of Child Psychology and Psychiatry, 46,* 598–611.

Jarvis, H. L., & Gathercole, S. E. (2003). Verbal and non-verbal working memory and achievements on National Curriculum tests at 11 and 14 years of age. *Educational and Child Psychology, 20,* 123–140.

Just, M. A., & Carpenter, P. A. (1992). A capacity theory of comprehension: Individual differences in working memory. *Psychological Review, 99,* 122–149.

Lindsay, G., & Desforges, M. (1999). Computerised baseline assessment of literacy. *Journal of Research in Reading, 22,* 55–66.

Miyake, A., Friedman, N. P., Emerson, M. J., Witzki, A. H., Howerter, A., & Wager, T. D. (2000). The unity and diversity of executive functions and their contributions to complex "frontal lobe" tasks: A latent variable analysis. *Cognitive Psychology, 41,* 49–100.

Montgomery, J. (1995). Sentence comprehension in children with specific language impairment: The role of phonological working memory. *Journal of Speech and Hearing Research, 38,* 187–199.

Montgomery, J. (2000). Verbal working memory in sentence comprehension in children with specific language impairment. *Journal of Speech, Language, and Hearing Research, 43,* 293–308.

Pickering, S. J., & Gathercole, S. E. (2001). *Working memory test battery for children.* London: Psychological Corporation UK.

Pickering, S. J., & Gathercole, S. E. (2004). Distinctive working memory profiles in children with special educational needs. *Educational Psychology, 24,* 393–408.

Strand, S. (1999). Baseline assessment, value-added and the prediction of reading. *Journal of Research in Reading, 22,* 14–26.

Towse, J. N., & Hitch, G. J. (1995). Is there a relationship between task demand and storage space in tests of working memory capacity? *Quarterly Journal of Experimental Psychology, 48,* 108–124.

Towse, J. N., Hitch, G. J., & Hutton, U. (1998). A re-evaluation of working memory capacity in children. *Journal of Memory and Language, 39,* 195–217.

Towse, J. N., Hitch, G. J., & Hutton, U. (2002). On the nature of the relationship between processing activity and item retention in children. *Journal of Experimental Child Psychology, 82,* 156–184.

Turley-Ames, K., & Whitfield, M. M. (2003). Strategy training and working memory task performance. *Journal of Memory and Language, 49,* 446–468.

CHAPTER 13

An Individual-Differences Approach to the Study of Reading Comprehension

CHRISTOPHER SCHATSCHNEIDER
ERIN RENEE HARRELL
JULIE BUCK

Recently, there has been a shift in educational research favoring experimental studies that employ random assignment to conditions (Levin, 2004). The idea is that experiments that employ random assignment and have control over a small set of variables to be manipulated will yield more causal information than will quasi-experimental and correlational studies (Shadish, Cook, & Campbell, 2002). Indeed, the hierarchy of studies that produce causal information appears to range from randomized control studies, which carry the most causal information, to correlational studies, which are thought to carry the least amount of causal information. In spite of the limitations of correlational research to yield much causal information, these studies nevertheless play an important role in educational research, including research into the processes of becoming a skillful reader (Stanovich & Cunningham, 2004).

One important role that correlational studies play in the research into reading development is that they are able to produce information about how individual differences in cognitive abilities relate to differences in reading outcomes. That is, they provide information about potential cognitive skills that may be targeted for intervention in randomized control trial studies to investigate whether targeting these skills for intervention will produce gains in reading ability. For example, early work in the area of phonological processing as it relates to reading was essentially correlative in nature (Calfee, Lindamood, & Lindamood, 1973; Bradley & Bryant, 1978). It wasn't until the "second and third wave" of research into phonological processing that we began to see actual experimental and intervention studies on the impact of phonological processing on reading development (Stanovich, 2000). Of course, not all correlational studies lead to causal relations. This is certainly true in the area of reading acquisition. Many constructs have been found to correlate with reading, including visiomotor, visiospatial, and other perceptual tests that when put through a more rigorous test have not proven themselves to be as important as their correlations suggest (Schatschneider, Fletcher, Francis, Carlson, & Foorman, 2004). In fact, numerous constructs have been investigated to determine their role in the development and acquisition of literacy skills. Sometimes these constructs become the target for intervention research in investigating ways of improving outcomes in reading. Strong correlative relationships provide the impetus needed to test these relations out in a causally meaningful design. Below we present an individual-differences study investigating the correlates of reading comprehension. By conducting studies such as these, it is our hope that meaningful cognitive processes can be uncovered that will lead to furthering our understanding of this complex cognitive task.

INDIVIDUAL DIFFERENCES IN READING COMPREHENSION

There have been numerous individual-differences studies investigating the relationship between various cognitive components and reading comprehension (Daneman, 1991). Constructs such as eye movement control (Pavlidis, 1981), perceptual span (Rayner & Duffy, 1988), phonological awareness (Wagner, Torgesen, Laughon, Simmons, & Rashotte, 1993), word recognition (Stanovich, 1986), working memory (Swanson, 1992), vocabulary (Beck & McKeown, 1991), listening comprehension (Daneman & Carpenter, 1980), background knowledge (Kahmi, 2005), and various other higher order thinking and reasoning skills (Oakhill & Yuill, 1986) have all been investigated as being potentially correlated with reading comprehension.

One limitation in many of the studies listed above is that they often do not simultaneously include other predictors thought to be important in reading comprehension. Studies that employ multiple predictors can employ a regression strategy that will allow a direct comparison of the relative impacts each predictor has upon a dependent variable. Additionally, including multiple predictors of various constructs in a single study allows for an investigation of potential interaction effects. That is, it's possible that some constructs are more or less predictive of reading comprehension at various levels of other variables. The goals of the present study were to identify and assemble a battery of cognitive measures that were shown to be highly related to reading comprehension from other studies of individual differences and to administer them to a large number of children that ranged widely in age. In this way, we could compete the most predictive predictors of reading comprehension against each other, explore potential interactive effects, and also investigate the changing nature of these relationships across a wide age range of students. Based upon a review of the literature, we chose the following constructs: oral reading fluency, vocabulary, listening comprehension, reasoning and inferential skills (IQ), and working memory.

ORAL READING FLUENCY

Oral reading fluency is the ability to accurately and efficiently read aloud a selected passage of text (Fuchs, Fuchs, Hosp, & Jenkins, 2001). Skill in oral reading fluency represents a

> complicated, multifaceted performance that entails, for example, a readers' perceptual skill at automatically translating letters into coherent sound representations, unitizing those sound components into recognizable wholes and automatically accessing lexical representations, processing meaningful connections within and between sentences, relating text meaning to prior information, and making inferences to supply missing information. (Fuchs et al., 2001, p. 240)

Studies of oral reading fluency and reading comprehension have shown moderate to high correlations between oral reading fluency and reading comprehension. In one study, Fuchs, Fuchs, and Maxwell (1988) obtained three measures of reading comprehension and one oral reading fluency measure from 70 middle- and junior-high-school students with reading disabilities and found a correlation of .91 between oral reading fluency and reading comprehension as measured by a group-administered nationally normed test. The relationship between reading fluency and comprehension has also been borne out in experimental studies. Interventions that increase reading fluency have been shown to produce gains in reading comprehension, even of new material not included in the intervention (Therrien, 2004).

VOCABULARY

Vocabulary, or word knowledge, usually refers to the ability to understand the meanings of words. But what does it mean to understand the meaning of words (Beck & McKeown, 1991)? It's clear that "to know" a word is not an all-or-none proposition. People can have various degrees of understanding of a word, from "never heard it before" to "heard it but can't quite define it" to "can't define it, but can use it in a sentence" to "knows it extremely well in all of its nuanced meanings." The estimation of how well one understands a word is often referred to as *depth* of vocabulary (Beck, McKeown, & Kucan, 2002). Another aspect of vocabulary is *breadth*, or simply how many words a person knows. Measures of vocabulary often tap both these domains to varying degrees. Regardless of whether a measure of vocabulary stresses depth or breadth, it appears that word knowledge is highly related to reading comprehension. It seems intuitively obvious that in order to comprehend a passage of text, it would be important to understand most, if not all, of the words in that passage. Therefore, it is not surprising that researchers have often found a strong correlation between vocabulary and reading comprehension (Stanovich, Nathan, & Vala-Rossi, 1986; Oakland, de Mesquita, & Buckley, 1988; Roth, Speece, & Cooper, 2002).

LISTENING COMPREHENSION

Listening comprehension is another construct that shows a strong relationship with reading comprehension. In the simple view of reading (Gough & Tunmer, 1986; Hoover & Gough, 1990), listening comprehension plays a key role. In this theory, reading comprehension is a sole product of the ability to decode words and listening comprehension. An implication of this theory is that if you are able to read the words of a passage, then the sole determinant of reading comprehension is listening comprehension. This view of reading is supported by correlational research that suggests that the relationship between listening and reading comprehension increases as children become more proficient readers, with correlations approaching .80 for high-school and college students (Daneman, 1991; Daneman & Carpenter, 1980; Sticht & James, 1984; Curtis, 1980). However, this large correlation is not surprising given the numerous subskills that are thought to comprise listening comprehension. Attention, vocabulary knowledge, inferential reasoning, and syntactic and semantic awareness, among others, play a role in the ability to effectively comprehend ideas and information presented orally.

IQ

There have been a plethora of studies indicating a strong relationship between IQ and reading ability (Kaufman, Lichtenberger, & McLean, 2001), with higher correlations reported between IQ and reading comprehension (Spear-Swerling & Sternberg, 1994) than IQ and decoding skill (Torgesen, 1989). The higher correlation between reading comprehension and IQ is understood to reflect the similar demands on "higher order" cognitive processes such as abstraction of background knowledge, integration of new information with existing information, and other strategic and inferential processes (van den Bos, Brand-Gruwel, & Lind, 1998). Although there is a current push in the field to remove IQ from the definition of reading disability (Fletcher et al., 2002), this effort is not due, by any means, to any question about the strong relationship between IQ and reading.

WORKING MEMORY

Implicit in many theories of reading comprehension is the idea that short-term memory plays an important part. Whether processing phonological information to form words, or holding a number of words in memory to identify syntactic structure, short-term memory is thought to be a critical component in many of these activities. However, many of the tasks used to assess simple memory span have not been shown to be strong correlates of reading comprehension (Daneman, 1991). While these tasks that tap "passive storage capacity" have not been strongly related to reading, more complex memory tasks that force people to process information while simultaneously holding information in storage appear to have a stronger relationship with reading comprehension (Swanson & Howell, 2001). Memory tasks that have both storage and processing components are often referred to as "working memory" tasks. Correlations of these types of memory tasks with reading comprehension have a higher relationship with reading comprehension, with some correlations approaching .70 being reported across a wide range of ages (Swanson & Howell, 2001).

METHOD

Participants

Participants were 585 students in grades 3, 7, and 10 (n = 218, 188, 180, respectively) attending low-, middle-, and high-socioeconomic-status schools in three school districts in Florida. These districts were selected to represent Florida demographics within the schools. Every student in classrooms where teachers agreed to participate was asked to return a consent form. Of the students who returned parent consents, participants were randomly selected.

Fifty-seven percent of participants were female. Forty-one percent of participants were white, 38% were African American, and 17% were Hispanic. Seventeen percent of participants indicated that they spoke Spanish, 5% Haitian–Creole, and 2% French. Student characteristics by grade are presented in Table 13.1.

Materials and Procedures

A 2-hour battery of tests was individually administered to participants after they had taken the Florida Comprehensive Assessment Test (FCAT) in March. Students were tested in April, May, or June. The assessments were conducted by testers who completed rigorous training and reached an acceptable level of proficiency in test administration. All protocols were checked by a second rater.

The testing battery included tests assessing oral reading fluency, listening and reading comprehension, word reading and decoding efficiency, working memory, verbal reasoning, and nonverbal reasoning. All of the measures, except for the measures of listening comprehension and working memory, were standardized tests.

Reading Fluency and Efficiency Measures

The Sight Word Efficiency and Phonemic Decoding Efficiency subtests of the Test of Word Reading Efficiency (TOWRE; alpha = .95) were ad-

TABLE 13.1. Demographics and Sample Characteristics

Demographics	Third grade (n = 215)	Seventh grade (n = 188)	Tenth grade (n = 182)
Gender			
Male	49%	37%	51%
Race/ethnicity			
Caucasian/white	39%	47%	37%
African American	42%	34%	36%
Hispanic	15%	13%	24%
Asian	1%	4%	2%
Other/multiracial	3%	2%	1%
Mother's education			
Not given	20%	10%	20%
Elementary	3%	1%	0%
Junior high	4%	5%	4%
High school/GED	37%	42%	39%
College degree	28%	28%	30%
Graduate degree	8%	14%	7%
Free/reduced lunch			
Did not qualify	55%	60%	76%
Free lunch	40%	34%	0%
Reduced lunch	5%	6%	4%

ministered (Torgesen, Wagner, & Rashotte, 1999). For the Sight Word Efficiency subtest, students read a list of words for 45 seconds. Their scores were based on the number of correctly pronounced words read. The Phonemic Decoding Efficiency subtest required students to read a list of nonwords. Again, their scores were based on the number of correctly read nonwords in 45 seconds.

Multiple types of oral reading fluency (ORF) measures were administered to students. Students read three standardized ORF passages (AIMSweb, 2002). Each passage was grade-specific, although 10th-grade students read eighth-grade ORF passages since AIMSweb does not provide passages for grades above eight. The median number of words read correctly in 1 minute on these three passages was the students' final score. Three passages extracted from textbooks on the state adoption list for each grade, and three passages taken from the practice items on the FCAT, were read. Each set of passages were administered and scored in the same manner as the AIMSweb ORF passages. Again, the median number of words read correctly was the students' final score for the textbook passages and the FCAT passages.

Vocabulary

Vocabulary was measured using the Vocabulary subtest of the Wechsler Abbreviated Scales of Intelligence (WASI). This 42-item task includes low-end picture items where items 1–4 require the examinee to name pictures that are displayed one at a time, while items 5–42 are orally and visually presented words that the examinee must define orally. The reliability coefficients reported for Vocabulary in the third, seventh, and 10th grade are .88, .86, and .90, respectively.

Listening Comprehension

Listening comprehension was assessed by orally presenting three passages to students that were previously used in Florida's statewide reading assessment test. Passages were shortened such that no passage took more than 2 minutes to read. When the passage was completed, the examiners read a series of multiple-choice questions that the students had to answer.

Intelligence

In addition to the Vocabulary subtest of the WASI, three other subtests were administered: Block Design, Similarities, and Matrix Reasoning. The WASI Block Design subtest is a measure of perceptual organization and general intelligence designed to tap abilities related to spatial visualization, visuomotor coordination, and abstract conceptualization. The reliability coefficients for Block Design in the third, seventh, and 10th grade are .92, .92, and .89, respectively. The WASI Similarities subtest is a measure of abstract verbal reasoning ability. The examinee is asked to identify relationships between pairs of words, either presented verbally or through pictures. The reliability coefficients for Similarities in the third, seventh, and 10th grade are .89, .85, and .83, respectively. The WASI Matrix Reasoning subtest is a measure of nonverbal fluid reasoning and general intellectual ability. It is a series of 35 incomplete patterns that the examinee completes by pointing to or stating the number of the correct response from five possible choices. The reliability coefficients for Matrix Reasoning in the third, seventh, and 10th grade are .93, .89, and .86, respectively.

Working Memory

To measure working memory, an adapted version of Gaulin and Campbell's (1994) Competing Language Processing Task was developed. The reading span measure involved the student reading a true or false sentence out loud (e.g., "Candy is sweet," "Triangles are round"). After reading each sentence, the student stated whether the sentence was true or false. After reading a group of sentences, ranging from only one sentence to six sentences, the student was asked to recall the last word in each sentence. Each sentence was three words long. If the student correctly recalled fewer than half of the words, then the task was stopped and the student's score was calculated. The listening span task was similar, except that each sentence was read to the student. The scoring and stop rules were the same for both the listening and the reading span tasks.

Reading Comprehension

Reading comprehension was assessed using the Reading Comprehension subtest of the Gray Oral Reading Test (GORT-4). The GORT-4 is a test of oral reading rate, accuracy, fluency, and comprehension. It is appropriate for individuals ages 6 to 18 years, 11 months. The GORT-4 contains 14 separate stories that increase in difficulty. Each story is followed by five multiple-choice comprehension questions. The reliability coefficients for the GORT-4 in the third, seventh, and 10th grade are .94, .91, and .85, respectively.

RESULTS

Statistical Analyses

Means, standard deviations, and numbers of subjects for the student assessment data are presented in Table 13.2. The assessment data from the third-, seventh-, and 10th-grade students were analyzed in two main stages. First, we conducted principal components analyses using an oblique rotation to reduce the number of variables for further analysis. Oblique rotation, which allows the rotated factors to correlate, was chosen because the cognitive constructs extracted from these factor analyses will undoubtedly be intercorrelated. In order to determine the number of factors to retain for subsequent analyses, we used three different criteria: Kaiser's rule (retain all factors with eigenvalues greater that 1.0), scree plots, and a minimum of at least 70% of the total variance from the original variables should be accounted for in the factors (Stevens, 1992). Once satisfied with the number of factors to retain, we interpreted the

TABLE 13.2. Means, Standard Deviations, and Numbers of Children by Grade in School

Measures	Third grade	Seventh grade	Tenth grade
TOWRE Sight Word Efficiency[a]			
Mean	103.34	102.05	91.96
SD	14.56	11.87	10.33
n	215	188	182
TOWRE Phonemic Decoding[a]			
Mean	100.49	100.60	91.17
SD	16.03	14.81	16.19
n	215	188	182
WASI Vocabulary[b]			
Mean	48.71	48.53	46.40
SD	11.81	9.25	9.27
n	210	184	177
WASI Similarities[b]			
Mean	53.28	49.39	47.43
SD	11.15	10.94	9.60
n	210	186	182
WASI Block Design[b]			
Mean	49.81	49.48	47.43
SD	10.62	10.94	9.60
n	213	186	182
WASI Matrix Reasoning[b]			
Mean	52.05	49.93	47.03
SD	10.87	8.98	8.98
n	210	186	182
ORF FCAT[c]			
Mean	95.58	124.25	155.16
SD	39.72	30.48	33.60
n	215	187	181
ORF Grade-Based[c]			
Mean	104.60	154.39	156.80
SD	41.92	37.05	34.49
n	215	187	181
ORF Text-Based[c]			
Mean	92.55	125.99	136.21
SD	41.35	32.38	28.60
n	215	188	182
Reading Span			
Mean	19.22	25.80	24.87
SD	8.05	6.54	7.16
n	214	186	182

TABLE 13.2. (continued)

Measures	Third grade	Seventh grade	Tenth grade
Listening Span			
Mean	19.68	25.18	24.94
SD	7.89	7.19	7.85
n	215	187	182
Listening Comprehension			
Mean	10.19	11.31	7.79
SD	3.11	3.20	2.18
n	213	186	182
GORT-Comprehension[d]			
Mean	9.10	9.03	8.06
SD	3.02	3.18	2.41
n	163	147	150

[a]Test of Word Reading Efficiency; [b]Weschler Abbreviated Scale of Intelligence; [c]Oral Reading Fluency; [d]Gray Oral Reading Test.

factors based upon the zero-order correlations of the variables with the factors. Variables with the highest correlations carried the most weight in determining the labeling of the factor.

Based upon the results of the factor analyses, we created unit-weighted composites of those factors. These composites were then used in a series of regression analyses to predict reading comprehension. All of the composites were z-scored prior to analyses to aid in the interpretation of the results and to decrease unnecessary collinearity among the predictor variables and the interaction terms (Aiken & West, 1991). Because of our interest in potential curvilinear and interaction effects, we decided to conduct our analyses in the following manner. First, we tested all of the constructs separately to see if any of them demonstrated a significant curvilinear (quadratic) relationship with reading comprehension. If any construct was found to have a significant quadratic relationship to reading comprehension, then this term was retained for further analyses of potential interaction effects with other constructs. This strategy gives a priority to polynomial terms over interactions. Because of the anticipated moderate correlation among the constructs, it is possible to observe a significant interaction between two correlated variables when no interaction exists (Lubinski & Humphreys, 1990). This can occur if one of the variables has a quadratic relationship with the outcome variable that is not modeled in the regression analyses. After potential quadratic relationships are investigated, we started to build regression models using all of the composites constructed from the factor analyses, and all possible *n*-way interaction terms. In the first step, we tested the significance of the highest order interaction term. If this term was found to be significant, we stopped the model building and attempted to interpret the interaction. However, if this term was found to be nonsignificant, the term was removed from the model, and the next level of *n*-way interactions was tested. If this next level of *n*-way interactions was nonsignificant, by both demonstrating no uniquely significant terms and by not being significant as a set, those terms were removed from the analyses and the next lower level of *n*-way interactions was examined in the same manner. This process was repeated until either a significant interaction term was detected or all of the potential interactions were eliminated from the model. This strategy is in alignment with the procedures proposed by Appelbaum and Cramer (1974) to investigate nonorthogonal effects. If any significant interaction terms were found to be significant, we followed them up with tests of simple effects proposed by Cohen, Cohen, West, and Aiken (2002).

Third Grade

Twelve variables were entered into a principal components analysis with oblique rotation: two subtests of the TOWRE (Sight Word Efficiency and Phonemic Decoding Efficiency), four subtests of the WASI (Vocabulary, Similarities, Block Design, and Matrix Reasoning), three composite measures of oral reading fluency, a measure of listening comprehension, and two measures of working memory (reading span and listening span).

The results of the principal components analysis indicated that either a three- or a four-factor solution would provide an adequate representation of the covariances among the 12 measures. Kaiser's rule indicated a three-factor solution (with eigenvalues of the four largest components being 6.3, 1.48, 1.01, and .91, respectively). The scree plot, however, showed a definite flattening at components 5 and 6 and beyond, with eigenvalues of .58 and .54, respectively. Additionally, a three-factor solution accounts for 74% of the covariation among the measures, while a four-factor solution accounts for 80% of the covariation. While either a three- or a four-factor solution could have been argued, we decided to retain four because the fourth component's eigenvalue was close to 1, and the scree plot indicated a four-factor solution.

The correlations of the four retained components with the original measures, along with the component intercorrelations, are presented in

Table 13.3. The first component had the highest correlations with the two subtests of the TOWRE and the three oral reading fluency composites. All of these measures tap the speed at which words (and nonwords) are read, either in isolation or in context. These measures are all thought to be measures of reading fluency (Fuchs et al., 2001). We therefore labeled this construct Fluency. The second component had the highest correlations with the Vocabulary and Similarities subtest of the WASI and the measure of listening comprehension. The Vocabulary and Similarities subtests represent the Verbal IQ component of the WASI, and all three of these constructs tap into a domain of verbal ability, broadly defined. This component was labeled Verbal Ability, or simply Verbal. The third and fourth components were each represented by two measures with high correlations. The third component had high correlations with the Block Design and Matrix Reasoning subtests of the WASI and was named Nonverbal Ability, or simply Nonverbal. The fourth composite had high correlations with reading span and listening span of our working memory subtest and was therefore called Memory. Finally, in addition to identifying these four composites, we also noted that these

TABLE 13.3. Factor Loadings (Correlations) and Factor Intercorrelations for the Third-Grade Battery

Measures	Fluency	Verbal	Nonverbal	Memory
Listening comprehension	.49	**.82**	.39	.41
TOWRE Sight Word Efficiency	**.92**	.51	.41	.26
TOWRE Phonemic Decoding Efficiency	**.88**	.46	.43	.25
WASI Vocabulary	.58	**.90**	.40	.44
WASI Block Design	.49	**.89**	.40	.28
WASI Similarities	.35	.37	**.90**	.27
WASI Matrix Reasoning	.42	.47	**.86**	.33
ORF Grade-Based	**.96**	.58	.34	.36
ORF FCAT	**.96**	.58	.35	.37
ORF Text-Based	**.95**	.55	.37	.35
Reading Span	.21	.34	.26	**.87**
Listening Span	.39	.39	.30	**.85**
Intercorrelations				
Fluency	1.00			
Verbal	.56	1.00		
Nonverbal	.40	.43	1.00	
Memory	.34	.41	.31	1.00

Note. n = 200.

constructs were moderately correlated with one another, with correlations ranging from .31 to .56. These sizable correlations were anticipated and further justify our use of an oblique rotation.

These four composites were then used in a series of multiple regressions outlined above. First, none of the composites showed evidence for a quadratic relationship with reading comprehension. Therefore, a full model was constructed with all four main effect terms, six two-way interactions, four three-way interactions, and one four-way interaction. Following the procedures outlined in Appelbaum and Cramer (1974), we tested a series of models that reduced in complexity as we examined the highest order interaction terms in each model and removed them if they did not demonstrate statistical significance. In these models, none of the n-way interaction terms achieved statistical significance and our final model consisted of simply four main effects.

The results of this final model along with the intercorrelations among the composites and reading comprehension are reported in Tables 13.4a and 13.4b. All of the composite variables were significantly correlated with reading comprehension. Fluency, Verbal Ability, and Nonverbal Ability all accounted for unique variance in reading comprehension, with 5%, 6%, and 2% of the variance uniquely accounted for, respectively. Memory was not uniquely related to reading comprehension. Finally, this model accounted for 45% of the total variance in reading comprehension.

Seventh Grade

The same 12 variables that were examined in the third-grade principal components analysis were used in the seventh-grade analysis. Kaiser's

TABLE 13.4a. Estimated Correlations for the Third-Grade Cognitive Composites and GORT Comprehension

Composites	Fluency	Verbal Ability	Nonverbal Ability	Memory	GORT Comprehension
Fluency	1.00				
Verbal Ability	.52	1.00			
Nonverbal Ability	.41	.44	1.00		
Memory	.34	.40	.38	1.00	
GORT Comprehension	.54	.58	.46	.41	1.00

Note. n = 163.

TABLE 13.4b. Estimated Parameters for the Third-Grade Regression Analyses

Parameter	Estimate	Standard error	t	p	Semipartial r^2
Intercept	7.74	.35	22.05	.0001	
Fluency	0.84	.22	3.73	.0003	.05
Verbal Ability	0.67	.16	4.23	.0001	.06
Nonverbal Ability	0.57	.25	2.28	.0237	.02
Memory	0.45	.24	1.89	.0610	.01
Total R^2	.45				

Note. n = 163.

rule and the scree plot both indicated that a three-factor solution would adequately represent the covariation among the variables, with the eigenvalues of the first five components being 5.9, 1.7, 1.3, .7, and .6, respectively. The first three components accounted for 74% of the covariation among the measures.

The correlations of the measures to the three components are shown in Table 13.5. The pattern of correlations for the first component was identical to the pattern found in third grade, with the three oral reading fluency measures and the two reading efficiency measures from the TOWRE showing the highest correlations. We retained the label of Fluency for this factor. The second component had the highest correlations with all four subtests of the WASI and with listening comprehension. The four subtests of the WASI represent the Full Scale IQ construct from that measure. All of these tests require some kind of higher order reasoning and inferencing. Therefore, we named this component Reasoning Ability, or Reasoning. This component represents the combining of components two and three from the third-grade analyses. The last component had the highest correlations with the working memory measures and was labeled Memory.

All three of these components were first examined separately to see if they exhibited a quadratic relationship with reading comprehension. Reasoning was found to have a quadratic relationship with the dependent variable, $F(1,144) = 4.63$, $p < .05$. Therefore, both the linear and the quadratic term for Reasoning were used in subsequent analyses. Following the same strategy as employed in the third-grade regression analyses, we fit a full factorial model in the prediction of reading comprehension, but we also included the quadratic term for Reasoning. No

TABLE 13.5. Factor Loadings and Factor Intercorrelations for the Seventh Grade Battery

Measures	Fluency	Reasoning	Memory
Listening comprehension	.45	**.72**	.30
TOWRE Sight Word Efficiency	**.87**	.36	.27
TOWRE Phonemic Decoding Efficiency	**.89**	.39	.20
WASI Vocabulary	.53	**.82**	.13
WASI Block Design	.49	**.85**	.06
WASI Similarities	.29	**.81**	.22
WASI Matrix Reasoning	.31	**.70**	.38
ORF Grade-Based	**.94**	.52	.18
ORF FCAT	**.95**	.55	.18
ORF Text-Based	**.94**	.51	.19
Reading Span	.22	.16	**.87**
Listening Span	.22	.35	**.82**
Intercorrelations			
Fluency	1.00		
Reasoning	.49	1.00	
Memory	.21	.23	1.00

Note. n = 179.

significant interactions among the cognitive components were detected. The results of the final model, along with the intercorrelations among the predictors and reading comprehension, are presented in Tables 13.6a and 13.6b. All of the composite variables were significantly correlated with reading comprehension. Reasoning and Fluency, along with the quadratic term for Reasoning, accounted for unique variance in reading comprehension, with 23%, 3%, and 2% of the variance uniquely accounted for, respectively. Memory was not uniquely related to reading comprehension. Finally, this model accounted for 56% of the total variance in reading comprehension. In comparing this model to the third-

TABLE 13.6a. Estimated Correlations for the Seventh-Grade Cognitive Composites and GORT Comprehension

Composites	Fluency	Reasoning	Memory	GORT Comprehension
Fluency	1.00			
Reasoning	.55	1.00		
Memory	.28	.32	1.00	
GORT Comprehension	.55	.71	.29	1.00

Note. n = 146.

TABLE 13.6b. Estimated Parameters for the Seventh-Grade Regression Analyses

Parameter	Estimate	Standard error	t	p	Semipartial r^2
Intercept	8.70	.24	36.13	.0001	
Fluency	.76	.24	3.11	.0023	.03
Reasoning	2.47	.29	8.63	.0001	.23
Memory	.11	.21	0.50	.6168	.00
Reasoning * Reasoning	.62	.28	2.20	.0291	.02
Total R^2	.56				

Note. n = 146.

grade model, it appears that Reasoning is playing a larger role in predicting unique variance in reading comprehension than the combination of Verbal and Nonverbal Ability did in third grade. In third grade, Verbal and Nonverbal Ability accounted for a combined 8% of the unique variance in reading comprehension, while in seventh grade, the Reasoning component, which is a composite of Verbal and Nonverbal Ability, accounts for 25% of the unique variance, when both the linear and the quadratic terms are combined.

To demonstrate the quadratic relationship between Reasoning and reading comprehension in the presence of Reasoning Ability, a series of graphs were created and appear in Figures 13.1a and 13.1b. Figure 13.1a shows a scatterplot of the relationship between Reasoning and reading comprehension after regressing out the influences of the other predictor variables in the final model. To further highlight the changing nature of the relationship between Reasoning and reading comprehension, students who scored a full standard deviation below the nationally normed average were represented by triangles, while those students above that point were designated with circles. As seen in Figure 13.1a, the relationship of Reasoning and reading comprehension increases as scores on reasoning and reading comprehension increase. This relationship can be expressed by the following equation:

$$\hat{Y}_{rc} = 8.70 + 2.47(\text{Reasoning}) + .62(\text{Reasoning}^2)$$

From this equation, we can estimate the relationship between Reasoning and reading comprehension at any given level of Reasoning. This is done by taking the first derivative of the above equation. The first derivative is represented by the equation below:

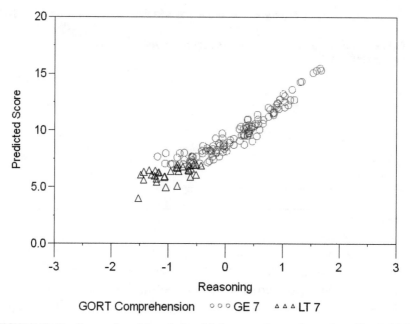

FIGURE 13.1a. Scatterplot of the relationship between Reasoning and predicted GORT Comprehension in seventh grade.

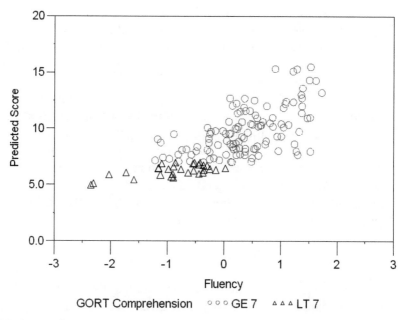

FIGURE 13.1b. Scatterplot of the relationship between Fluency and predicted GORT Comprehension in seventh grade.

Relationship of Reasoning and Reading Comprehension
= 2.47 + 1.24(Reasoning).

We can also test for statistically significant relationships between Reasoning and reading comprehension at any given level of Reasoning. Using the procedures outlined in Aiken and West (1991), we estimated that the relationship between Reasoning and reading comprehension at 1 standard deviation below normal was equal to $2.47+(1.24)(-1) = 1.23$. This translates into a 1.23 standard score point increase on GORT comprehension (which has a mean of 10 and an SD of 3 in the normed reference sample) for every 1 standard deviation increase in reasoning. Using a test of simple slopes, the relationship between Reasoning and reading comprehension was found to be statistically significant, $t(141) = 2.01$, $p = .0463$. Converting the t-value into an estimate of effect size, using the formula presented in Lipsey and Wilson (2001), we estimated that the effect size of Reasoning on reading comprehension at this level was $d = .34$. At 1 standard deviation above the mean, the relationship between Reasoning and reading comprehension was estimated to be equal to $2.47 + (1.24)(+1) = 3.71$ standard score points on the GORT Comprehension test, which is also significant, $t(141) = 5.78$, $p < .0001$. The estimated effect size of this relationship was $d = .97$. Figure 13.1b shows the relationship of Fluency and predicted reading comprehension controlling for the other variables in the model. The relationship between Fluency and reading comprehension is not as strong as it is for reasoning, as shown by the increased scatter of points. It's also interesting to note that for both Reasoning and Fluency, no student scored above a 7 on GORT comprehension that did not have a reasoning or fluency score above average (z-score greater that 0 on the x-axis of Figures 13.1a and 13.1b).

Tenth Grade

Again, the same variables that were examined in the third- and seventh-grade principal components analysis were used in the analysis of the tenth-grade data. Kaiser's rule and the scree plot both indicated that a three-factor solution would adequately represent the covariation among the variables, with the eigenvalues of the first five components being 5.5, 1.9, 1.1, .7, and .7, respectively. The first three components accounted for 71% of the covariation among the measures.

The correlations of the measures to the three components are shown in Table 13.7. The pattern of correlations of the measures with the three

TABLE 13.7. Factor Loadings and Factor Intercorrelations for the Tenth-Grade Battery

Measures	Fluency	Verbal	Memory
Listening comprehension	.38	**.68**	.16
TOWRE Sight Word Efficiency	**.89**	.35	.22
TOWRE Phonemic Decoding Efficiency	**.87**	.31	.21
WASI Vocabulary	.46	**.79**	.24
WASI Block Design	.27	**.78**	.37
WASI Similarities	.33	**.78**	.15
WASI Matrix Reasoning	.26	**.75**	.36
ORF Grade-Based	**.95**	.50	.25
ORF FCAT	**.95**	.47	.28
ORF Text-Based	**.93**	.41	.27
Reading Span	.25	.29	**.83**
Listening Span	.23	.27	**.83**
Intercorrelations			
Fluency	1.00		
Reasoning	.43	1.00	
Memory	.25	.32	1.00

Note. n = 176.

retained components was identical to the pattern found for seventh grade. As in the seventh-grade principal components analysis, the first component was labeled Fluency, the second component Reasoning, and the third component Memory.

All three of these components were first examined separately to see if they had any quadratic relationship with reading comprehension. Reasoning was found to have a quadratic relationship with the dependent variable, $F(1,147) = 11.00$, $p < .001$. Therefore, both the linear and the quadratic term for Reasoning were used in subsequent analyses. We then fit a full factorial model in the prediction of reading comprehension, and we also included the quadratic term for Reasoning. This model yielded a significant three-way interaction between Fluency, Reasoning, and Memory, along with main effects for Fluency and Reasoning (see Tables 13.8a and 13.8b for correlations and regression weights for this model). An inspection of the unique variances accounted for by each predictor revealed that Reasoning accounted for 19% of the unique variance (17% from the main effect, 2% from the quadratic effect), Fluency accounted for 7% of the unique variance, and Memory accounted for no unique variance by itself. The total variance accounted for from the final model was 55%.

TABLE 13.8a. Estimated Correlations for the Tenth-Grade Cognitive Composites and GORT Comprehension

Composites	Fluency	Reasoning	Memory	GORT Comprehension
Fluency	1.00			
Reasoning	.53	1.00		
Memory	.31	.36	1.00	
GORT Comprehension	.55	.65	.27	1.00

Note. n = 150.

Figures 13.2a and 13.2b display scatterplots of the relationships between Reasoning and predicted reading comprehension and Fluency and predicted reading comprehension, respectively. Figure 13.2a shows a dramatic change in the relationship between Reasoning and reading comprehension as a function of overall level of Reasoning. Employing the same simple slopes analyses used in the seventh-grade analyses, we estimated the relationship between Reasoning and reading comprehension to be 2.06 + 1.33(Reasoning), and the relationship between Reasoning and reading comprehension at 1 standard deviation below the mean of reasoning to be 2.06 + 1.33(–1) = .73, $t(141) = 1.54$, $p = .1256$, which is a nonsignificant effect. This simple slope has an effect size of $d = .25$. For 1 standard deviation above the mean on Reasoning, we estimated the relationship between Reasoning and reading comprehension to be 2.06 + 1.33(1) = 3.39, $t(141) = 4.44$, $p < .0001$, with an effect

TABLE 13.8b. Estimated Parameters for the Tenth-Grade Regression Analyses

Parameter	Estimate	Standard error	t	p	Semipartial R^2
Intercept	7.83	.175	44.66	.0001	
Fluency	0.99	.215	4.59	.0001	.07
Reasoning	2.06	.279	7.40	.0001	.17
Memory	−0.029	.192	−0.15	.8779	.00
Reasoning * Reasoning	0.667	.285	2.33	.0210	.02
Fluency * Reasoning	0.326	.304	1.07	.2860	.00
Fluency * Memory	0.285	.233	1.22	.2238	.00
Reasoning * Memory	−0.535	.314	−1.70	.0915	.01
Fluency * Reasoning * Memory	0.752	.329	−2.28	.0238	.02
Total R^2	.55				

Note. n = 150.

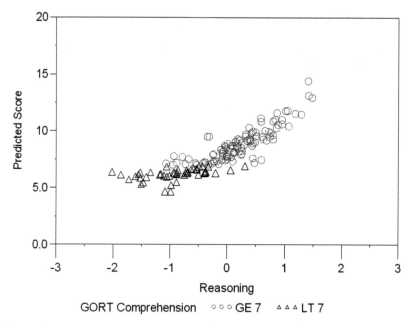

FIGURE 13.2a. Scatterplot of the relationship between Reasoning and predicted GORT Comprehension in tenth grade.

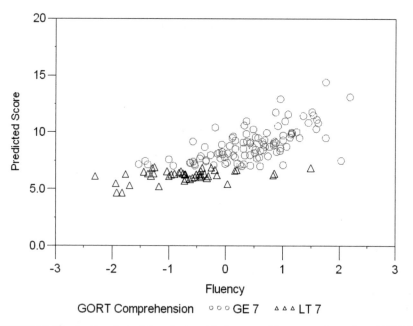

FIGURE 13.2b. Scatterplot of the relationship between Fluency and predicted GORT Comprehension in tenth grade.

size of $d = .73$. Figure 13.2b shows the relationship between Fluency and reading comprehension, controlling for all other variables in the model. The relationship between Fluency and reading comprehension appears to be linear and not as strong as the relationship between Reasoning and reading comprehension.

CONCLUSION

The results of this individual differences study of potential predictors of reading comprehension extend our knowledge in a number of ways. First, the results from this study indicate that oral reading fluency and reasoning skills are strong predictors of reading comprehension. Both of these constructs are strongly related to reading comprehension and both account for a significant portion of unique variance controlling for the effects of other predictors in the study. This result is not surprising given the strong correlations found in other studies of fluency and reasoning skills. But by measuring these constructs together in a single study, we were able to assess their joint and unique impacts upon reading comprehension. Memory span (as measured by listening and reading span assessments) did not show any unique predictive utility once fluency and reasoning skills were partialled-out. This is not to say that memory is unimportant to reading, but that perhaps its effects may be more indirectly related to reading comprehension.

Second, it appears that the unique importance of reasoning skills increases in the later grades. The unique variance associated with reasoning ability was 8% in third grade (with verbal and nonverbal reasoning combined), increased to 25% in seventh grade, and was 19% in 10th grade. This is due almost completely to the increased zero-order correlations of reasoning with reading comprehension, with correlations of .58 and .46 for verbal and nonverbal reasoning in third grade, and correlations of .71 and .65 with reasoning and reading comprehension in seventh and 10th grades, respectively. The correlation between fluency and reading comprehension remained relatively constant across the three grades, with correlations of .54, .55, and .55 in third, seventh, and tenth grade, respectively.

Third, the relationship between reasoning and reading comprehension was found to be curvilinear in seventh and 10th grade. That is, reasoning was less correlated with reading comprehension at lower levels of reasoning than at higher levels of reasoning ability. This was an unanticipated finding. One possibility for this outcome is that the multiple-choice questions administered after reading the GORT-4 passages may vary in the amount of inferential ability needed to correctly answer the question. Questions that can be directly ascertained from the passage would be easier to answer than those that require more inferential skills. So those students with lower reasoning skills would be able to answer the less inferential questions, but would be less likely to correctly answer the more demanding passages. If some of the easier questions on the GORT-4 were less likely to tap inferential reasoning skills, then this would explain the lower relationship between reasoning and reading comprehension at the lower end of ability.

Finally, these results seem to suggest that training studies that include a fluency-building component may have its greatest impact across all ability levels in the lower grades, but may still have an impact on older students with poor comprehension abilities in 10th grade. Reasoning skills appear to take on greater importance in our measures of reading comprehension as the students become older.

REFERENCES

Aiken, L. S., & West, S. G. (1991). *Multiple regression: Testing and interpreting interactions.* Thousand Oaks, CA: Sage.

Aimsweb. (2002). *Reading curriculum based measurement oral reading fluency.* Retrieved January 15, 2002 from www.aimsweb.com.

Appelbaum, M. I., & Cramer, E. M. (1974). Some problems in the nonorthogonal analysis of variance. *Psychological Bulletin, 81,* 335–343.

Beck, I. L., & McKeown, M. G. (1991). Conditions of vocabulary acquisition. In R. Barr, M. Kamil, P. Mosenthal, & P. D. Pearson (Eds.), *Handbook of reading research* (Vol. 2, pp. 789–814). Mahwah, NJ: Erlbaum.

Beck, I. L., McKeown, M. G., & Kucan, L. (2002). *Bringing words to life: Robust vocabulary instruction.* New York: Guilford Press.

Bradley, L., & Bryant, P. E. (1978). Difficulties in auditory organization as a possible cause of reading backwardness. *Nature, 271,* 746–747.

Calfee, R. C., Lindamood, P., & Lindamood, C. (1973). Acoustic–phonetic skills and reading: Kindergarten through twelfth grade. *Journal of Educational Psychology, 64,* 293–298.

Cohen, P., Cohen, J., West, S., & Aiken, L. (2002). *Applied multiple regression/ correlation analysis for the behavioral sciences.* Mahwah, NJ: Erlbaum.

Curtis, M. E. (1980). Development of components of reading skill. *Journal of Educational Psychology, 72,* 656–669.

Daneman, M. (1991). Individual differences in reading skills. In R. Barr, M. Kamil,

P. Mosenthal, & P. D. Pearson (Eds.), *Handbook of reading research* (Vol. 2, pp. 512–538). Mahwah, NJ: Erlbaum.

Daneman, M., & Carpenter, P. (1980). Individual differences in working memory and reading. *Journal of Verbal Learning and Verbal Behavior, 19,* 450–466.

Fletcher, J. M., Lyon, G. R., Barnes, M., Stuebing, K. K., Francis, D. F., Olson, R. K., et al. (2001). *Classification of learning disabilities: An evidence-based evaluation.* Paper presented at the 2001 Learning Disabilities Summit in Washington, DC. Retrieved March 8, 2005, from www.nrcld.org/html/information/articles/ldsummit/fletcher.doc.

Fuchs, L. S., Fuchs, D., Hosp, M. K., & Jenkins, J. R. (2001). Oral reading fluency as an indicator of reading competence: A theoretical, empirical, and historical analysis. *Scientific Studies of Reading, 5,* 239–256.

Fuchs, L. S., Fuchs, D., & Maxwell, L. (1988). The validity of informal reading comprehension measures. *RASE: Remedial and Special Education, 9,* 20–28.

Gaulin, C. A., & Campbell, T. F. (1994). Procedure for assessing verbal working memory in normal school-age children: Some preliminary data. *Perceptual and Motor Skills, 79,* 55–64.

Gough, P. B., & Tunmer, W. E. (1986). Decoding, reading, and reading disability. *RASE: Remedial and Special Education, 7,* 6–10.

Hoover, W. A., & Gough, P. B. (1990). The simple view of reading. *Reading and Writing, 2,* 127–160.

Kahmi, A. G. (2005). Finding the beauty in the ugly facts about reading comprehension. In H. W. Catts & A. G. Kahmi (Eds.), *The connections between language and reading disabilities* (pp. 201–212). Mahwah, NJ: Erlbaum.

Kaufman, A. S., Lichtenberger, E. O., & McLean, J. E. (2001). Two- and three-factor solutions of the WAIS-III. *Assessment, 8,* 267–280.

Levin, J. R. (2004). Random thoughts on the (in)credibility of educational–psychological intervention research. *Educational Psychologist, 39,* 173–184.

Lipsey, M. W., & Wilson, D. B. (2001). *Practical meta-analysis.* Thousand Oaks, CA: Sage.

Lubinski, D., & Humphreys, L. G. (1990). Assessing spurious "moderator effects": Illustrated substantively with the hypothesized "synergistic" relation between spatial and mathematical ability. *Psychological Bulletin, 107,* 385–393.

Oakhill, J., & Yuill, N. (1986). Pronoun resolution in skilled and less-skilled comprehenders: Effects of memory load and inferential complexity. *Language and Speech, 29,* 25–37.

Oakland, T., de Mesquita, P., & Buckley, K. (1988). Psychological, linguistic and sociocultural correlates of reading among Mexican American elementary students. *School Psychology International, 9,* 219–228.

Pavlidis, G. T. (1981). Do eye movements hold the key to dyslexia? *Neuropsychologia, 19,* 57–64.

Rayner, K., & Duffy, S. A. (1988). On-line comprehension processes and eye movements during reading. In M. Daneman, G. E. MacKinnon, & T. G. Waller (Eds.), *Reading research: Advances in theory and practice* (Vol. 6, pp. 13–66). San Diego, CA: Academic Press.

Roth, F. P., Speece, D. L., & Cooper, D. H. (2002). A longitudinal analysis of the connection between oral language and early reading. *Journal of Educational Research, 95*, 259–272.

Schatschneider, C., Fletcher, J. M., Francis, D. J., Carlson, C., & Foorman, B. R. (2004). Kindergarten prediction of reading skills: A longitudinal comparative analysis. *Journal of Educational Psychology, 96*, 265–282.

Shadish, W. R., Cook, T. D., & Campbell, D. T. (2002). *Experimental and quasi-experimental designs for generalized causal inference.* Boston: Houghton Mifflin.

Spear-Swerling, L., & Sternberg, R. J. (1994). The road not taken: An integrative theoretical model of reading disability. *Journal of Learning Disabilities, 27*, 91–103, 122.

Stanovich, K. E. (1986). Matthew effects in reading: Some consequences of individual differences in the acquisition of literacy. *Reading Research Quarterly, 21*, 360–407.

Stanovich, K. E. (2000). *Progress in understanding reading.* New York: Guilford Press

Stanovich, K. E., & Cunningham, A. E. (2004). Inferences from correlational data: Exploring associations with reading experience. In N. K. Duke & M. H. Mallette (Eds.), *Literacy research methodologies* (pp. 28–45). New York: Guilford Press.

Stanovich, K. E., Nathan, R. G., & Vala-Rossi, M. (1986). Developmental changes in the cognitive correlates of reading ability and the developmental lag hypothesis. *Reading Research Quarterly, 21*, 267–283.

Stevens, J. (1992). *Applied multivariate statistics for the social sciences* (2nd ed.). Hillsdale, NJ: Erlbaum.

Sticht, T. G., & James, J. H. (1984). Listening and reading. In P. D. Pearson (Ed.), *Handbook of reading research* (pp. 293–317). New York: Longman.

Swanson, H. L. (1992). Generality and modifiability of working memory among skilled and less skilled readers. *Journal of Educational Psychology, 84*, 473–488.

Swanson, H. L., & Howell, M. (2001). Working memory, short-term memory, and speech rate as predictors of children's reading performance at different ages. *Journal of Educational Psychology, 93*, 720–734.

Therrien, W. J. (2004). Fluency and comprehension gains as a result of repeated reading: A meta-analysis. *RASE: Remedial and Special Education, 25*, 252–261.

Torgesen, J. K. (1989). Why IQ is relevant to the definition of learning disabilities. *Journal of Learning Disabilities, 22*, 484–486.

Torgesen, J. K., Wagner, R. K., & Rashotte, C. A. (1999). *Test of word reading efficiency.* Austin, TX: PRO-ED.

van den Bos, K. P. (1998). IQ, phonological awareness and continuous-naming speed related to Dutch poor decoding children's performance on two word identification tests. *Dyslexia, 4*, 73–89.

van den Bos, K. P., Brand-Gruwel, A., & Lind, E. A. (1998). Text comprehension strategy instruction with poor readers. *Reading and Writing, 10,* 471–498.

Wagner, R. K., & Stanovich, K. (1996). Expertise in reading. In K. A. Ericsson (Ed.), *The road to excellence: The acquisition of expert performance in the arts and sciences, sports, and games* (pp. 189–225). Hillsdale, NJ: Erlbaum.

Wagner, R. K., Torgesen, J. K., Laughon, P., Simmons, K., & Rashotte, C. A. (1993). Development of young reader's phonological processing abilities. *Journal of Educational Psychology, 85,* 83–103.

CHAPTER 14

Promising Avenues for Better Understanding Implications of Vocabulary Development for Reading Comprehension

RICHARD K. WAGNER
ANDREA E. MUSE
KENDRA R. TANNENBAUM

Nearly all of the chapters in this volume address promising avenues for future research on the implications of vocabulary development for reading comprehension. Rather than attempt a summary of what is better said by the chapter authors, our purpose in this chapter is to highlight two additional promising avenues for future research that were not featured in the previous chapters. We do not intend to suggest that they are of more, or even equal, importance compared with some of the promising avenues described in previous chapters. We feature them merely because they were not covered previously. The two promising avenues we discuss are research that examines the underlying dimensions of the constructs of vocabulary and of reading comprehension for the purpose of informing a new generation of measures, and research that directly tests alternative hypotheses of relations between developing vocabulary and reading comprehension.

UNCOVERING THE UNDERLYING DIMENSIONS
OF VOCABULARY AND READING COMPREHENSION

Most common measures of vocabulary assess either receptive or expressive vocabulary. Performance on measures of receptive and expressive vocabulary is highly correlated, with the distinction between receptive and expressive vocabulary perhaps reflecting task requirements as opposed to genuine underlying dimensions of individual or developmental differences. Receptive vocabulary measures typically present a series of pictures. The examinee hears a word and points to the correct picture. Expressive vocabulary measures typically involve having the examinee hear a word, then provide a verbal definition.

Turning to measures of reading comprehension, a variety of measures exist, ranging from cloze procedures that require filling in missing words in paragraphs to providing a summary of a passage or answering questions that test one's comprehension of what was read. Perhaps the most consistent reaction to the current crop of reading comprehension measures is that they fall short of assessing the full range of activities that are considered to be included in the construct of reading comprehension (Snow, 2002).

The refinement and growing popularity of analytical techniques such as confirmatory factor analysis makes it possible to test alternative models of the latent structure of constructs such as vocabulary or reading comprehension. We present two examples of using confirmatory factor analysis to investigate underlying dimensions in vocabulary knowledge.

Underlying Dimensions of Morphological Knowledge

Within the domain of linguistics, *morphology* refers to the structure of words in terms of *morphemes*, or "minimal meaningful elements" (Bloomfield, 1933), that is, prefixes, roots, and suffixes. The meaning of a word is derived from the combined meanings of the morphemes of that particular word. An awareness of morphology can be helpful in determining, for example, that the -*er* in *teacher* denotes "one who teaches" and the *un-* in *unhappy* indicates "not happy."

The same morpheme often has the same spelling even when it is pronounced differently in two words (*sign/signature*), and the same sound often has two or more different spellings when it represents different morphemes (*there/their/they're*). Such spellings only make sense when the morphological structure of words and their morphological relations to other words are taken into account.

Morphological awareness, which refers to a conscious awareness of or the ability to use the smallest units of meaning in a language, may be important in learning to read English (Carlisle, 1995, 2000; Carlisle & Fleming, 2003; Carlisle & Nomanbhoy, 1993; Deacon & Kirby, 2004; Mahony, Singson, & Mann, 2000; Nagy, Berninger, Abbott, Vaughan, & Vermeulen, 2003; Tyler & Nagy, 1989). This is due in part to the fact that although the English writing system is alphabetic, it is also morphological (Chomsky & Halle, 1968; Shankweiler et al., 1995).

Muse (2005) used confirmatory factor analysis to test alternative models of the nature of individual differences in morphological knowledge. One potential underlying dimension that was investigated was that of morphological awareness versus use of morphological knowledge. For the purpose of this study, *morphological awareness* referred to an individual's ability to reflect upon and manipulate morphemes. Use of *morphological knowledge*, on the other hand, referred to an individual's ability to correctly employ morphological units, but without necessarily having a conscious awareness of how or why these units were used in a particular way. For example, morphological use may be demonstrated when a participant correctly responded to items in which the answer could be obtained partially by using context. A model that represented use and awareness as two separate latent variables was compared to a model that assumed use and awareness were not theoretically separable and were in fact representative of the same construct.

Method effects are a potential source of error in most types of assessment. Therefore, the general model described above was extended to assess the influence of response format. A model that included two latent variables representing two types of response formats, production and multiple choice, was compared to a model that had one latent variable to represent both types of response formats.

Because some researchers have argued that morphological knowledge is simply a by-product of vocabulary, two models were designed to test this possibility. A model in which morphological knowledge and vocabulary were represented as two separate latent variables was compared to a model that collapsed these two constructs into one latent variable. Finally, the degree to which morphological knowledge predicted reading comprehension also was addressed.

The participants were 99 fourth graders recruited from local elementary schools. All participants were native speakers of English. The measures that were given were the following.

Tests of Morphological Structure (Carlisle, 2000)

These measures were designed to assess students' awareness of the relations of base and derived forms. The base and derived forms were equivalent in word frequency on the two tasks. The two tasks contained equal numbers of word relations that were transparent (i.e., the sound of the base form is intact in the derived form) and shift words (i.e., the phonological representation shifts from base to derived form). There were two types of morphological structure tasks: decomposition and derivation. The decomposition task, which was comprised of 30 items, required the decomposition of derived words in order to finish sentences. An example of an item included in this task was: "The word is *driver*. The sentence is: *Children are too young to* _____." The derivation task, which was comprised of 30 items, required the production of a derived word in order to finish a sentence. An example of an item included in this task was: "The word is *farm*. The sentence is: *My uncle is a* _____."

Derivational Suffix Choice Test

There were three derivational suffix choice tests. The items for these tests were constructed based on prior research by Mahony (1994), Singson, Mahony, and Mann (2000), Nagy, Diakidoy, and Anderson (1993), and Tyler and Nagy (1989).

The derivational suffix choice with real words task contained 25 items. The participant was required to choose among four options (all using real words in the stems), each of which had a different derivational suffix that signaled part of speech (e.g., *directs, directions, directing,* or *directed*), the one that fit the context of a sentence composed of real words (e.g., *He listened carefully to the* _____.).

The derivational suffix choice using real words with improbable suffixes task, also referred to as the morphological signals task, contained five items. The participant was required to choose which of four sentences correctly used a plausible but improbable derivational suffix attached to a real word stem (e.g., *dogless*). A correct response indicated understanding of the grammatical information signaled by the suffix (e.g., *When he got a new puppy, he was no longer dogless*, but not *He was in the dogless*).

The derivational suffix choice with nonwords task was comprised of 14 items. The participant was required to choose which of four options (e.g., *jittling, jittles, jittled, jittle*) fit the context of a sentence composed of real words (*Our teacher taught us how to _____ long words*). A correct response indicated understanding of grammatical information conveyed by derivational suffixes independent of their semantic content. All items were presented visually for the child to read silently while the experimenter read them aloud to the child; thus correct responding did not require decoding ability.

Bee Grass Test (University of Washington, 1999)

This task, which consisted of 14 items, was based on the research of Elbro and Arnbak (1996) and Fowler and Liberman (1995). Children decided which of two options was a better answer to a riddle. For example, *Which is a better name for a bee that lives in the grass? A grass bee or a bee grass?* Another example would be, *Which is a better name for grass where lots of bees like to hide? Bee rass or grass bee?* The items were presented visually while the experimenter read the items to the child.

Comes From Task (University of Washington, 1999)

This task, which consisted of 12 items, was based on tasks used by Berko (1958), Carlisle (1995), Derwing (1976), Mahony (1994), and Mahony, Singson, and Mann (2000). This version of the task was different from versions used in previous research in that it was shorter and used high-frequency words. This task required the child to decide if the second word was derived ("comes from") the first word. An example of a correct yes response was *quick* and *quickly*. An example of a correct no response was *moth* and *mother*. Items were presented visually for the child to look at while the experimenter read the items to the child.

Morpheme Identification

The morpheme identification task consisted of 13 items. This task assessed the ability to distinguish different meanings across homophones.

For each item, two different pictures were presented simultaneously to the child and each of the pictures was labeled orally for the child by the experimenter. The child was then given a word or phrase containing the target morpheme and was asked to choose from between the two pictures the one that best corresponded to the meaning of that morpheme. For example, in one test item, the child was asked to select from the two pictures showing *the color blue* and *he blew out some air*, respectively, the one that contained the meaning of the morpheme *blue* in *blueberries*. Another item contrasted *a picture of my son* with *the sun* and asked the child to select the picture that best represented the meaning of *son* in *grandson*.

Morphological Construction

This task, which consisted of 20 items, required children to create new meanings by combining morphemes and thus tested the ability to construct new meanings from knowledge of previously learned morphemes. In the morphological construction test, 20 scenarios were orally presented in two- to four-sentence stories. Children were then asked to come up with words for the objects or concepts presented by each scenario. Fourteen of the stories required responses involving morpheme compounding, while the remaining six items involved syntactic manipulations. One example of the compounding items was: *Early in the morning, we can see the sun coming up. This is called a sunrise. At night, we might also see the moon coming up. What could we call this?* The correct response for this item was *moonrise*. An example of an item requiring a syntactic response was this: *This is a musical instrument called a hux. Now we have three of them. These are three _____* (the correct response was *huxes*). The maximum score for this task was 20.

Florida Comprehensive Assessment Test
Reading Comprehension Subtest

Florida Comprehensive Assessment Test (FCAT) Reading Comprehension measured students' ability in four areas: words and phrases in context; main idea, plot, and purpose; comparisons and cause/effect; and reference and research. This subtest was composed of reading selections and questions about each selection. The narrative and informational selections reflected the kinds of fiction and nonfiction students read in school. Two different types of scores were obtained for the students in the sample. The first was the criterion-referenced test, which measured how well students were meeting the Sunshine State Standards (FCAT SSS). The Sunshine State Standards were the skills and competencies that Florida students should be able to learn, as defined by practicing classroom teachers, educational specialists, businesspeople, and Florida citizens. The second type of score obtained was the norm-referenced test (FCAT NRT), which is the Stanford Achievement Test Series—Tenth Edition (SAT 10). This allows the performance of Florida students to be compared with the performance of students nationwide.

The results were straightforward. The underlying structure of individual differences in morphological knowledge was characterized by a single underlying latent ability. There was no support of a meaningful distinction between morphological awareness and use of morphological knowledge, nor was there evidence of method effects associated with multiple-choice versus free-response item types. This general model fit the data quite well, yielding a chi-square with 27 degrees of freedom of 28.45, p = .39, with a CFI of .97, a Tucker–Lewis index of .99, and a root mean square error of approximation of .02.

Models that examined the magnitude of relations between morphological knowledge and vocabulary, and between morphological knowledge and reading comprehension, were tested next. These models also yielded excellent fits to the data. The model including morphological awareness and vocabulary is presented in Figure 14.1. Note the very strong correlation between these two constructs of .91. A comparison between this model and a nested model that forced the correlation to be a perfect 1.0 indicated that the obtained value of .91 is not significantly different from a correlation of 1.0. In other words, a single underlying dimension accounted for individual differences on both morphological knowledge and vocabulary.

Turning to morphological knowledge and reading comprehension, a model including these constructs is presented in Figure 14.2. The correlation between morphological knowledge and reading comprehension was remarkably strong at .86, although this value was significantly different from a perfect correlation of 1.0.

In summary, all of the morphological measures examined were measures of the same underlying construct of morphological knowledge. A single underlying dimension accounted for individual differences on both morphological knowledge and vocabulary. Morphological knowledge was strongly related to reading comprehension performance.

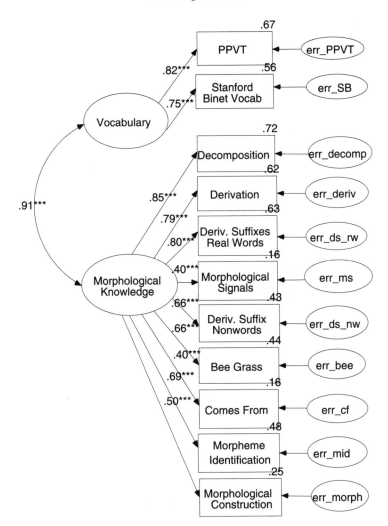

FIGURE 14.1. Relations between morphological knowledge and vocabulary.

Underlying Dimensions of Vocabulary

In this study, three possible underlying dimensions of vocabulary knowledge were investigated (Tannenbaum, Torgesen, & Wagner, 2005): breadth, depth, and fluency. *Breadth of vocabulary* refers to the size of the mental lexicon. An *index of breadth* of vocabulary is the number of words that have some level of meaning to an individual. *Depth of vocabulary* knowledge refers to the richness of meaning. An *index of depth*

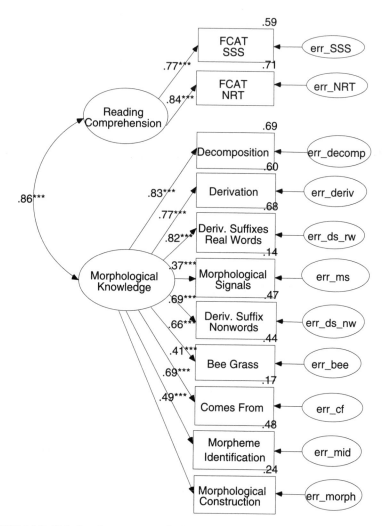

FIGURE 14.2. Relations between morphological knowledge and reading comprehension.

of vocabulary knowledge is knowledge of multiple meanings of words. *Fluency of access* to vocabulary knowledge is defined as the rate at which the individual accesses the meaning of a word.

Multiple measures of breadth, depth, and fluency were given to a sample of 203 third-grade students. The measures of breadth were the Peabody Picture Vocabulary Test—Third Edition (PPVT-III; Dunn & Dunn, 1997) and the Vocabulary subtest of the Wechsler Intelligence Scale for Children—Third Edition (WISC-III; Wechsler, 1991). The measures of depth were the Multiple Meanings and the Attributes subtests of the Language Processing Test—Revised (LPT-R; Richard & Hanner, 1995). Finally, the measures of fluency were the Word Use Fluency (WUF) subtest of the Dynamic Indicators of Basic Early Literacy Skills (DIBELS; Good & Kaminski, 2002) and an experimenter-developed Semantic Category Fluency test. Finally, reading comprehension was assessed by performance on the FCAT.

A model that distinguished between breadth and both depth and fluency, but not between depth and fluency, fit the data quite well. This model of vocabulary knowledge, along with the construct of reading comprehension, is presented in Figure 14.3. The results of this study

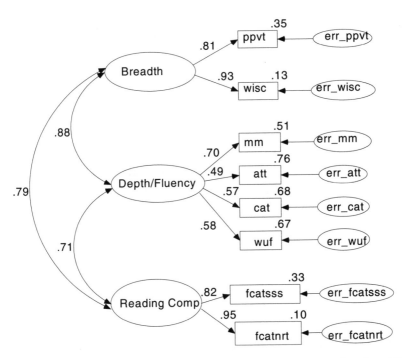

FIGURE 14.3. Two-factor measurement model with reading comprehension. All regression weights and covariances are significant ($p < .001$); ppvt, Peabody Picture Vocabulary Test—Third Edition; wisc, Vocabulary subtest of Wechsler Intelligence Scale for Children—Third Edition; mm, Multiple Meanings subtest of Language Processing Test—Revised; att, Attributes subtest of Language Processing Test—Revised; cat, semantic category fluency; wuf, Word Use Fluency subtest of Dynamic Indicators of Basic Early Literacy Skills; fcatsss, Florida Comprehensive Assessment Test—Sunshine State Standards; fcatnrt, Florida Comprehensive Assessment Test—Norm Referenced Test.

indicated that breadth of vocabulary knowledge was more strongly related to reading comprehension than were the combined construct of
depth and fluency. However, these two underlying dimensions of vocabulary knowledge have significant overlapping variance that contributes to the prediction of reading comprehension.

Underlying Dimensions of Reading Comprehension

We are in the initial stage of a similar investigation of underlying dimensions in reading comprehension. We have been developing items that
correspond to several frameworks for understanding reading comprehension including proposed classifications of inferences (Graesser, Singer,
& Trabasso, 1994) and the assessment framework proposed for the 2009
National Assessment of Educational Progress in Reading. After we have
administered the items to a substantial number of students, we will use
a strategy similar to that described in the investigations of morphology
and vocabulary to test alternative models of the nature of individual and
developmental differences in reading comprehension.

COMPARING ALTERNATIVE MODELS OF RELATIONS BETWEEN DEVELOPING VOCABULARY AND READING COMPREHENSION

With development and instruction, vocabulary and reading comprehension typically improve from year to year. Performance on measures
of vocabulary is highly correlated with performance on measures of
reading comprehension (e.g., Nagy et al., 2003). But might there be a
causal relation between the development of vocabulary and reading
comprehension?

Anderson and Freebody (1981, cited in Nagy, Chapter 4, this volume)
suggested three possible ways that vocabulary and reading comprehension could be related causally. Their *instrumental hypothesis* was that
knowing more words makes you better at reading comprehension. Their
knowledge hypothesis was that individual differences in both vocabulary
and reading comprehension are caused by individual differences in knowledge. On this view, vocabulary and reading comprehension are both indicators or manifestations of individual differences in the richness of
conceptual knowledge. Finally, their *aptitude hypothesis* is similar to their
knowledge hypothesis with the exception that vocabulary and reading

comprehension are correlated because individual differences in both are caused, at least in part, by individual differences in a fundamental ability such as general verbal ability: high verbals have better vocabularies and are better at reading comprehension than low verbals.

Nagy (Chapter 4, this volume) makes a convincing case for a specific version of the knowledge hypothesis. He argues that individual differences in metalinguistic awareness (of which phonological awareness, morphological awareness, and syntactic awareness are examples) are causally related to individual differences in both vocabulary and reading comprehension. Thus individual differences in vocabulary and reading comprehension are correlated because both are caused by individual differences in metalinguistic awareness. Carlisle (Chapter 5, this volume) makes a related case for morphological processing, arguing that it leads to increased breadth and depth of word knowledge, which in turn impacts reading comprehension. Here, individual differences in morphological processing exert a direct causal influence on individual differences in word knowledge and an indirect influence on individual differences in reading comprehension via word knowledge.

Structural equation modeling, and its special case of path analysis, can be used to test alternative causal models. However, when measures of vocabulary, reading comprehension, and other variables of interest are obtained simultaneously, or even cross-sectionally, the data rarely are sufficient to distinguish alternative causal models. A reason for this state of affairs is the problem of equivalent models (Lee & Hershberger, 1990). In a nutshell, for saturated models in which some kind of link—correlational or causal—exists between all variables in a set, one can merrily reverse the direction of causal arrows, or replace causal arrows by correlations or vice versa, and generate a large set of very different models that nevertheless cannot be distinguished empirically because all of the models provide an identical fit to the data. Longitudinal data provide a way to rule out many equivalent models for causal models without feedback loops, because nothing at time 2 can be a cause of anything at time 1.

In the present study, we tested four alternative causal models of developmental relations between vocabulary and reading comprehension by fitting path analytic models to longitudinal data provided by 216 students for whom annual assessments of vocabulary and reading comprehension were available from second through fifth grade.

1. The first model posits that individual differences in reading comprehension exert a causal influence on vocabulary development because

many new vocabulary words are learned by inferring meaning from context when reading as opposed to being taught them directly. Children who are better at reading comprehension are more likely to figure out the meanings of new vocabulary words. If so, there will be a causal influence of individual differences in reading comprehension on subsequent individual differences in vocabulary.

2. The second model posits that individual differences in vocabulary exert a causal influence on the development of reading comprehension skills. The idea, related to Anderson and Freebody's (1981) instrumental hypothesis, is that a large vocabulary might provide a richer comprehension experience when reading, which over time improves reading comprehension. This idea also is implicit in Carlisle's (Chapter 5, this volume) view that individual differences in vocabulary, which arise in part because of individual differences in morphological awareness, lead to individual differences in reading comprehension.

3. The third model posits that causal relations are bidirectional. In other words, both model one and model two are operating simultaneously.

4. The fourth model posits that vocabulary and reading comprehension are correlated because they jointly are caused by some third variable. Examples of this model include Anderson and Freebody's (1981) knowledge and aptitude hypotheses, and Nagy's (Chapter 4, this volume) metalinguistic awareness hypothesis.

A fifth, logically possible, model that vocabulary and reading comprehension are unrelated, was not entertained because of the overwhelming evidence of correlations between them.

Each path analytic model included both vocabulary and reading comprehension as variables at two time points. The measure of vocabulary was the Vocabulary subtest from the Stanford–Binet. The measure of reading comprehension was Passage Comprehension from the Woodcock–Johnson. These models also included an autoregressor variable. Taking vocabulary, for example, the best predictor of vocabulary in fifth grade is vocabulary in fourth grade. The same variable at an earlier point in time is called an *autoregressor variable*. It is necessary to have the autoregressor variable in the model to rule out spurious effects that mimic causal relations. For example, if one tests a path analysis model that has fourth-grade reading comprehension as a predictor of fifth-grade vocabulary and the autoregressor variable of fourth-grade vocabulary is left out, a spurious "causal" influence can result: fourth-grade reading comprehension is likely to be correlated with the unmeasured fourth-grade vocabulary, and the only real causal influence might be between fourth- and fifth-grade vocabulary.

Results for the time period of fourth to fifth grade are presented in Figure 14.4. The results for the time periods second to third grade, and third to fourth grade, were highly similar to the results presented in Figure 14.4. In this figure, the four coefficients of interest are on the arrows in the center of the figure. Each of these path coefficients is significant. The causal influence of fourth-grade reading comprehen- sion on fifth-grade vocabulary is represented by the path coefficient of .18. The causal influence of fourth-grade vocabulary on fifth-grade reading comprehension is represented by the path coefficient of .34. The autoregressive effect for reading comprehension is represented by the path coefficient of .72, and that for vocabulary is represented by the path coefficient of .45.

The bidirectional model was supported for every time point exam- ined. However, the high degree of initial correlation between vocabu- lary and reading comprehension observed for each of the models is unlikely to be accounted for by the magnitude of observed causal rela- tions, suggesting the additional influence of third variables that jointly cause both vocabulary and reading comprehension.

ACKNOWLEDGMENTS

This research was supported by Grant No. R305G030104 from the Institute for Education Sciences and by Grant No. HD23340 from the National Institute of Child Health and Human Development.

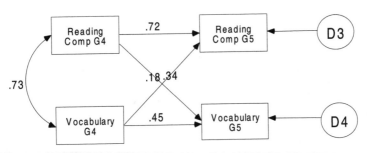

FIGURE 14.4. Path analysis of development of vocabulary and reading comprehen- sion from fourth to fifth grade.

REFERENCES

Anderson, R. C., & Freebody, P. (1981). Vocabulary knowledge. In J. T. Guthrie (Ed.), *Comprehension and teaching: Research reviews.* Newark, DE: International Reading Association.

Berko, J. (1958). The child's learning of English morphology. *Word, 14,* 150–177.

Bloomfield, L. (1933). *Language.* New York: Holt.

Carlisle, J. F. (1995). Morphological awareness and early reading achievement. In L. Feldman (Ed.), *Morphological aspects of language processing* (pp. 189–209). Hillsdale, NJ: Erlbaum.

Carlisle, J. F. (2000). Awareness of the structure and meaning of morphologically complex words: Impact on reading. *Reading and Writing: An Interdisciplinary Journal, 12,* 169–190.

Carlisle, J. F., & Fleming, J. (2003). Lexical processing of morphologically complex words in the elementary years. *Scientific Studies of Reading, 7,* 239–253.

Carlisle, J. F., & Nomanbhoy, D. (1993). Phonological and morphological awareness in first graders. *Applied Psycholinguistics, 14,* 177–195.

Chomsky, N., & Halle, M. (1968). *The sound pattern of English.* New York: Harper & Row.

Deacon, S. H., & Kirby, J. R. (2004). Morphological awareness: Just "more phonological?" The roles of morphological and phonological awareness in reading development. *Applied Psycholinguistics, 25,* 223–238.

Derwing, B. (1976). Morpheme recognition and the learning of rules for derivational morphology. *Canadian Journal of Linguistics, 21,* 38–66.

Dunn, L. M., & Dunn, L. M. (1997). *Peabody picture vocabulary test—Third edition.* Circle Pines, MN: AGS.

Elbro, C., & Arnbak, E. (1996). The role of morpheme recognition and morphological awareness in dyslexia. *Annals of Dyslexia, 46,* 209–240.

Fowler, A. E., & Liberman, I. Y. (1995). The role of phonology and orthography in morphological awareness. In L. B. Feldman (Ed.), *Morphological aspects of language processing* (pp. 157–188). Hillsdale, NJ: Erlbaum.

Good, R. H., & Kaminski, R. A. (2002). *Dynamic indicators of basic early literacy skills.* Eugene, OR: Institute for the Development of Educational Achievement.

Graesser, A. C., Singer, M., & Trabasso, T. (1994). Constructing inferences during narrative text comprehension. *Psychological Review, 101,* 371–395.

Lee, S., & Hershberger, S. (1990). A simple rule for generating equivalent models in covariance structure modeling. *Multivariate Behavioral Research, 25,* 313–334.

Mahony, D. (1994). Using sensitivity to word structure to explain variance in high school and college level reading ability. *Reading and Writing: An Interdisciplinary Journal, 6,* 19–44.

Mahony, D., Singson, M., & Mann, V. (2000). Reading ability and sensitivity to morphological relations. *Reading and Writing: An Interdisciplinary Journal, 12,* 191–218.

Muse, A. E. (2005). *The nature of morphological knowledge.* Unpublished doctoral dissertation, Florida State University.

Nagy, W., Berninger, V., Abbott, R., Vaughn, K., & Vermeulen, K. (2003). Relationship of morphology and other language skills to literacy skills in at-risk second-grade readers and at-risk fourth-grade writers. *Journal of Educational Psychology, 95*(4), 730–742.

Nagy, W., Diakidoy, I., & Anderson, R. (1993). The acquisition of morphology: Learning the contribution of suffixes to the meanings of derivatives. *Journal of Reading Behavior, 25,* 155–170.

Richard, G. J., & Hanner, M. A (1995). *Language processing test—Revised.* East Moline, IL: LinguiSystems, Inc.

Shankweiler, D., Crain, S., Katz, L., Fowler, A. E., Liberman, A. M., Brady, S. A., et al. (1995). Cognitive profiles of reading-disabled children: Comparison of language skills in phonology, morphology, and syntax. *Psychological Science, 6,* 149–156.

Singson, M., Mahony, D., & Mann, V. (2000). The relation between reading ability and morphological skills: Evidence from derivational suffixes. *Reading and Writing: An Interdisciplinary Journal, 12,* 219–252.

Snow, C. E. (2002). *Reading for understanding: Toward an R&D program in reading comprehension.* Santa Monica, CA: Rand.

Tannenbaum, K. R., Torgesen, J. K., & Wagner, R. K. (2005). *Relationships between word knowledge and reading comprehension in third-grade children.* Manuscript submitted for publication.

Tyler, A., & Nagy, W. (1989). The acquisition of English derivational morphology. *Journal of Memory and Language, 28,* 649–667.

Wechsler, D. (1991). *Wechsler intelligence scale for children—Third edition.* New York: Psychological Corporation.

Index

Index of breadth of vocabulary
  measures of, 284–286, 285*f*
  overview, 283
Index of depth of vocabulary
  measures of, 284–286, 285*f*
  overview, 283–284
Individual-differences approach. *see also*
    Individual differences in vocabulary
    learning
  comprehension skills and, 250–251
  IQ and, 253
  listening comprehension and, 252–253
  oral reading fluency and, 251–252
  overview, 249–250
  study of reading comprehension with,
    254–257, 258*t*–259*t*, 259–265, 266*f*,
    267–269, 270*f*, 271, 271–272
  word knowledge and, 252
  working memory and, 253–254
Individual differences in vocabulary
    learning. *see also* Individual-differences
    approach
  causal models of, 287–288, 289*f*
  knowledge hypothesis and, 287
  metalinguistic awareness and, 54–61
Infancy
  family environment and, 42–43
  overview, 1–5
  parent–child interactions during, 33–34
Inferences about word meaning
  causal models of, 288
  difficulties in, 87–88
  incidental learning and, 7
  morphological processing and, 83, 84–
    87, 93–99, 96*t*
Infinitival complement argument structure
  fast mapping and, 164–166, 164*t*, 165*f*, 166*f*
  reading skills and, 172, 172*t*
Inside-out skills, 18
Instruction. *see also* Intervention
  bilingualism and, 146–149
  comprehension instruction and, 69–71
  contextual word learning and, 59–60,
    213–215
  English language learners and, 130–131
  improving, 185–189
  increasing metalinguistic awareness and,
    68–69, 71–72
  metalinguistic awareness and, 71–72
  morphological processing and, 90–99, 96*t*
  in older and updated basals, 184–185

  overview, 6–7
  in the primary grades, 189–192
  research regarding, 206–222
  selecting words to teach, 192–201, 199*t*
  Spanish–English cognates in science
    curriculum and, 149–154, 152*t*
  vocabulary instructional flooding
    hypothesis and, 222–226
  working memory and, 241–245, 243*t*
Instruction, cognate-focused
  English language learners and, 130–131
  learning and instruction and, 146–149
  nature of English and, 145–146
  science vocabulary and, 142–145
  vocabulary gap and, 141
Instruction in Beijing
  compared to reading instruction in Hong
    Kong, 110–115, 111*t*, 112*t*, 114*t*
  vocabulary knowledge and, 116–118, 117*t*
Instruction in Hong Kong
  compared to reading instruction in
    Beijing, 110–115, 111*t*, 112*t*, 114*t*
  vocabulary knowledge and, 116–118, 117*t*
Instruction, keyword method of
  overview, 6
  research regarding, 212, 222
Instruction, rich. *see also* Instruction
  overview, 185–189
  research regarding, 217–218
  selecting words to teach and, 196–197
  vocabulary instructional flooding
    hypothesis and, 222–226
Instrumental hypothesis, 52, 286
Intention-reading skills, 4
Intentional contextual analysis, 216–217
Intentionality in language learning, 208–209
Interrelatedness aspect of word
    knowledge, 10
Intervention. *see also* Instruction
  collaborative strategic, 66, 69
  comprehension skills and, 65–66
  contextual word learning and, 59–60
  enhancing responsive caregiving and, 36–
    37, 37–40, 40–43, 44*t*–45*t*, 45–47, 46*t*
  metalinguistic demands on, 67–68
  phonological awareness and, 25–27, 26*f*, 27*f*
  vocabulary gap and, 55
  working memory and, 241–245, 243*t*
Intervention, collaborative strategic
  comprehension instruction and, 69
  metalinguistic awareness and, 66